The Laws of the Markets

A selection of previous *Sociological Review* Monographs

Life and Work History Analyses[†]
ed. Shirley Dex

The Sociology of Monsters[†]
ed. John Law

Sport, Leisure and Social Relations[†]
eds John Horne, David Jary and Alan Tomlinson

Gender and Bureaucracy*
eds Mike Savage and Anne Witz

The Sociology of Death: theory, culture, practice*
ed. David Clark

The Cultures of Computing*
ed. Susan Leigh Star

Theorizing Museums*
ed. Sharon Macdonald and Gordon Fyfe

Consumption Matters*
eds Stephen Edgell, Kevin Hetherington and Alan Warde

Ideas of Difference*
eds Kevin Hetherington and Rolland Munro

[†] Available from The Sociological Review Office, Keele University, Keele, Staffs ST5 5BG.
* Available from Marston Book Services, PO Box 270, Abingdon, Oxon OX14 4YW.

The Laws of the Markets

Edited by Michel Callon

Blackwell Publishers/The Sociological Review

First published in 1998

Blackwell Publishers
108 Cowley Road, Oxford OX4 1JF, UK

and
350 Main Street
Malden, MA 02148, USA

British Library Cataloguing in Publication Data

A CIP catalogue record for this book is available from the British Library

Library of Congress Cataloging-in-Publication Data applied for

ISBN 0 631 20608 6

Printed and bound by Whitstable Litho Ltd.

This book is printed on acid-free paper.

Contents

For Bruno and John

Introduction: the embeddedness of economic markets in economics

Michel Callon

Even as the market seems triumphant everywhere and its laws progressively and ineluctably impose themselves worldwide, we cannot fail to be struck by the lasting topicality of the following well-known quotation from D. North:

'It is a peculiar fact that the literature on economics . . . contains so little discussion of the central institution that underlies neoclassical economics—the market' (North, 1977).[1]

How can this surprising shortcoming be explained? How can this self-proclaimed failure of economic theory be accounted for? By distinguishing the thing from the concept which refers to it, the marketplace from the market, the English language suggests a possible answer. While the market denotes the abstract mechanisms whereby supply and demand confront each other and adjust themselves in search of a compromise, the marketplace is far closer to ordinary experience and refers to the place in which exchange occurs. This distinction is, moreover, merely a particular case of a more general opposition, which the English language, once again, has the merit of conveying accurately: that between economics and economy, between theoretical and practical activity, in short, between economics as a discipline and economy as a thing. If economic theory knows so little about the marketplace, is it not simply because in striving to abstract and generalize it has ended up becoming detached from its object? Thus, the weakness of market theory may well be explained by its lack of interest in the marketplace. To remedy this shortcoming, economics would need only to return to its object, the economy, from which it never should have strayed in the first place.

The matter, however, is not so simple. The danger of abstraction and unrealism which is supposed to threaten every academic discipline—and which time and again has been exposed and stigmatized,

Michel Callon

notably by economic sociology—is certainly real; it is the formulation of this danger that is suspect. It takes at face value a conception of science which the anthropology of science and techniques (AST) has undermined over the past few years. Saying that economics has failed by neglecting to develop a theory of real markets and their multiple modes of functioning, amounts to admitting that there does exist a thing—the economy—which a science—economics—has taken as its object of analysis. The point of view that I have adopted in this introduction, and which the book strives to defend, is radically different. It consists in maintaining that economics, in the broad sense of the term, performs, shapes and formats the economy, rather than observing how it functions (Latour, 1987) (Callon, 1994).

In order fully to assess the contribution of economics to the constitution of the economy we would need to write a history which has yet to be invented. What we do have are separate stories, of economic thought, presented according to a purely disciplinarian logic, on the one hand, and of economic activities, carefully separated from economics, on the other; on the one hand a history of ideas showing the progressive development of the theory and its concepts (reconstituting for example the genealogy of the market concept)[2] and on the other a social history of the economy (which relates, for example, the evolution of the different forms of market organization). That a degree of interdependence exists between these two histories is hardly questionable, even if this has not been systematically studied. That is why it would be fascinating to construct a social history of economics which would show how abstract notions such as that of supply and demand, or those of interconnected markets[3] (à la Walras (Walras, {1926} 1954)), imperfect competition (as proposed by Chamberlin (Chamberlin, 1933)) or incentives, have been formulated in constant relation to practical questions which, in turn, they help reformulate (Dumez, 1985). Karl Polanyi brilliantly demonstrates in *The Great Transformation* that this type of history is both possible and filled with lessons. His book is often used to criticise the myth of the self-regulating market. But it is also, and above all, one of the rare attempts to link up economics and economy, with a convincing analysis of the role of economic theories, such as that of Ricardo, in the establishment of a labour market.

The aim of the present book is to contribute to the analysis and understanding of the subtle relationships between economics and the economy; not within an historical perspective, although some chapters do include historical material, but within a deliberately anthropological one. To give a broad outline of this perspective, the

2   © The Editorial Board of The Sociological Review 1998

most convenient starting point is the general definition of the market proposed by Robert Guesnerie in his attempt explicitly to raise the question of relations between the market and the market-place (Guesnerie, 1996). According to Guesnerie, a market is a co-ordination device in which: a) the agents pursue their own interests and to this end perform economic calculations which can be seen as an operation of optimization and/or maximization; b) the agents generally have divergent interests, which lead them to engage in c) transactions which resolve the conflict by defining a price. Consequently, to use Guesnerie's words, 'a market opposes buyers and sellers, and the prices which resolve this conflict are the input but also, in a sense, the outcome of the agents' economic calculation.'

This definition has the advantage of stressing the essential:

- a market implies a peculiar anthropology, one which assumes a calculative agent or more precisely what we might call "calculative agencies';[4]
- the market implies an organization, so that one has to talk of an organized market (and of the possible multiplicity of forms of organization) in order to take into account the variety of calculative agencies and of their distribution;[5]
- the market is a process in which calculative agencies oppose one another, without resorting to physical violence, to reach an acceptable compromise in the form of a contract and/or a price.[6] Hence, the importance of the historical dimension which helps us to understand the construction of markets and the competitive arrangements in which they are stabilized, for a time and in a place.

The point that needs to be borne in mind is that the agents enter and leave the exchange like strangers. Once the transaction has been concluded the agents are quits: they extract themselves from anonymity only momentarily, slipping back into it immediately afterwards.[7] This sudden metamorphosis is not self-evident; it is highly paradoxical. As Mitchel Abolafia points out in his contribution, it is not easy to make this relationship of strangeness compatible with the unavoidable fact that the agents are in touch with each other during the transaction.

The threefold characterization of the market proposed by Guesnerie leads us to the formulation of our first question: what is a calculative agency?

What calculative agencies are not

Under which conditions is calculativeness possible? Under what conditions do calculative agents emerge?

In order to write and conclude calculated contracts—that is to say, to go into the content of goods and their prices—the agents need to have information on the possible states of the world. More specifically, for calculative agents to be able to make decisions they need at least to be able to: (i) establish a list of the possible states of the world (each state of the world being defined by a certain list of actors and goods, and by a certain distribution of these goods amongst the actors); (ii) rank these states of the world (which gives a content and an object to the agent's preferences); (iii) identify and describe the actions which allow for the production of each of the possible states of the world.

An essential point in this general definition needs to be noted. For an agent to be able to calculate—ie to rank—her decisions, she must at least be able to draw up a list of actions that she can undertake, and describe the effects of these actions on the world in which she is situated. This presupposes the existence in organized form of all the relevant information on the different states of the world and on the consequences of all conceivable courses of action and the access of all this information to the agent. Thus she will not only be able to get an idea of possible goals and rank them, but also mobilize the resources required to attain them.[8]

Before going on, in the following section, to address the conditions under which decisions are calculable, we need to discuss two classical points of view: that of cognitive psychology and that of cultural influences.

Cognitive psychology presumes that individual economic agents are capable of mental calculation. Now, this hypothesis is far too demanding. One can not attribute to the agents the capacity of mental calculation. This has been shown with regard to scientists who, since Locke and throughout the history of classical economics, have served as models. Cognitive anthropology has, however, brilliantly confirmed it and extended it to all ordinary agents (d'Andrade, 1995). Calculating—we shall limit ourselves here to this point—is a complex collective practice which involves far more than the capacities granted to agents by epistemologists and certain economists. The material reality of calculation, involving figures, writing mediums and inscriptions—and I shall return to this

4

point—are decisive in performing calculations. From the fact that calculations are made in the quasi-laboratories of calculative agencies (the word agent places too much weight on the individual) we should not infer that there are calculative beings, no matter how well or poorly informed they may be.[9] From collective performance we cannot induce individual mental competence.[10]

The other explanation, symmetrical in relation to the first one, consists of looking at cultural frames for the origin of the agents' calculative competence. Rather than postulating that the ability to calculate is an intrinsic property of *homo sapiens*, it is the culturally or socially constructed dimension of this competence which is emphasized. Irrespective of the mediations through which this influence is supposed to be exercised, it is asserted that in all cases certain social structures or cultural forms favour calculation and selfish interests while others induce agents to be altruistic, disinterested, generous and even to give freely. The socio-cultural context functions as an injunction, sometimes silent but always effective: 'to survive, to exist, thou shalt calculate!'. DiMaggio has synthesized this approach very well in addressing the question of the role of culture in the constitution of market societies. Culture, he explains, is frequently called upon to explain the appearance of rational actors, the atoms of the market economy, because agents, in their behaviour and calculative capacities, differ from one society to the next: 'Some person concepts (those entailing much agency and individuality) arguably render persons better equipped to operate in market contexts than others'. This difference of equipment—the word is well chosen—is frequently invoked, notably in studies of developing countries or of so-called transitional economies. If the agents resist calculative rationality and hence the market, it is because they are 'embedded' in the social or cultural frames which turn them away from it (DiMaggio, 1994).

Bai Gao, in his contribution, draws upon the Japanese case to show that this culturalist approach, which claims to explain why some societies block the emergence of calculative agencies, is so weak that it fails to account for an even simpler problem: that of the shift from one modality of calculative agency to another. In the case of Japan it is not a question of explaining why, suddenly, economic agents started calculating, but of why they changed their ways of doing so. The transformation which gripped the Japanese economy at the end of the Second World War consisted essentially of the appearance of new criteria for evaluating economic efficiency and profitability, which favoured co-operation and the long term. What

Gao proves is the impossibility of placing the origins of this little shift, of this substitution of one type of calculation for another, in culture. Since culture cannot explain this minor evolution, it is even less apt to account for a major transformation such as the one which makes uncalculative agencies calculative.

In order to become calculative, agencies do indeed need to be equipped. But this equipment is neither all in the brains of human beings nor all in their socio-cultural frames or their institutions. What is it then? How on earth does one become calculative, since this competence is neither in human nature nor in institutions?

In search of possible sources of calculativeness

How can we clarify and then characterize this equipment which is so easily overlooked and yet without which no calculation is possible? One strategy consists in considering situations of extreme uncertainty, those in which the limits of the solutions proposed by cognitive psychology and culturalism are most obvious. How does an atomized agent manage to start calculating when the information she needs to calculate is inexistent or contradictory, or when there are no institutional guidelines which are sufficiently stable and legitimate both to allow for shared expectations and to make an unknown future manageable?

Modern economic theory has devoted significant efforts to explaining the possibility of calculation in situations of radical uncertainty or even ignorance. As a start, I shall recall the main solutions put forward (Eymard-Duvernay, 1996). I shall then point out their limits—owing to the closeness of these solutions to the cognitive psychological paradigm—and introduce social network analysis. This, in turn will lead me, after several reformulations, to the sought-after solution.

Market co-ordination encounters problems when uncertainties on the states of the world, on the nature of the actions which can be undertaken and on the expected consequences of these actions, increase. Problems are at their worst when the uncertainties leave room for pure and simple ignorance.[11] Now, such situations are the rule and not the exception. This is even more obvious with the uncertainties generated by technosciences. The general question is thus the following: how can agents calculate when no stable information or shared prediction on the future exists?

In order to maintain the possibility of co-ordination, economists

6

have proposed several solutions which—they assure us—are, or ought to be, applied in concrete market situations. The most 'orthodox' solution is that of contingent contracts. Contingent contracts are revisable contracts; their renegotiation is planned, thus taking into account the occurrence of events specified beforehand (Hart and Moore, 1988).[12] The greater the uncertainties, the more difficult it is to implement this solution. It implies, to a certain extent, that the agents spend their time renegotiating their contracts, that is to say, interacting and exchanging information as it is produced. In this case market co-ordination as such disappears, leaving room for uninterrupted social interaction involving many different agents. These agents, no matter how much they wish to do so, are no longer able to become strangers; they are entangled.[13] I shall revert to this notion a little further.

Another solution is that of a focal point. In this case we presume that the agents share common knowledge or have the same points of reference which guarantee the co-ordination. The nature of these references known to each agent is highly variable. It may pertain to a shared culture, rules, procedures, routines or conventions which guarantee the adjustments and predictability of behaviour. Socioeconomics has studied in detail these intermediate realities to explain the co-ordination of market action. But it is easy to show that these different solutions suffer from the same limits. Whether we talk about a common culture or of shared rules or conventions, we encounter the same stumbling block: a rule, convention or cultural device does not govern behaviour completely since it entails irreducible margins of interpretation. These margins of interpretation can be removed only during interaction, negotiation or discussion.

All these solutions have the common feature of providing autonomous—over-autonomous—and isolated—over-isolated—agents with the social relations which, by opening them up to their environment, enable them to co-ordinate their action with those of other agents. Why not take this dependence of their environment as a starting point? Why not consider that one solution to the question of co-ordination, in a situation of radical uncertainty, is to admit that beneath the contracts and the rules there is a 'primitive' reality without which co-ordination would not be possible? An understanding of this ultimate basis is the purpose of the notion of a social network or, more broadly, the notion of embeddedness as initially formulated by Polanyi and later refined by Granovetter. If agents can calculate their decisions, irrespective of the degree of uncertainty concerning the future, it is because they are entangled in a web of relations and connections; they do not have to open up to the world because they contain their world. Agents are actor-worlds (Callon, 1986a).

At this point it is useful to recall Granovetter's solution, for it has been the source of many misinterpretations preventing us from seeing its originality and its true limits as well as, more generally, those of social network analysis (Granovetter, 1985). The solution lies in his definition of the notion of a network. Granovetter first does away with the classical opposition between *homo sociologicus* and *homo economicus*. He convincingly shows that beyond their oft-asserted differences, the two conceptions both assume the existence of individual agents with perfectly stabilized competencies. The thesis of over-socialization, like that of under-socialization, rests on a common hypothesis: that of the existence of a person closed in on himself—a *homo clausus*, to use Elias' expression. This hypothesis precludes any solution to the problem of co-ordination in a situation of radical uncertainty . For Granovetter the only possible solution is that provided by the network; not a network connecting entities which are already there, but a network which configures ontologies. The agents, their dimensions, and what they are and do, all depend on the morphology of the relations in which they are involved.

This crucial point warrants clarification. The network, in this sense, does not link agents with an established identity (that is to say, endowed with a set of fixed interests and stable preferences) to form what would be a rigid social structure constituting the framework in which individual actions are situated. It is on this point that embeddedness in a network of social relations, as defined by Granovetter, is different from embeddedness according to Polanyi. The latter assumes the existence of an institutional frame constituting the context in which economic activities take place.[14] In the social network as defined by Granovetter, the agents' identities, interests and objectives, in short, everything which might stabilize their description and their being, are variable outcomes which fluctuate with the form and dynamics of relations between these agents (Callon, 1986b), (Smith, 1994).

This means that the agent is neither immersed in the network nor framed by it; in other words, the network does not serve as a context. Both agent and network are, in a sense, two sides of the same coin. Either one enters the network through the agents and one is immediately tempted to characterize them by the shape of their relationships; or one focuses on the network itself, in which case one uses the associations of its constitutive agents to describe it. The best way to explain the radical nature of this approach—which amounts to replacing the two traditionally separate notions of agent and network by the single one of agent-network—is through examples drawn from the now substantial literature on the subject.

The equivalence between agency and form of network was clearly explained in one of Granovetter's seminal articles: 'The strength of the weak ties' (Granovetter, 1973). The capacity of an agent to make autonomous choices, that is to say, to make decisions which do not merely fall in line with the decisions made by other agents, is not inscribed in her nature; it coincides with the morphology of her relationships. When she finds herself at the intersection of two networks which scarcely, if at all, overlap, the range of available options affords her with a large margin of manœuvre. She is even endowed with the possibility of considering action in terms of alternative choices and her faculty for arbitration is enhanced. If, however, the relations are redundant, the agent is deprived of all ability to make choices. This example shows that it is possible to characterize the different types of agency through the distribution of relationships. Studies by Burt on structural holes uphold and generalizes this thesis. In a network, a structural hole corresponds to the points, and hence the agents, whose contacts are not related to one another. Burt shows that structural holes are associated with agencies capable of strategic combinations and manipulation. Following the same approach, he suggests that entrepreneurial action is linked to certain relational configurations. 'When you take the opportunity to be the tertius you are an entrepreneur in the literal sense of the word— a person who generates profit from being between others' (Burt, 1993). We could thus review the different types of configuration and show that each of them corresponds to a particular type of agency, that is to say, a particular mode of action. However, to make the point, it would be simplest to consider the elementary unit of the network: the triangular relationship. The bilateral relationship, so strongly emphasized by interactionism, teaches us nothing about the social dimension. Simmel said so long ago: relations between **A** and **B** are not enough to explain their actions and identities. These become intelligible only when embedded in the indirect and sometimes invisible relations bearing on them. One need simply add a third party, **C**, and adopt its point of view, for the relationship between **A** and **B** to become analysable and comprehensible. Burt describes three possible strategies for **C**: that of the *mediator* where

9

in case of conflict between **A** and **B**, **C** acts as an intermediary and helps them to negotiate; that of *tertius gaudens* where **C** takes advantage of conflict between **A** and **B** whose forces balance out; and, finally, that of the *despot* (*divide per impere*) where **C** creates conflict to preclude coalition and align the interests of **A** and **B** with his own. As we can see, without bringing **C** into the picture, whatever happens between **A** and **B** remains incomprehensible (Hatchuel, 1995). Inversely, the possibilities for action of **C** remain unintelligible if we fail to take into account both **A** and **B**. This elementary algebra of social relations, starting with the triad, becomes increasingly complex as other relations are added to it. The logic remains, however: it identifies the action with a sort of positional calculation.

This similarity between network and action, rooted in the three-party game, knows no bounds. Granovetter shows, for example, by comparing two Philippine towns, that there is a correlation between the degree of personalization of credit and the size and density of the social networks. Baker, in a bold analysis of financial future markets, shows that the very status of money—why, for example, a financial asset should be considered as closest to money—in industrialized societies where numerous currencies proliferate, depends on the positions of the holders of these assets in their network (Baker, 1984).[15] David Stark (this monograph) provides a cogent illustration of this point: talking of ownership rights in the absolute, and thus of possibilities for agents to engage in certain courses of action, without taking into account the ties binding them, makes little sense. To understand what property rights consist of in a concrete socio-economic context, in other words, to reconstitute the set of rights and obligations incumbent on each agent, there is no alternative but to analyse relationships. This 'swing-wing' ontology of the agency, which changes with the changing shapes of the network, is shared by so-called evolutionary economics simply because 'in an organicist ontology relations between entities are internal rather than external and the essential characteristics of any element are seen as outcomes of relations with other entities' (Hodgson, 1994). We would be hard pressed to find a better definition of agent-network.

What benefits accrue from social network analysis? Answer: a simple explanation of the possibility that agents have of calculating, when caught up in situations of extreme uncertainty. They do not have to open up to their environment in order to exchange or get information, or to negotiate and co-ordinate their decisions so as to lay the foundations of a possible order. They are open and connected; it is from these connections that they derive their ability to calculate. *Homo clausus* of economic theory is replaced by *homo apertus* of social network analysis, and the degrees and forms of opening of the latter depend on the form of the relationships. Whether the situation is uncertain or not, the only thing that counts for *homo apertus*, and which he takes into account, is the network of direct and indirect relations surrounding him. This calculative logic is clearly expressed in the triangular games mentioned above, where the elementary action consists of a calculation of alliances and conflicts. Irrespective of whether the states of the world and the causal links between decisions and their effects are known or not, the agency follows its combinatorial logic, that of connection and disconnection, which is entirely relational.

This solution seems neat. It eliminates the insurmountable problem posed by *homo clausus* who in situations of uncertainty has no alternative but to open up in order to re-establish the co-ordination. Is it not, however, a bit too easy? Before answering this question it would be relevant here briefly to mention and discuss the usual critiques exposing the reductionist nature of social network analysis. DiMaggio, for example, very subtly points out that it is hardly convincing to deduce the strategy of an agent from her position in a network of relations (DiMaggio, 1994). Between a position and an action, is it not necessary, he asks, to interpose values, preferences and projects; in short, everything which defines the agency and avoids reducing action to structural determinations? Is it not excessive, he adds, to consider that an agent in a structural hole has no objectives and projects other than constantly building up more non-redundant relationships with the aim of increasing her capacity for control? This criticism, which reintroduces the dualism of structures and agency, or positions and dispositions, is by no means groundless. Many social network analysts lay themselves open to it by introducing the notion of social capital. Burt, for example, considers that an agent's relationships with other agents, whether direct or indirect, are all comparable to a social capital which she mobilises for the purpose of developing her own relational strategies. This social capital is greater when the agent finds herself in a very obvious position of a structural hole. Each relationship, owing to its non-redundancy, provides her with information and opportunities for specific action. This concept, pervasive in sociology (Coleman, 1988), (Bourdieu, 1979), thoroughly undermines the strength of social network analysis. By dissociating agency and network, it widens the gap between agency and structure. The agent, simply because she mobilizes a capital—of which the form and volume do of course depend on the form of the network and on her position therein—escapes, at least in part, from the network. Cast aside, freed from the network to which she is attached only by the resources it provides, the agent regains her autonomy. The monism of social network analysis is thus substituted for the traditional dualism of agencies and structures. The notion of social capital is the Trojan horse of dualism since it severs the formal identity between agent and network; it splits the agent-network again by introducing the usual opposition between the action and the resources of that action.

If we are to avoid the temptation of dualism, we need to banish any explanation separating the agency from the network and, in particular, avoid the usual concepts of resources or social capital so as to maintain, against all odds, what some denounce as impoverishing reductionism. But is this intransigence sufficient? Does it enable us satisfactorily to explain the emergence of calculating agencies in situations of radical uncertainty? Should we settle for a pure social network analysis, cleansed of all dualistic influence?

Gift giving and framing

To answer this question we need to revert to the notion of calculation. We have seen that in order to maintain the *homo clausus* of economic theory in a state of calculativeness when faced with uncertainty, we have to agree to open him out onto his environment and to grant him the ability to develop complex interactions with other agents. In order to be calculative the agent must be open and, according to social network analysis, once open and caught up in the triangular game he is *de facto* calculative. The assumption of openness of social network analysis thus transforms the problem into a solution: the agent-network is by construction calculative, since all action is analysed in terms of combinations, associations, relationships and strategies of positioning. The agent is calculative because action can only be calculative.

Should we stop there and say that social network analysis exhausts the questions of calculation and of the emergence of calculative agencies, dismissing the usual distinction between certain and uncertain situations and, consequently, replacing the notion of information by the notion of relation? No, because ever since Mauss, social sciences have been confronted with the question of the gift, that is to say, the existence of uncalculated, disinterested actions (Mauss, [1925] 1969). Social network analysis explains what Mauss finds so self-evident that he does not even try to explain it: the existence of calculative agencies. But how does social network analysis account for the existence of disinterestedness to which Mauss grants utmost importance? It is once again by examining this ever-relevant question of the gift and disinterested giving which will allow us to proceed further. If we wish to explain the emergence of calculative agencies, we will also have to explain the emergence of non-calculative ones, which in turn will lead us to amend social network analysis substantially, without, however, overlooking its contribution.

The analysis of disinterestedness or, in other words, of the absence of calculativeness, generally wavers between two extreme interpretations.[16] The first emphasizes the subjective dimension of disinterestedness. The action is disinterested if the agent wittingly avoids introducing any element of calculation. The second, by contrast, highlights the objective dimension: disinterestedness is an illusion. This illusion may, in turn, have two origins: (i) the agent is generous and, despite believing herself to be altruistic, she only inscribes her action in networks of reciprocity which transcend her—here disinterestedness is merely the driving force enabling each agent to play his or her part in a system of exchange, since a gift is always followed by a counter-gift which cancels out the asymmetry created by the gift;[17] (ii) disinterestedness, often likened to trust, is considered as a consequence of a more primitive calculation of which the agent is not aware: 'If I abandon myself, if I trust without any calculation, that is because it's the most rational solution when, in situations of uncertainty, I try to maximise my gain expectations'.[18]

The first explanation depends on the subject's lived experience, whereas the second takes apart its mechanisms and springs to show that this experience is merely an illusion. Between these two extreme solutions (is it better to grant everything to the subject or to take everything away from it?), which one is to be preferred? The latter cannot be chosen because it dissolves the agency in the structures and resolves the problem before posing it. The former warrants closer examination, however, for we cannot reduce social science to a mere recording of the states of the subject's conscience. To avoid these two extremes, the most moderate authors adopt a middle course. Williamson, for example, maintains that most actions and decisions are calculated, even when they resemble trust

(Williamson, 1993). Yet he recognizes the existence of behaviours associated with the family, love and friendship, from which calculation is absent. As Pascal put it, man is neither all beast nor all angel, he is capable of switching from calculativeness to disinterestedness depending on the circumstances. However, Williamson would add, the part that is beast, that of calculativeness, is by far the greater of the two.

Moderation is praiseworthy. But is it satisfactory from a theoretical point of view? Obviously not. Asserting that there do exist spheres of activity and types of behaviour in which the agent does not calculate, and others in which he becomes a calculator, is too easy an answer to the question we posed—that of the conditions of the emergence of non-calculative agencies. That agents refrain from calculating when they are engaged in relations from which calculation is absent is a solution that hardly helps to solve the problem.

To my knowledge there exists on the social science market only one answer to the question asked which reconciles the subjective experience of disinterestedness with the practical observation that, in the absence of conscious calculation, the results of the action initiated by the agent—that is to say, the return in the form of a counter-gift—can nevertheless reasonably be anticipated by the observer. This is the solution (which makes the actions that the agent does not calculate, calculable for the observer), proposed by Bourdieu. It is based on two elements. The first is the interval between the gift and the counter-gift. This interval makes it possible to 'mask the contradiction between the intended truth of the gift as a generous, free and one-way gesture, and the truth that makes it a moment in a relationship of exchange which transcends the singular acts of exchange' (Bourdieu, 1997). The time which passes and which, in the moment of giving, the agent has in front of himself like an obscure space hiding the future counter-gift, remains unrealized, allows for the subjective experience of disinterestedness. Amnesia, socially structured by the time lag between the gift and its return gift, generates generosity as a subjective experience. But— and this is where the second element comes in—the return gift does end up coming, thus forming a true gift-and-counter-gift economy. The generous disposition of agents—that is to say, their propensity to give, receive and give back, to use the famous triple obligation described by Mauss—is encouraged by institutional incentives. These ensure that generosity is recognized as such and is socially viable. This solution has an immense advantage. It spares our argument from all essentialism. There is nothing in human nature, there are no sectors of activity, which impose, exclusively or successively, either disinterested or calculative actions. The fact that an agent calculates or does not has nothing to do with its inherent selfishness or altruism; nor is it due to the nature of the relationships in which it is engaged (a market transaction or, by contrast, love, friendship or the family). It is, and this is the solution suggested by Bourdieu, the formatting of these relationships which will orientate the agent towards calculativeness or disinterestedness.

The analysis which Bourdieu offers us of this formatting has the merit of putting us on the right track towards a solution to the more general question of the emergence of calculative agencies. The time lag, says Bourdieu, is the decisive factor behind the switch from one regime to another, from calculativeness to non-calculativeness. The longer this interval, that is to say, the more time the return gift or counter-gift takes to arrive, moving further and further out of the giver's field of vision, the more the giver will experience herself as disinterested. The shorter the interval, the more the gift will be experienced as calculative. P. Bourdieu, to stress this point, cites the following admirable maxim by La Rochefoucauld: 'Being in too much of a hurry to pay a debt is a form of ingratitude'. When the beneficiary is in a hurry to release herself, she makes it clear that she has opted for a market transaction and therefore that she has calculated her decision. When, on the other hand, she lets time pass, effacing even the memory of the initial decision, she switches to the regime of non-calculative action.

The emergence of a calculative agency, says Bourdieu, depends on a time frame. Either the return gift is in the frame, and the agency is calculative, or it is beyond the frame and she is not. In the first instance the decision takes into account the return gift, in the second it ignores it. This taking into account depends only on the framing, the tracing of a boundary between relationships and events which are internalized and included in a decision or, by contrast, externalized and excluded from it. This analysis is compatible with that proposed by social network analysis: calculation does indeed concern relationships and combinations. But it also enables one to explain what social network analysis cannot explain, ie uncalculated action, by introducing the notion of framing. Framing demarcates, in regards to the network of relationships, those which are taken into account and those which are ignored. The difference between calculated action and uncalculated action is thus reduced to its simplest expression: it is encompassed in the taking into account or not of the return gift. The analysis of this mechanism of inclusion or exclusion, that is to say, the examination of the notion of framing, merits our further attention.

Framing as a process of disentanglement

To explain the absence of calculation, Bourdieu reduces framing to its time dimension. **A** calculates her action when she includes in her decision the most probable subsequent decisions of the other agents: **B**, **C**, etc. Either **B**'s counter-gift is anticipated, placed in the frame, and **A** calculates; or, and this is the virtue of time, it is ignored, placed outside the frame, and the action switches over to disinterestedness. In this section I shall broaden this definition of framing by stressing its multidimensionnality.

I shall show that if calculations are to be performed and completed, the agents and goods involved in these calculations must be disentangled and framed. In short, a clear and precise boundary must be drawn between the relations which the agents will take into account and which will serve in their calculations and those which will be thrown out of the calculation as such.

The extreme case of framing is that in which, as Bourdieu describes it, no relationship whatsoever is taken into account. The frame is empty—which is another way of saying that no framing has taken place—and the agent finds himself faced with his decision alone. He consequently switches to pure generosity for all possibilities of calculation, which implies that at least two terms relate to each other, are eliminated. However, to explain this extreme case we need to consider the question of framing mechanisms in all their generality. How can we account for the fact that the openness of the *homo apertus* of social networks can be made variable, so that it passes through all the forms of agency from the most purely non-calculative to the most purely calculative? How is the delimiting, or framing, of relationships at a point in the network achieved? This is the question to which we will now turn.

Economic theory has already addressed this question very specifically through the notion of externality which allows the introduction of the more general question of disentanglement (Callon, his contribution).

Economists invented the notion of externality to denote all the connections, relations and effects which agents do not take into account in their calculations when entering into a market transaction. If, for example, a chemical plant pollutes the river into which it discharges its toxic waste, it produces a negative externality. The interests of fishermen, bathers and other users are harmed and in order to pursue their activity they will have to make investments for which they will receive no compensation. The factory calculates its decisions without taking into account the effects on the fishermen's activities. Externalities are not necessarily negative, they may also be positive. Take the case of a pharmaceutical company which wants to develop a new drug. To protect itself it files a patent. However, in so doing, it divulges information which becomes available to competitors and can be used by them to develop their own research and development.

The notion of externalities is essential in economic theory because it enables us to emphasize one of the possible shortcomings of the market, one of the limits of its effectiveness. But it is also very useful for understanding the meaning of the expression 'constructing a market'. This is where the joint notions of framing and overflowing fit in, which I shall come back to shortly.

Social network analysis as promoted by Granovetter reminds us that any entity is caught up in a network of relations, in a flow of intermediaries which circulate, connect, link and reconstitute identities (Callon, 1991). What the notion of externality shows, in the negative, is all the work that has to be done, all the investments that have to be made in order to make relations visible and calculable in the network. This consists of framing the actors and their relations. Framing is an operation used to define agents (an individual person or a group of persons) who are clearly distinct and dissociated from one another. It also allows for the definition of objects, goods and merchandise which are perfectly identifiable and can be separated not only from other goods, but also from the actors involved, for example in their conception, production, circulation or use. It is owing to this framing that the market can exist and that distinct agents and distinct goods can be brought into play. Without this framing the states of the world can not be described and listed and, consequently, the effects of the different conceivable actions can not be anticipated.

What economists say when they study externalities is precisely that this work of cleansing, of disconnection, in short, of framing, is never over and that in reality it is impossible to take it to a conclusion. There are always relations which defy framing. It is for these relations which remain outside the frame that economists reserve the term externalities. The latter denotes everything which the agents do not take into account and which enables them to conclude their calculations. But one needs to go further than that.

When, after having identified some of these externalities, the agents, in keeping with the predictions of Coase's famous theorem, decide to reframe them—in other words to internalize the externalities—other externalities appear. Callon, in his contribution, suggests the term 'overflowing' to denote this impossibility of total framing. Any frame is necessarily subject to overflowing. It is by framing its property rights by means of a public patent that a pharmaceutical firm produces externalities and creates overflowing. It is by purifying the products that it markets that a chemical firm creates the by-products which escape its control.

The impossibility of eliminating all overflowing has, in reality, a profound reason discussed by Callon in his chapter. To ensure that a contract is not broken, to delimit the actions than can be undertaken within the framework of this contract, the agents concerned have to mobilize a whole range of elements, called, to use Leigh Star's expression, boundary-objects (Star and Griesemer, 1989). These objects allow the framing and stabilization of actions, while simultaneously providing an opening on to other worlds, thus constituting leakage points where overflowing can occur.

Let us take the most simple example, that of a market transaction concerning a motor car. The transaction is possible because rigorous framing has been performed. This framing has reduced the market transaction to three distinct components: the buyer, the producer-seller, and the car. The buyer and the seller are identified without any ambiguity, so that property rights can be exchanged. As for the car, it is because it is free from any ties with other objects or human agents, that it can change ownership. Yet even in this extreme, simple case, not all ties can be cut. Something passes from the seller to the buyer: the car, which conveys with it the know-how and technology of the producer. All the property rights in the world cannot prevent this overflowing, except by eliminating the transaction itself. If the buyer is a firm, reverse engineering becomes possible. This is a general point which can be expressed as follows: the simple fact of framing the transaction because it mobilizes or concerns objects or beings endowed with an irreducible autonomy, is a source of overflowing. Complete framing is a contradiction in terms, whereas complete externalization is possible, as suggested, in the case of pure gifts.

The framing/overflowing duo suggests a move towards economic anthropology and more specifically towards the entangled objects of Thomas and the careers of objects of Appadurai (Appadurai, 1986). The latter shows that the status of goods can change, that they can be commoditized, decommoditized and then recommoditized, etc.: one is not born a commodity, one becomes it. Thomas's thesis expands on and enhances Appadurai's, describing precisely what constitutes this process of merchandization. Thomas gives the best theoretical explanation for this reconfiguring in his discussion of the distinction between market transactions and gifts. His argument is fairly complex and subtle but I think that it can be summed up in the following passage:

> Commodities are here understood as objects, persons, or elements of persons which are placed in a context in which they have exchange value and can be alienated. The alienation of a thing is its dissociation from producers, former users, or prior context (Thomas, 1991).

The last sentence of this quotation is obviously the important one. To construct a market transaction, that is to say, to transform something into a commodity, and two agents into a seller and a consumer, it is necessary to cut the ties between the thing and the other objects or human beings one by one. It must be decontextualized, dissociated and detached. For the car to go from the producer-seller to the customer-buyer, it has to be disentangled. It is on this condition that the calculation can be looped and that the deal can be closed; that the buyer and the seller, once the transaction has been concluded, can be quits. If the thing remains entangled, the one who receives it is never quit and cannot escape from the web of relations. The framing is never over. The debt cannot be settled.[19]

This notion of entanglement is very useful, for it is both theoretical and practical. It enables us to think and describe the process of 'marketization', which, like a process of framing or disentanglement, implies investments and precise actions to cut certain ties and to internalize others. The advantage is that this analysis applies to anything and enables one to escape the risk of essentialism. To entangle and to disentangle are two opposite movements which explain how we move away from or closer to the market regime. No calculation is possible without this framing which allows one to provide a clear list of the entities, states of the world, possible actions and expected outcome of these actions.

Strawberry story

To my knowledge, few scholars have focused on analysing this work of framing which allows for calculation and consequently makes possible the emergence of calculative agencies. One of the best studies I know is that of Marie-France Garcia on the transformation of the table strawberry market in the Sologne region of France (Garcia, 1986). This transformation occurred in the early 1980s and resulted in the constitution of a market with characteristics corresponding to those described in political economy manuals:

- existence of a perfectly qualified product;
- existence of a clearly constituted supply and demand;
- organization of transactions allowing for the establishment of an equilibrium price.

Garcia analysed all the investments required to produce the frames allowing for the construction of this market. First material investments were needed. Uncoordinated transactions between producers and intermediaries engaged in interpersonal relationships were henceforth held in a warehouse built for this purpose. The producers took their product there daily, packed in baskets, and exhibited it in batches in the warehouse. Each batch had a corresponding data sheet which was immediately given to the auctioneer. The latter entered the data into his computer and compiled a catalogue which was handed out to the buyers. Producers and shippers then went into the auction room which was designed in such a way that buyers and sellers could not see one another but nevertheless had a clear view of the auctioneer and the electronic board on which prices were displayed. The display of the strawberries in the hall and the catalogue enabled all parties concerned to have precise knowledge of the supply in terms of both quality and quantity. Moreover, the fact that the different batches were displayed side by side highlighted differences in quality and quantity between producers. The latter could compare their own production with that of their competitors, something which had not been possible formerly when collections were made locally. As Garcia notes: 'those growers who had been caught up in personal relationships with intermediaries and shippers entered into impersonal relationships'.

All of these different elements and devices contributed to the framing of transactions by allowing for the rejection of networks of relations, and thus by constructing an arena in which each entity was disconnected from the others. This arena created a space of calculability: the technique of degressive bidding, the display of transactions on the electronic board, the relative qualification of batches of strawberries on their data slips, and knowledge of the national market all made the transactions calculable. As this example clearly shows, the crucial point is not that of the intrinsic competencies of the agent but that of the equipment and devices (material: the warehouse, the batches displayed side by side; metrological: the meter; and procedural: degressive bidding) which give his or her actions a shape.

To these elements of framing, so often overlooked and without which no overflowing could be contained, must be added those the importance of which economic theory has constantly—and rightly so—stressed. The first in line are property rights which define the right to use certain assets, to derive an income from them and to sell or transfer them definitively to a third party. Without the existence of such rights it goes without saying that calculation becomes meaningless, since the actions and their results cannot be imputed to anyone at all. For agencies to exist, there have to be procedures of attribution of actions and of their effects. Of course, in the establishment and evolution of these property rights, the state and the legal system have an irreplaceable role.[20]

The existence of one or several currencies also facilitates the emergence of calculative agencies. The most decisive contribution of money is not, however, where one would expect it to be. To be sure its main contribution was to provide a unit of account without which no calculation would be possible. However the essential is elsewhere. Money is required above all—even if this point is often overlooked—to delimit the circle of actions between which equivalence can be formulated. It makes commensurable that which was not so before. The case of negative externalities, for example the effects of pollution produced by a chemical plant, clearly illustrates this point. Once identified and acknowledged, overflowing, if it is to be framed and thus internalized, has to be measured (Callon, this volume). This measuring involves the establishment of a metrology, anchored in techno-scientific instruments, which enables the agents concerned to establish quantitative correspondences between a cause (eg, the discharge of dioxin) and an injury (eg, a probability of cancer). This correlation between a risk of death and the activity of a factory, established by means of laboratory experiments and epidemiological research, creates a link between two distinct series of events. But if this relationship (between a discharge and deaths) becomes calculable by the agents, it is not enough merely to prove its existence; it has to be expressed in the same units. This is where money comes in. It provides the currency, the standard, the common language which enables us to reduce heterogeneity, to construct an equivalence and to create a translation between a few molecules of a chemical substance and human lives. Money comes in last in a process of quantification and production of figures, measurements and correlations of all kinds. It is the final piece, the keystone in a metrological system that is already in place and of which it merely guarantees the unity and coherence. Alone it can do nothing; combined with all the measurements preceding it, it facilitates a calculation which makes commensurable that which was not so before: grams of dioxin and a human life. Thanks to it the agents can measure the investments required to reduce the risk of death below a certain threshold. Money establishes an ultimate equivalence between the value of a human life and that of investment in pollution abatement.

Furthermore what Garcia suggests, and what we shall be looking at in the following section, is that beyond the material, procedural, legal and monetary elements which facilitate the framing and construction of the space of calculability, there is a capital, yet rarely mentioned, element: economic theory itself.

In the construction of the strawberry market, a young counsellor of the Regional Chamber of Agriculture played a central part. Remarkably his actions were largely inspired by his university training in economics and his knowledge of neo-classical theory. The project which he managed to launch, through alliances and skill, can be summed up in a single sentence: the construction of a real market on the pure model of perfect competition proposed in economics handbooks. As Garcia says, it is no coincidence that the economic practices of the strawberry producers of Sologne correspond to those in economic theory. This economic theory served as a frame of reference to institute each element of the market (presentation on the market of batches which account for only a small portion of the supply; classification of strawberries in terms of criteria which are independent of the identity of their producers; unity of time and place which makes the market perfectly transparent; and, finally, the freedom of wholesalers and producers alike who are not obliged to buy or sell).

This case provides an outstanding example in that it enables us to follow the birth of an organized market. Above all, it is the purest and most perfect example of market organization. The conclusion that can be drawn from it is extremely simple yet fundamental: yes, *homo economicus* does exist, but is not an a-historical reality; he does not describe the hidden nature of the human being. He is the result of a process of configuration, and the history of the strawberry market shows how this framing takes place. Of course it mobilizes material and metrological investments, property rights and money, but we should not forget the essential contribution of economics in the performing of the economy.

The embeddedness of economy in economics

The groundwork is now complete for a presentation of the core argument of this volume: the role of economics as a discipline, in the broad sense of the term, in the formatting of calculative agencies. In a sense this argument takes up and pursues the assertion of Max Weber for whom accounting methods were the key prerequisites of modern capitalism (Weber {1992}, 1978) (Weber {1923}, 1981).[21] To show the capacity of economics in the performing (or what I call 'performation') of the economy, we have to start between the two with the set of calculating tools without which calculative agency would not be possible. It is on this point that the chapter by Peter Miller provides a decisive contribution.

Calculativeness couldn't exist without calculating tools. Consequently and in order to understand how they work, full significance has to be restored to that humble, disclaimed and misunderstood practice: accounting and the tools it elaborates. That notions such as cost and profit depend directly on accounting tools is obvious but not of prime importance here. The most interesting element is to be found in the relationship between what is to be measured and the tools used to measure it. The latter do not merely record a reality independent of themselves; they contribute powerfully to shaping, simply by measuring it, the reality that they measure. That is what Miller shows by analysing the role of accounting tools in the production of zones of calculability in the framing of decisions.

In his demonstration, Miller considers the evolution and transformation in time of these tools and their related practices. His first observation concerns the collective nature of this process which is carried out by a host of professionals of all kinds, including the accountants themselves but also businessmen, professional associations and even the foremost economists. During the past decades this collective work has grown to such an extent that a real performance measure industry has developed (Meyer, 1994). It is by following the dynamics of the conception, reconception and diffusion of these tools that we are able to discover what makes them powerful and indispensable for internalizing overflowing. Miller shows, for example, how accounting tools progressively frame time by allowing for calculations of equivalence between events occurring at different dates. He also describes recent developments in management accounting which increasingly call on 'a wide range of non-financial measures, including set-up times, inventory levels, defect and rework rates, material and product velocity within the factory, and much else besides'. In short, the tools are constantly reconfigured to take into account in more and more detail a set of entities and relationships which were hitherto excluded from the framework of calculation. The framing becomes more refined, richer, delving into the complexity of relationships, and in so doing it authorizes decisions which are more and more calculated or (to use the commonly-accepted word) more and more rational.

The existence of calculative agencies correlates closely with that of accounting tools. The relationship does not, however, end there, for the nature and content of calculations made by agencies depend largely on the characteristics of the tools used. Gao shows the variety of the measurement tools and the diversity of their effects on economic dynamics. The choice of accounting tools prioritizing the short term caused Japan to embark on a trajectory which it could leave only by changing its measurement tools. Countless studies have demonstrated that accounting tools and, more generally, management tools influence agents behaviours. These effects never appear so clearly as when tools induce strategies of adaptation. Meyer recalls, for example, the effect produced by the generalization of EPS (earning per share) intended as an incentive for managers: 'managers adapted to it by finding ways to improve reported earnings, by deferring maintenance, depreciation, research and development, expenditures and the like' (Meyer, 1994). Not only do accounting tools constitute spaces of calculability and define the way the calculation is made up, but also, through the reactions they provoke, new calculative strategies emerge which lead to the changing of goals. An analysis that fails to take these tools into account would be unable to understand the emergence and logic of calculative agencies, for all decisions are the outcomes of this complex calculating system.

These different tools are not isolated; whether compatible or adjusted to one another or not, they are connected to one another and are collectively carried along by the dynamic so well described by Miller. It is hardly surprising that in these conditions the possibility of establishing a link between micro and macro calculations depends entirely on the existence and availability of tools allowing for this connection. The aggregation of behaviours and calculations is not a theoretical problem; it is a problem of accounting technology.

In this vast accounting system, a true metrological infrastructure in which economic activities are embedded, some areas are more robust and solid than others. Paradoxically, it is in those sectors which seem most subject to a calculative logic that the development of highly efficient accounting tools is most problematical. This is the case of the future markets studied by Abolafia in his contribution. He presents traders whose only obsession is to make calculated decisions, yet who cannot resolve themselves to framing their decisions once and for all, because the relevant information—that which counts and which they have to take into account—generally comes from outside the frame, from an unpredictable place. What strange calculative agencies who, in order to calculate, constantly have to have an eye on the incessant overflowing which redefines the framework of decisions. The problem of the trader is that of being able at any moment to grasp the state of the overflowing, to identify those agents whose decisions will have an effect on the one he intends to make or who, inversely, will react to his own decisions. In order not to be caught unawares, he must be capable of following the connections, the unexpected links, without however being submerged in the mass of relations and events. How can one perform framing when one has to be attentive to all this overflowing? How is it possible to become *homo clausus* when survival requires one to be *homo apertus*? This question is at the heart of the stock market and the speculative behaviour which it spawns. Nowhere is the tension between framing ad overflowing so intense and so difficult to control.

Measurement tools, designed to manage this tension, are necessarily highly singular because they must be capable of tracking down the incessant overflowing without leaving their frame. When what counts is having an all-embracing view of the network, monitoring all the relations and events, recording the movement of each point (for each point may count), the only suitable tool is a network analyser—one which provides a synthetic, summarized and framed image of the network. Hence chartism, that strange calculative practice, that proto-instrument so to speak which, starting with the aggregated curve which records prices, analyses its shape and attempts at revealing the hidden dynamic of the different individual decisions behind it. The tool is an analyser of form intended to establish an intelligible link between a framed price (and the decision stemming from it) and the set of countless connections and relations which have been framed.

We might be tempted to add that, from a Foucauldian perspective, this vast metrological accounting system, made of tools, calculation procedures and incorporated competencies, contributes to the 'disciplining', of behaviour and decisions.[22] Miller clearly shows—and his surpassing of Foucault warrants emphasis—that this disciplining is in no way mechanical, irreversible or irrevocable. It evolves and transforms itself since the tools, those solid points in the system, are themselves plastic, open, reconfigurable and, moreover, constantly reconfigured. As framing and calculating tools they have the property, through transforming themselves, of varying the modalities of framing and calculation. They are exchangers which stabilize certain procedures but simultaneously help them to evolve. To explain both the effects of 'disciplining' and the constant reconfiguring of these effects, there is no need to involve agents who defy the implacable logic of institutional devices and arrangements. Tools are at the heart of this dynamic and are responsible for formatting the calculating agencies. Due to their plasticity and their position as mediators they simultaneously allow this formatting to be reconfigured.

Stark (his contribution) takes another step forward by linking this accounting system to forms of justifying action: 'We are all bookkeepers and storytellers. We keep account and we give account, we can all be called to account for our action'. Not only do accounting tools contribute very largely to the performation of calculative agencies and modes of calculation, while allowing the constant reconfiguring of these agencies, they also contribute directly to the shaping of a discourse through which these agencies account for their action. A profit rate measures the result of the action calculated by a manager and when it is redefined it induces transformations of manager behaviour; it also provides the same manager with justification for his action vis-à-vis the shareholders.

Marketing, the history of which is recounted by Franck Cochoy in his contribution, has contributed powerfully to the setting up and deployment of the framing devices of calculative agencies. Take for example the concept of a marketing mix. As we know, this concept substitutes a quadruple reality—the fundamental 4Ps—for a product considered as an indivisible entity: a product is a Price, it is the object of a Promotion, it is a Place where it is available and, lastly, it is the target of a Product strategy. The product is therefore a multidimensional reality, an entanglement of properties that the marketing mix disentangles. The tool thus facilities a more detailed analysis of buying decisions, as well as the preferences which they express or reveal. The seller, instead of settling for a rough calculation, has an instrument which enables him, by varying each of the four dimensions, to distinguish in detail all the relations involved and to calculate each one independently. The framing of decisions proves to be greatly enhanced, as it is by the use of econometrics mobilized by marketing management. The latter makes it possible to construct sub-populations of consumers and to link them to certain characteristics of products. And, thanks to econometrics, the analytical work is thus amplified, which helps to identify the more and more complex and differentiated causal links. When the concept of social marketing is introduced, a new step in increasing of the power of framing is taken. Marketing tools become capable of absorbing the actors and decisions which formerly defied them: those of the non-profit sector or even, in certain cases, the social protest movements themselves. By enhancing the inventory of relations and events to be taken into account, marketing tools promote calculations which constantly involve more and more elements and relations.

The formulation of these instruments which substantially increase the ability of producers and sellers to frame and internalize consumers and their preferences, helps to disrupt even trading practices. Like accounting tools, marketing tools perform the economy. Cochoy describes the tireless work done by the founding fathers of marketing and how they painfully recorded and then transported, formatted and compiled the concealed knowledge of practitioners; he also describes how this knowledge, once formalized and generalized, has been returned to these same practitioners through teaching. Marketing as a set of tools and practices taken from practitioners and reconfigured by 'academic' marketing specialists, fell, after numerous transformations and generalizations, on the head of the practitioners. This is how the progressive standardization of marketing people and the simultaneous constitution of the discipline of marketing can be explained. The same movement also establishes practices, particularly material ones, which have an impact on the consumers themselves. The consumer who, to calculate her preferences, distinguishes the four different dimensions behind the unity of a product (price, position, etc.), is the consequence of the marketing mix rather than the cause. Similarly, social marketing, by extending the spaces of calculability, contributes powerfully to the emergence of calculative agencies where they are least expected, ie in those areas where profit had till then been prohibited.

Is it not excessive to refer to economic theory when discussing the role of accounting tools or marketing management in the performation of calculative agencies? Obviously not. These instruments are mediators between economics and economy. Not only are they responsible for the cross-relations between the two but, like any mediator, they actively promote the construction and constitution of each of them (on mediation see: Hennion, 1993). Without mediators like accounting tools and marketing management it would be impossible to distinguish between economics and an economy, just as it would be impossible to explain their interdependency. Moreover, the history of accounting tools features some of the greatest economists. They launch into battle dialoguing with practitioners, debating on the best way to determine and measure costs and at other times to define the calculative agent—a radical innovation—as a 'decision-making' agent. But accounting and marketing do not content themselves merely with providing economics and economists with access to the economy. They feed back to economics for, as Miller and Cochoy note, through all their collecting, comparing, generalising and integrating, these humble practitioners, simultaneously involved in several worlds and institutions, end up compiling an entire body of knowledge. Although hybrid, this knowledge is both original and very general. It is thus able to influence existing academic disciplines by mixing and combining them. By following this complicated history, we witness the birth and development of a *homo economicus* whose characteristics evolve and become increasingly complex. S/he inhabits two worlds simultaneously: that of economics (including, amongst others, disciplines and practices like accounting or marketing) with its manuals, and that of the economy with its organizations—two worlds which are stakeholders in one and the same adventure.

Among those mediators which bind economics to economy while constituting each as an independent entity, law, together with accounting metrology and marketing management, is well situated. Of course it provides a powerful tool for framing, or more precisely for enacting, calculative agencies[23] but what we wish to emphasize here is that it is an essential link, an irreplaceable coupling device between theoretical work and economic practices, for it organizes real experiments. The contribution by Hervé Dumez and Alain Jeunemaître provides convincing evidence. It shows that we can directly transpose onto social science in general and economics in particular the main results of the anthropology of science and techniques (AST) which has hitherto been concentrated primarily on the natural and life sciences. The cement industry is to competition theory what the drosophila is to genetic theory: a model which, owing to its crystal-clear simplicity, enables economists to ask some fundamental questions and to evaluate the different possible solutions. As a true laboratory the cement industry has, over several decades, provided the material for testing a whole series of arguments on the effects of certain forms of pricing (such as the basing point system) or organization (such as vertical integration). On each of these points heated controversies have developed, involving eminent economists, professional syndicates, public administrations (FTC) and businessmen in complicated alliances. The by-products of these controversies have been numerous and diverse, for instance outstanding academic articles (eg, by J.M. Clark—who was involved in the debate on accounting techniques and on the notion of workable competition), administrative regulations and pricing systems. Some concepts in the controversy, such as that of market closure, when put to the test were shown to lack robustness and were rapidly rejected because unable to mobilize allies and satisfactory proof. Remarkably, throughout this history real experiments were organized: hypotheses have been put forward, measures—in all senses of the word—have been taken, and results have been evaluated. As in all experiments, the temporal dimension which leaves mechanisms the time to settle, has been essential. But these experiments have the peculiarity of taking place on a large scale, involving numerous actors while not being confined to a laboratory or research center. The numerous characteristics of this experimentation include the following:

– as AST came to admit for the natural sciences, there is no reason to imagine an end to these debates and controversies; no theory or concept can provide a final solution, simply because economic activities constantly spawn new problems, creating new overflowing. The frames which are conceived and enforced (for example the basing price system) to enable agents to calculate, are overflowed by new transport techniques which require new reflection and new solutions to restore calculability.

– experimentation closely links economics as a discipline and the economy as a thing. It would thus be meaningless to distinguish between an existing reality (economy) and the analytical discourse explaining it. Social science is no more outside the reality it studies than are the natural and life sciences. Like natural science, it actively participates in shaping the thing it describes. The cement industry provides a striking example. The agents engaged in the sector are not the only ones to play a role in its evolution. Above all, their strategies are not of their own making since these depend largely on the work of economists and civil servants who intervene directly in the debates and the choice of procedures and regulations. The cement market is more like an unfinished building, an eternal work site which keeps changing and of which the plans and construction mobilize a multitude of actors participating in the development, by trial and error, of analytical tools, of rules of the game, of forms of organization and pricing principles. It would be wrong to distinguish in this overall construction—the practice of its own theory and the theory of its own practice— between the thing and the theory of the thing. This can be summed up in the following noteworthy phrase: economy is embedded not in society but in economics, provided one incorporates within economics all the knowledge and practices, so often denigrated, that make up for example accounting or marketing. Gao illustrates this very well with the famous Japanese model which, he shows, owes more to Schumpeter than to a hypothetical national tradition whose authenticity is constantly re-evaluated by the actors. We see why we have to be wary of the catch-all that socio-economics likes to use as a rallying cry: the market is socially constructed. What is under construction is precisely this heterogeneous collective, populated by calculating agencies. Society is not a starting point, a resource or a frame; it is, along with the market, the temporary outcome of a process in which social sciences—economics in this case—are the stakeholder.

– the knowledge produced by these experiments, the elements of economic theory formulated by the different protagonists, are not the fruit of efforts to abstract and theorize by specialists in the calm of their cabinets. They are collective achievements in which non-specialists (businessmen, civil servants, etc.) play an essential role. Thus, the social field in which economic theory is produced resembles the hybrid forums Callon refers to in his chapter, hybrid forums in which non-experts actively participate in debates, tests and attempts at interpretation—in short, in experimentation and collective learning.[24]

This performance of the calculative agencies—ie, of the economy by economics—is largely carried out through the intervention of professional economists. The study of the strategies developed by this profession is thus indispensable for an understanding of the variety of mediations through which this gigantic enterprise of formatting takes place. Unfortunately very few studies exist on the subject.

The classical study by McCloskey on the rhetoric of economics is nevertheless worth mentioning, although its definition of rhetoric remains so classical that it is obviously limited (McCloskey, 1985, 1990). As the sociology of science has shown, we cannot detach rhetoric, its forms and effects, from the controversies, theoretical or political, in which the protagonists are engaged. Dumez and Jeunemaître illustrate this point so well. For an economist, convincing a colleague during a conference organized by a scientific association is a Pyrrhic victory if he can not convince an FTC commission or a court. Rhetoric, defined as the art of building alliances to establish a favourable balance of power whether in science or politics, cannot be reduced to an excess of mathematization or generalizing abstraction intended to terrorize the opponent. Mathematics has never terrorized anyone but those who have let themselves be terrorized by it! On the other hand, the infinitely more classical and simple rhetoric of Fetter in his struggle against the basing price system, is formidably effective. He denounces his opponents by accusing them of being bought off by the cement producers, and therefore of blindly defending their interests. At the same time he presents himself as a 'mere theorist' out only to defend the general interest: 'my interest in this or any other subject of this kind is imply the same as any citizen would have'. There is no need for equations or abstract concepts to reduce the opponent to silence; one need only manipulate interests, promote collusion and become the spokesperson of the general will. What good, true rhetoric it is, that becomes fully meaningful and significant only when attached to the debates and controversies in which the actors—in this case the economists with their arguments and counter-arguments, their theories and counter-theories—are involved.

In the construction of trials of strength which enable certain arguments and tools and, thus, certain ways of framing calculative agencies to triumph—and consequently economics to perform the economy, the dissemination of students trained in economics is of prime importance. These actors become the partners and intermediaries enabling economic theory to dialogue with practitioners and thus to shape them (Fligstein emphasizes, for example, the role of former economics students in business (Fligstein, 1990)).

More generally, the strength of economics derives largely from its heterogeneity and the fact that it is constantly the scene of conflict and internal debate. There is probably not a single theoretical argument defended by any economist, which has not been severely

31

criticized by another economist. This internal diversity endows economics with an amazing ability to respond, adjust and react (Lebaron, 1997). This ability seems even greater when we remember that the economists' profession constitutes a whole spectrum from the 'purest' theoreticians to the specialists closest to the business world. Everything is set up so that these incessant movements through which economics and the economy inform and perform each other might be produced.

Economization

In our initial definition of the market, we indicated the prime importance of the existence and hence the formatting of calculative agencies. Without them no market transactions are possible. But, as we have seen, the market, although it needs calculative agencies, is also characterized by multiple forms of organization. Several types of organized market exist, depending in particular on the nature of the calculations of the calculative agencies. There are countless ways of calculating and we have already noted the diversity of their modalities, explicable to a large extent by the tools used and the frames created. A market in which the agencies are, for example, reluctant to introduce time equivalence, to consider products as homogeneous entities and to exclude from their calculation the possibility of vertical integration, is profoundly different from a market in which all these operations are technically possible. Another important variable is the number and the distribution of calculative agencies.

Finally, the market is a process in which the calculative agencies compete and/or co-operate with one another. This simply means that once framed, each agency is able to integrate the already framed calculations of the other agencies into its own calculations. It is these cross-related calculations that contribute to defining the market as a dynamic process.

The examination of these two dimensions (the organization and the process) alone warrants far more attention. I shall however confine myself here to a few considerations intended solely to clarify the subject of this book. First, I shall consider the question of the extension of the market, examining in turn the problem of the merchandization of goods and of state-market relations. Secondly, I shall consider competition as a confrontation between agencies endowed with calculating tools of differing levels of efficiency.

Extension of the market

Modernity is considered by some to be the twofold rise in importance of technosciences and the market. The fall of the Berlin Wall, the striking growth of the NICs and the rising pre-eminence of finance markets, in short, what is generally called globalization, seem to provide unquestionable proof of this inoxerable destiny. According to these commentators, and contrary to what Polanyi argued in *The Great Transformation*, the global market society is marching on. Archaic cultures and traditional societies are disappearing in the face of the unavoidable ascendancy of the modern world.

This extreme view does of course have its detractors who deny the very existence of such globalization (Fligstein, forthcoming), (Callon and Cohendet, 1997) and emphasize the composite, heterogeneous nature of the economies being established and becoming more closely linked to one another (Appadurai, 1996).

Beyond this debate, and even before proposing elements of an answer to the questions underlying it, it may be useful to revert to what must be the anthropological starting point of this reflection: how, if at all, does the proliferation and dissemination of calculative agencies work? In other words, is it feasible to conceive of a disentangling process which, through being deepened and generalized, ends up creating this community of strangers and strangers only, the sociological possibility of which Polyani vehemently denied?

To reply theoretically to this theoretical question, it is best to start with examples. The contribution by Viviana Zelizer provides the most striking and definitive one. We are all familiar with the attacks by Marx and Simmel against money and their denunciation of its destructive and alienating power. Marx saw money as the fetish *par excellence* of the modern world; one that concealed the reality of relationships between the people that lay behind relationships between things. In his famous text on the philosophy of money, Simmel took over where he had left off. Money dissolves social ties, founds a society based on pure rationality and kills personal relationships; responsible for the foreignness between agents, it seals the triumph of *gesellschaft* over *gemeinschaft*. The depersonalizing power of money seems even stronger and more implacable with the constant struggle, since the beginning of the century, of public authorities to oust private and false currencies and to guarantee the universality of an official one. This struggle seems easily won. Money is one of the goods without any usage value since its main function is to provide equivalence. Does this simple property, which enables it to circulate without being set anywhere and to be indefinitely substitutable, not make disentanglement easier?

Disentangling a service relation, the realization of which frequently requires the effective co-presence of the supplier and the consumer, is obviously a brain-teaser. The interpersonal links, the attachment, are so to speak inscribed in the service relation, so that the framing is costly, necessitating very specific equipment. On the other hand framing money, that is to say disentangling it, seems to require little effort since money is by construction already framed: cold, circulating, constantly changing hands, going from account to account. Yet for a long time anthropologists have tried to show that this is not so. Money, contrary to widespread belief, is constantly diverted and thus re-entangled. For example, French money in New Caledonia may be treated in exactly the same way as the shells used in ritual exchange (Bensa and Freyss, 1994); or the monetary debts between bikers can be seen as the basis of highly complex personal relations (Portet, 1994). In the nineteenth century in the Landes in France, the various currencies in circulation were so similar that the craftsman who produced his own coins was not really considered in the village to be a forger (Traimond, 1994). Currencies are continually being reinvented at a local, private level. But the true demonstration of the impossible disentanglement of money is given by Zelizer who raises the only question that counts: can one give a gift in money? Or put another way: can one organize overflowing and multiply ties with money, that epitome of framing and forcing out? The answer is yes, and Zelizer multiplies the examples showing the generality and universality of this reply.

At the center of the constantly renewed, never failing resistance of money to disentanglement, lies a crucial practice: that of ear-marking. This capital concept provides us with the key to understanding entanglement.

Money, whatever its degree of abstraction and dematerialization, by the mere fact that it circulates and that its circulation is calculated by agencies engaged in transactions, leaves traces: those of its successive attachments, the points through which it passed, the agents in whose hands it landed at a given moment, only to move on again. When the money is a material object—a bank note, metal coin or shell—these traces merge with the different positions occupied by the object itself as it circulates from hand to hand—positions which describe a trajectory a little like tracer bullets used by soldiers in training. When it is plastic money, these traces are attached like a wake to the card in the form of receipts, bank records, and so on. Finally, when it is reduced to transactions and operations directly between two bank accounts, these traces are recorded on long listings—inscribed in ink or in the silicon chip—which provide the identities of the beneficiaries and issuers next to the amounts involved. Money has no use value, but it is a trail, a wake, a visible, materializable, traceable trajectory.

This means that money, as an operator of equivalence, cannot be dissociated from its trajectory or at least from a part of it; in other words, from its spaces of circulation.[25] If the trajectory were not legible, money would lose its quality as money. Total disorder would settle in since, being able to identify neither issuers nor receivers, agencies would be unable to do accounts, make transfers, impute profits and losses, and so on. It is precisely because money can not exist as a currency without the inscriptions telling us who used it, and when, that makes entanglement not only possible but even probable. Earmarking denotes all the practices through which agents particularize these inscriptions, by fixing trajectories, assigning movements, and simultaneously embedding money in a specific space of circulation, ie, by attaching it to certain issuers and beneficiaries.

In its most simple form earmarking consists of overloading bank notes, which in themselves are already saturated with inscriptions describing their official attachments, with new, private, messages. This practice, the object of interesting analyses,[26] is facilitated by the fact that the bank note is an excellent medium for the exercise of rewriting. Zelizer goes beyond these known practices and shows the variety, multiplicity and, in fact, universality of these strategies of re-inscription or earmarking which characterize trajectories and privatize money. For open lists of positions—which means that money is attached to none of them since it can occupy them all—earmarking substitutes closed, bounded lists which force it to pass through certain points. Earmarking is deployed as much in the domestic sphere, with silver coins which a grandmother gifts to her grandchildren to put in their piggybanks in memory of her, as in systems of mass distribution, with vouchers, fidelity or credit cards and other such devices. Zelizer's conclusion is altogether logical when she exposes the misinterpretation popularized by Marx and Simmel. What she shows without difficulty is that advanced societies proliferate earmarking and differentiation: 'To the extent that it (money) does become more prominent in social life, people will segregate, differentiate, label, decorate, and particularize it to meet their complex social needs'. The fact that there are goods which are widely available without any particular attachments opens paradoxically the possibility of an endless process of earmarking.

We note in passing that in certain cases the process follows the inverse path consisting of departicularizing a currency entangled in its networks of circulation and bearing the marks of the attachments binding it. This is what happens with the laundering of money earned through illegal activities such as those developed by Mafia networks. This laundering, as the word suggests, consists of erasing all traces so as to make the reconstitution of singular trajectories impossible. It is, however, as difficult for a financier to launder money as it was for Lady Macbeth to remove the spot of blood which incriminated her in the murder she committed; it requires specialized know-how and heavy investments, particularly in coding. The laundering, that is to say the disentanglement, of money is never complete because it remains possible to reconstitute lists even if they have errors or are incomplete. The affair of gold deposited by Jews in Swiss banks proves that when ordered to do so, it is possible to find the origin of the deposits and to publish the list (even if riddled with mistakes) of depositors.

The fact that the possibility or even the necessity of its entanglement is built into money, and that real money is consequently a variable compromise between entanglement and disentanglement, leads us to predict that the same process can, *a fortiori*, be observed for any other good.

A demonstration would be easy, given the number of studies supporting this argument. The case of organs is interesting because it is symmetrical to that of money. How is it possible to circulate a liver, a kidney or a heart, between a donor—generally dead—and a recipient—generally in danger of death—when the organ is entangled in the body of a potential donor and through him in his family or circle of friends? The transfer of the organ is a forcing out in the true sense of the term; its success depends on that of disentanglement. The difficulty of this disentanglement explains why the transfer is most often in the form of a gift which, as we have seen, reconciles circulation and entanglement. However, in some countries we witness what Fox calls a process of 'degifting', that is to say, a concerted and systematic attempt to disentangle organs so as to transform them into something which makes them more like goods than gifts (Fox and Swazey, 1992). It is at this cost—that of a successful forcing out—that a true organ market becomes possible, even if this market does not necessarily mean the formulation of prices. But how can an organ be definitively disentangled? The question is interesting because it is symmetrical to that proposed in respect of money: how does one entangle money?

Hoyle provides valuable elements of an answer (Hoyle, 1994). Faced with the increasing demand for transplants, an attempt is made to organize a market in which the organs that circulate are not only of high quality but may also be used by any recipient (barring immunological incompatibility). In short, the organ has to be transformed into a good free of all attachments. The procedure to frame the organ and thus disentangle it, requires the constitution of a file on the donor. For this purpose a standardized form is filled out, where all relevant information is noted (circumstances of death, medical history, family context). A file is thus constituted in relation to the organ for the purpose of transforming it into a half-good. This file reviews the relations in which the organ was entangled before the death of the potential donor. It is, however, in this file intended for disentanglement and through it, that the forces of re-entanglement—and this is the paradox—are freed and exhibited. The co-ordinators responsible for the file, for framing the organ by listing all the relations that have to be taken into account in the decision to transplant, are required in carrying out their work to interact with the donor's friends and family. They may also have to interact with the medical providers who cared of the donor during the last minutes of her life. They will thus gradually build up a 'narrative' which will enrich and complicate the form, adding new layers of interpretation, transforming into a thick description what should only have been a cold statement. Because nothing eludes the investigation—a human life is a ball of entangled threads: drugs, alcoholism, sexuality, which are difficult to unravel—the co-ordinators end up becoming tangled in the biography of the donor. The lesson is clear: the more investments increase to disentangle the organ and frame it by listing the relations that attach it to the donor—the better to detach it—the more the ties proliferate and multiply. This dynamic is in no way abstract, it is inscribed in the heart of the framing process and is its obvious outcome. Here, as in the case of money, it is spawned by a long process of inscriptions and re-inscriptions.

These two symmetrical examples amply serve our demonstration.[27] They suggest the following conclusion: the disentanglement which in its material realization implies the establishment of lists of positions and relations that, once established, allow calculation, opens the way to entanglement. This generalizes the argument defended by Callon in this book: framing requires the mobilization of entities, while their irreducible autonomy is a source of new overflowing.

Zelizer helps us to evaluate the inappropriateness of the reasoning usually employed to demonstrate the impossible generalization of the market. It is not traditional society which resists the market; it is not values which serve as a bastion to the infinite extension of calculation; it is not the necessary development of relations of trust at the heart of the market which sets the limits of the market. The mechanics are both simpler and more fundamental. Any framing produces overflowing, and any procedure of disentanglement produces new attachments. It is one and the same movement which causes calculative agencies to proliferate, while reinscribing them into spaces of non-calculability. The fact that these spaces—of calculability and of non-calculability—are organized in impervious spheres as in the political philosophy proposed by Michael Walzer, is neither necessary nor evident (Walzer, 1983). The economy is not a universe whose expansion is contained by other universes.

The idea that there exist orders of reality, social spaces organized according to incommensurable and antagonistic logics, is amusingly illustrated by Maupassant in a short story called *Le condamné à mort* (de Maupassant, 1987). Having sentenced a man to death, the Monacan state, possessing neither an executioner nor a guillotine, turned to the French state to sub-contract the execution. However, the Monacan authorities shrank back at the price: 'Sixteen thousand francs for a rascal! Oh no', and decided not to execute the sentence but rather to commute it to life imprisonment. But the cost of constructing the prison and maintaining the prisoner again seemed exorbitant. The state therefore offered the prisoner 'freedom' on the condition he be exiled. The prisoner, guessing the strength of his position, refused. 'So it was decided to offer the prisoner a rent of six hundred francs to go and live abroad. He accepted'. Since each party's interests were served in the compromise, all was well that ended well. Maupassant showed, through the absurd and the comical, that the order of the courts cannot rely on market calculation. He thus anticipated Walzer thesis and, indeed, of all those who maintain that the social link cannot be reduced to the market, that society is made of spheres or institutions, and that each one serves as a bastion against the expansion of the others. However charming the short story may be, it comes up against the same difficulty as the explanation proposed by Walzer. How can the existence of the separated areas of non-calculatability be explained? The hypothesis of independent spheres or that of 'incompatible' logics (DiMaggio, 1994) leaves the question of the emergence and formatting of non-calculative or calculative agencies untouched.[28] This is reassuring but explains nothing and ends up, moreover, causing concern: what institutional barriers are strong enough to contain the forces of a market which, although enclosed in its own sphere, is supposed to exist in its purest form? Won't the Monacan state (followed by many others) finish by choosing the market contract as the most convenient solution?

This concern disappears when we agree that the opposing forces are created in the same movement and that they are disseminated, that all framing creates overflowing, and that all disentanglement provides the opportunity for new entanglement. To understand the differentiation there is no need to explain it by the spheres or logics which mutually limit its expansion. Differentiation is spawned by a single recurring process. Simmel, in his own way, saw that irreducible ambivalence: 'Innumerable times (competition) achieves what usually only love can do: the divination of the innermost wishes of the other, even before he himself becomes aware of them,' (Simmel, {1908}, 1955).

The anthropological solution proposed, which has the advantage of being extremely simple, also allows us easily to account for an observation repeated so often: there is no Great Divide between societies populated by calculative agencies and societies in which the agents do not calculate. Even Deleuze and Guattari were on the wrong track with their concept of deterritorialization, that extraordinary faculty bestowed on capitalism for breaking all ties and undoing solidarity (Deleuze and Guattari, 1972). So-called traditional societies are populated—sometimes even over-populated—with calculative agencies. Thomas' entire book consists of a long and detailed demonstration of the impossibility, in Melanesian societies, of separating a gift economy and a market economy since the two are entangled right to the heart of the Kula. Strathern, with her analysis of so-called compensation mechanisms in highlander societies in New Guinea, reaches exactly the same conclusions: the highlanders spend their time calculating and establishing equivalences (Strathern, forthcoming). This explains their amazing faculty for understanding the theme of biodiversity and for taking part in scholastic debates on Intellectual Property Rights. When collecting rare species in New Guinea, multinationals encounter peoples who are more used than they are to framing, calculating and playing on the formal abstraction of property rights. These are conceived, and

Strathern stresses this point, not in the traditional perspective of Roman law (which implies that thing is physically shared between its different owners) but from a viewpoint of common law which associates, in an abstract way, a thing with a bundle of rights that can easily be distributed between several agents, making easier sophisticated calculations.

As for so-called modern societies, they are endowed with as many non-calculative agencies as calculative ones. This inextricable mixture can be found where we least expect it: at the very heart of financial institutions.[29] Abolafia shows us traders obsessed by networking, multiplying entanglements to put themselves in a position to calculate. Moreover, in our modern societies technosciences add their peculiar capacity for amplification, to the general movement in which entanglement arises from disentanglement. As Callon recalls in his chapter, technosciences multiply unexpected connections and overflowing, constantly making the work of reframing more necessary, more difficult, more expensive and more uncertain. Like Sisyphus in his futile attempt to push a boulder to the top of a hill, they continuously find themselves back at square one. Finance and technoscience form an alliance to open the way to the forces of entanglement.

The advantage of this anthropology of entanglement is that it frees us from the irritating and sterile distinctions between state and market, or between global economy and national economies.

How can relations between these two entities, the state and the market, politics and economics, be described? Block suggests the distinction between two paradigms (Block, 1994). In the first one the state and the market are considered to be two analytically separable realities, placed at the two ends of a continuum. A particular form of economy can be defined as mixed, a combination of two pure types. This paradigm has, to a large extent, proved to lack realism both historically and theoretically. The state does not intervene in the market; according to the second paradigm it participates—and its role is always essential—in the constitution of the economy. A way of showing this is to provide a list, obviously partial and purely indicative, of these constituent activities: rules governing the use of productive assets, legal frameworks governing recurring relations such as those between employers and employees, means of payment, managing the boundary with the rest of the world. It is easy to verify that each of these activities contributes directly to the framing of calculative agencies. They do not organize the actions and economic behaviours which already exist, outside of state action; they format these actions. Could we say that the waffle exists independently of the waffle-iron? Of course not. Similarly, we cannot say of an organized market activity that it exists without the state. The true question concerning the state is this: how and with what methods and efficiency does it contribute to the performation of calculative agencies and the organization of their relations? This simple question shows the existence of a wide range of possible contributions; a range which is as wide as that of forms of market organization. Before rushing for definitive classifications,[30] it seems wiser and more fruitful to make detailed individual case studies of observable configurations (Dobbin, 1994). The reconstruction in East European countries and China constitute, from this point of view, valuable laboratories and experiments from which Stark draws some conclusions. That the term transitional economy could be used in their case shows the weight of the old paradigm, and the extent to which market mechanisms are misunderstood, even among economists. There is nothing of a transition in the developments observed nor in their diversity which mark an extreme contrast between countries such as Poland, Hungary, Bulgaria or China (Nee, 1996). In each case reconfigurations, recombinations and rearrangements are at play and mix material peculiar to the history of each country. In these rearrangements the state often plays a crucial part and the dynamics in place impact, in turn, on its own position and contribution to the economy. Stark clearly shows that these recombinations have the effect of remodelling the calculative agencies and their relations. Based on a study of the process of redistribution of property rights and its networking effects, and after a detailed statistical analysis, he easily shows that the resulting type of organization, which he aptly calls recombinant property, is built on a threefold process of blurring: blurring of public and private, blurring of firms' boundaries, and blurring of the boundedness of legitimation principles. The mixed Hungarian economy, that of the second half of the 1990s, which recombines and blurs, certainly has a limited lifespan. This is a transitory economy, mixed like any economy, but not a transitional one. It corresponds to a stage on a singular trajectory; it was shaped by framings, related to state action in particular, which produce a unique situation in which losses are socialized and profits privatized.

That the state constitutes, rather than intervenes in, the economy, leads us to relativize the thesis of globalization which is, moreover, a subject of heated debate among economists. Fligstein shows convincingly that this worldwide extension of the market may simply be interpreted as the growing domination of a form of organized market, that of the United States, over other forms of organization (Fligstein, 1996). The organized American market favours the conception that the only people who have the right to inspect the activities of a firm are the shareholders, and the only preoccupation of firms must be to maximize the shareholder-value. That this form of domination is only partial and is constantly opposed, is a direct result of what has just been said on the constituent role of the state in economic life. The phenomena of path dependency recalled by Stark are so strong that there is no reason for the States of the dominated economies to align themselves with the role of the American state in the American economy. But other factors explain the existence of limits to any domination of any form of organization, whatever may be. The analysis of the Japanese economy by Gao shows this. A particular form of organized market (which obviously includes the public policies contributing to its constitution), although well-suited to solving certain problems and supporting certain forms of calculated action, may prove to be particularly ineffective when the circumstances change. The American model is efficient when situations are unstable, owing notably to the sophistication of financial techniques and the quick short-term calculations they allow. But when the significance (scope) of change increases and the actions to be undertaken have a more long-term perspective, other types of market and other calculating tools may be required.

Competition

The organized market cannot be reduced to a mere system of trade and transaction. It is also, above all, a process in which agents who design and produce goods enter into competition to capture a demand which they help to (re)define.

Max Weber is certainly among those who has grasped this agonistic dimension of the market most fully:

> A market may be said to exist wherever there is a competition even if only unilateral, for opportunities of exchange among a plurality of potential parties. Their physical assemblage in one place, as in the local market square, the fair (the 'long distance' market) or the exchange (the merchant's market), only constitutes the most constant kind of market formation. It is, however, only this physical assemblage which allows the full emergence of the

market's most distinctive feature, viz, dickering (Weber, {1922} 1978 quoted in: Swedberg, 1994).

This definition is reflected in our theory of the formatting of calculative agencies, and in the significance granted by it to material and metrological equipment. It has, moreover, the merit of recalling that the market is a pacific arena in which agents enter into competition with one another to secure positions of monopoly and domination. This tradition in which the market is a competitive process and device has obviously been developed by the neo-Austrian school and is illustrated in the work of authors such as Chamberlin, Schumpeter and Galbraith. Let me not be misunderstood. It is not enough to talk of imperfect competition to do justice to this dimension of the market. We have to go—as Chamberlin, among others, dared to—so far as to agree to consider that one of the weapons of competition, in fact its main weapon, is precisely for an economic agent to refuse disentanglement—that process which frees actors and produces agencies free of commitments—so that it can, by contrast, produce entanglement. Any self-respecting economic agent reweaves again during the night the framework undone by the market during the day.

Chamberlin put it marvellously in his definition of imperfect competition: 'It is to be recognized that the whole is not a single market, but a network of related markets, one for each seller' (Chamberlin, 1933, p.69). Schumpeter repeats the same lesson when he defines the entrepreneur—in a perspective similar to that of social networks—as the one who unexpectedly connects two hitherto unrelated populations of agents: on the one hand the engineers or researchers who work on the design and creation of new goods and, on the other, the customers and consumers who express a demand related to these goods.

This enables us to surpass Weber's indications, without rejecting them. The market is not a two-step process with a competition phase followed by an exchange phase. The type of representation puts the creation process of products and demand for these products in parenthesis, a process which we know involves a web of close connections between designers, producers, distributors and consumers. Preparing the final transaction, that is to say, capturing a customer and engaging her in an exchange from which each party leaves as a stranger involves—and this is obviously one of the paradoxes that has to be noted—a long process of networking.

It is to the understanding of this counter-intuitive mechanism (in order to prepare the market relationship, it is first necessary to relate, connect and associate) that Patrick McGuire and Mark Granovetter's chapter provides a powerful contribution. Their aim is to follow the early evolution of the electricity industry. Each decision on which the structure of the fledgling market will depend, the content of the goods offered and the modalities of competition are all analysed simply in terms of connections and networking. Whether it concerns the choice between central stations and isolated systems, between AC and DC or between 25 and 60 cycles, the same logic is always present, that of existing networks into which the industry fits and which, in turn, it rearranges. The agents who manage to occupy key positions draw the boundaries of competition, eliminate competitors, select technologies and thus capture the demand. We witness the creation of what ANT (Actor-Network Theory) called a socio-technical network which, by dint of exclusion, managed to organize highly regulated competition allowing a few agents to derive sustainable profits. In this struggle—in which the structure of the industry, the forms of competition and the technologies were shaped simultaneously—anything goes when it comes to strengthening ties: creation of professional associations, enrolment of the trade press, leadership of occupational or professional clubs, corporate welfare and employee clubs, lobbying the public authorities and even—ANT prepared us for this—the constitution of a collective laboratory which imposes technical standards for the production of lamps. We cannot show more clearly that the very nature of competition is to rarefy competition. One can refer here to the work of Burt ('the substantive richness of competition lies in its imperfection') and the subtle analysis of firms niche strategies by White (White, 1981, 1988). Defining imperfect competition by comparing it to a model of perfect competition (as for example in neoclassical theory), is totally justifiable when we view economics as a device intended to perform the economy, that is to say, to establish calculative agencies detached from one another. However, this position is misleading when our aim is to construct an anthropology of the markets. What McGuire and Granovetter show, in the case of electricity although there is no reason not to believe in the generality of the statement, is that perfect or imperfect competition—defined as a situation in which 'a set of firms produce the same or related products'—can emerge only in a highly structured industry. The more or less imperfect competition prevailing in organized markets is a latecomer in a long-lasting process. Competition, whether perfect or imperfect, is not a starting point but a finishing point. It can exist and really does exist—and that is what makes it so valuable. However, it occurs only when the boundaries, the technical options, have been selected and stabilized, ie in a world that is already highly structured and shaped. Now—and this is where McGuire and Granovetter are so important—this structuring is the last step in a long process dominated from the beginning to the end by rivalry between calculative agencies.

How are the dynamics of this rivalry to be described? Why are certain calculative agencies able to impose the events, actions and relations that other calculative agencies have to take into account in making their decision? One answer is that the power and modalities of calculation are not equally distributed among all the agencies: there is no reason why the metrological instruments and equipment available to each one should be identical. The calculative power of an agency depends on that of its calculating tools. These are characterized above all by the number and variety of relations and agents which they are able to take into account.[31] We showed this for accounting tools and marketing management: a tool which breaks down the unity of the product, which integrates the preferences of diverse sub-populations of consumers, and which takes into account the quality of the service provided, the volume of stocks and the changes of opinion in favour of or against a particular controversial technology, is more likely to result in successful actions. The more an agency is able to complicate and broaden the network of entities and relations to be taken into account, the greater is its capacity to create asymmetries between itself and other agencies. Competition between calculative agencies, focused on their ability to have their decisions recognized and accepted (for example to propose a given product on a given market segment), is largely determined by the respective qualities of the calculating devices. The probability of gain is on the side of the agency with the greatest powers of calculation, that is to say, whose tools enable it to perform, to make visible and to take into account the greatest number of relations and entities.

The struggle between two agencies is therefore rarely equal; it is reminiscent of the match between Kasparov and the IBM Deeper Blue. Calculative agencies engage in power struggles which are measured by the tools with which they are equipped. In certain cases these power struggles may lead to a situation of dependency. The most obvious form of this dependency corresponds to the 'parasiting' of one calculative agency by another which imposes (a part of) its calculation tools and rules, and consequently forces the host agency to engage in its own calculation. It is almost as if Kasparov—and this is not far from what happened—had to start calculating his moves not by playing like Kasparov but by imagining himself in the computer's position, that is to say, by borrowing from it its algorithms and calculation rules. The game would then no longer be between Kasparov, an autonomous and independent agency, a player in his own right formulating his own strategies, and the computer, also an independent and autonomous agent. It would be a game in which Kasparov was transformed into an appendix, a mere branch of the computer, as if the latter had delegated the execution of a part of its own calculation to the former. Engaging in one's opponent's game by entering into his calculating power means accepting dependency.

This type of situation is frequent in economy. Imposing the rules of the game, that is to say, the rules used to calculate decisions, by imposing the tools in which these rules are incorporated, is the starting point of relationships of domination which allow certain calculating agencies to decide on the location and distribution of surpluses. That is how the predominance of some forms of organization—for example the American form—is explained. The extension of a certain form of organized market, an extension which ensures the domination of agents who calculate according to the prevailing rules of that particular market, always corresponds to the imposition of certain calculating tools.

Market laws

As we reach the end of this long detour it is time to return to the original question.

By ridding ourselves of the cumbersome distinction between economics (as a discipline) and the economy (as a thing) and showing the role of the former in the formatting of markets, we find ourselves free from a positivist or, worse still, a constructivist conception of law. Market laws are neither in the nature of humans and societies—waiting for the scientist, like a prince charming, to wake and reveal them—nor are they constructions or artefacts invented by social sciences in an effort to improvise simple frameworks for explaining an opaque and complex reality. They account for regularities progressively enforced by the joint movement of the economy and economics, a movement that we have attempted to describe in this introduction. These regularities perform behaviours and therefore have the obduracy of the real; yet in turn they are performed by these behaviours and therefore have the contingency of an artefact.

These regularities, related to the stabilization of particular forms of organization of market relations, remain limited in time and space. It is therefore wrong to talk of laws or, worse still, of the law of the market. There exist only temporary, changing laws associated with specific markets.

The examples of the Hungarian and Japanese economies perfectly illustrate this point. Each of these economies is a particular historical and contingent—yet perfectly explicable—form of market organization. There is no other way of describing the Hungarian economy than that proposed by Stark: 'Parallel to the decentralized reorganization of assets . . . the centralized management of liabilities'. This arrangement shapes a network of assets and liabilities as well as a network of calculating agencies which develop hedging strategies.[32] These strategies in turn contribute to the emergence of regularities which, by allowing calculations and what economists would call expectations, lead to their own reinforcement. Not only are these regularities local and genuinely Hungarian, what is more, no general underlying or meta law—for example, a presumed optimizing behaviour of agents, whether Hungarian or Persian—can account for it. This is because the behaviour of the agents and their calculations are so embedded in the local reality that the mere transposition of financial tools imported without any other process leads straight to economic and political collapse. Gao confirms this absence of a founding, underlying law which, in its fine simplicity, would explain the diversity of forms and organizations. There exists no infrastructure which as a last resort might explain the social order. In the cosmos of the Japanese archipelago, in the space of a few decades, the laws governing the economy have changed completely. No simple explanation—and it is on this point that the demonstration revolves—can account for this phenomenon. The market laws of the first period, laws which themselves were local and historical, can at a pinch be considered as the driving forces behind the change, without however explaining the content of this change. The economic agents of the first period calculated their decisions, but in so doing they did not engender the market of the second period. We can see here the significance of the thesis of variability of forms of calculation and calculative agencies. It is not enough to have calculative agencies to explain a given evolution. The reason is simple: calculation can not take into account all the relations and actions since it exists only when framed, that is to say, closed off to overflowing which it tolerates and which acts obscurely, so contributing to the emergence of an unexpected reality. We cannot explain one form of market by another; however, what we do explain without anthropology is how we shift from a certain formatting of calculative agencies to another.

This point of view is at one with the old and sound intuition of anthropology supported by Sahlins among others (Sahlins, 1976) and recalled in this respect by Abolafia: rationality is always situated and the anthropologist strives to explore decision-making in natural settings. It is also akin to the classical analysis of Polanyi and his classification of economic institutions (reciprocity, redistribution, market). But beyond these (too) general classifications and *petitio principii*, the anthropology that we have proposed has the immense advantage of opening the field to empirical studies in order to reconstruct the diversity of formatting.

The recognition of the existence of local and transitory regularities is not unrelated to one of the mechanisms carefully studied by economic theory: that of lock-in and path dependency (David, 1984). Lock-in denotes all the mechanisms through which the evolution of a market or an institution becomes more and more irreversible. The choices and decisions made during the first period play a part in limiting the range of possible choices and decisions during the second period. Progressively the range of possible options narrows down, closes and locks, so that the agents have no alternative but to renew the choices made earlier. They are prisoners, trapped in networks from which they have neither the resources nor the desire to escape; they are submerged in the very structures they helped to set up. The role of technology in the construction of these interdependancies, these cases of lock-in, is capital. The simple decision to invest in a given technology sets off a dynamic of learning and accumulation which rapidly leads to unequal development. The chosen technology becomes increasingly attractive and profitable, not by virtue of its intrinsic qualities, but because substantial investments have been devoted to its improvement. This theory of lock-in has been the subject of an abundant literature, aimed in particular at accounting for the permanently open possibility of lock-out.

The notion of lock-in is rich but ambiguous; ambiguous because it takes as a reference the model of the flexibility of decisions and the openness of choices and scope of action. Lock-in is a deteriorated form of the market yet, as we have already mentioned, from an anthropological point of view the opposite is true. Organization of the market and the openness of choices vary inversely. McGuire and Granovetter show that the opening of options, particularly technical, is maximal at the outset when the market does not yet exist or, rather, is at its zero degree of organization. This opening, an outcome of the non-existence of the market, is situated not at the level of the agents but at the level of a virtual collective. Some agents opt for decentralized systems, others continue to fight for gas and yet others are keen on direct current, but each one sticks to his own course. To reconstitute the options as alternative ones, we need to imagine a social planner gathering all the relevant information and embarking on opportunity calculations. We thus get a glimpse of one of the possible reasons to justify planned economies: they are the only ones to make concurrent decisions comparable and calculable, at least on paper, when the options are still open. It is only when certain options have been eliminated and that the range of options has been drastically reduced, that the market is finally organized (firms are similarly structured, occupational categories are standardized and extra-organizational structures are created to manage competition and articulate common goals), and that individual agents can calculate the comparative merits of the options which remain open. Lock-in is not a deteriorated form of the market, it is its compulsory companion, a necessary symptom of it. However, the lock-in in question and the interdependancies it implies should not be likened to the abstract lock-in of North which reduces it to the mere institutional rigidification of initial game rules (North, 1990), or even to the more material lock-in of David who took into account the role of technology. It is deployed and unfolds in heterogeneous arrangements (which are solid because heterogeneous) where one finds, knit together—McGuire and Granovetter provide their quasi-exhaustive inventory—not only technology but also forms of organization and governance, relations between firms and public authorities, both local and national, associations and clubs, research centres, bribes, accommodating journalists, and so on.

It is thus under the condition of a double reversal that the notion of lock-in manifests its richness. Firstly lock-in is not the progressively deteriorated form of perfect flexibility; it is, on the contrary, the condition of a manageable flexibility which, if it exists, can only be limited. Secondly lock-in consists of a hetereogeneous arrangement which frames the calculative agencies against a background of visible interdependancies. It is thus as varied and multiple as the forms of market organization.

Once organized and hence locked-in, the market becomes calculable by the agents. Once the work of standardization (at least partial) of calculating tools is well on its way, each agency is in a position not only to calculate her decision but also, by construction, to include, at least partially, in her calculations the calculations of the other agencies. This integration, which is the material side of what we call anticipation, is far easier when, during the process of market organization, a calculative agency manages to impose directly her instruments and mode of calculation (here, the anticipation is perfectly rational because each agency makes the same calculations and follows the same procedures). In this case the calculated decisions produce the anticipated effects, aside from opportunistic behaviour, which is another way of saying that the market considered obeys certain laws which may be formulated in mathematical language. If mathematical economics can be realistic under certain conditions, it is not because human behaviour is naturally 'mathematizable''; it is because the calculative agencies are there to introduce interrelated calculations in decisions and in the formulation of actions.[33]

For an anthropology of markets

With this theory of the formatting of calculative agents we also avoid another difficulty, that of the impossible choice between the denunciation and the celebration of the market. This concerns social sciences to the highest degree. We have seen the positive and performative role of economics and its contribution to organizing markets. Sociology is implicated as well on the condition it avoids two pitfalls. The first corresponds to a strategy of enriching the economic theory of the agent. Economic sociology has rarely been able to resist this temptation. Underscoring the complexity of economic phenomena, a complexity to which economic theory with its cold and disincarnated view of *homo economicus* cannot do justice, sociology strives to give this abstract agent a bit more soul—the life and warmth he lacks—by mobilizing notions such as those of value, culture, rules or passions. Pareto dreamed it, economic sociology makes it. Yet, as we suggested, economic agents do not need be enriched. If they manage to become richer it is because, on the contrary, they were cooled, reduced and framed, particularly by economics! What we expect from sociology is not a more complex *homo economicus* but the comprehension of his simplicity and poverty.

The second pitfall for the sociology of markets is that of denunciation, which is not unrelated to the previous one. Let us heed Durkheim's warning:

> Political economy . . . is an abstract and deductive science which is occupied not so much with observing reality as with constructing a more or less durable ideal: because the man (sic) that the economists talk about, this systematic egoist, is little but an artificial man of reason. The man that we know, the real man, is so much more complex, he belongs to a time and a country, he lives somewhere, he has a family, a religious faith, and political ideas (Durkheim, {1988} 1970 quoted in: Smelser and Swedberg, 1994).

The fuel of this denunciation is again the acknowledgement of the impoverished and abstract character of *homo economicus*, that being of reason, severed of all ties. But this acknowledgement does not lead Durkheim to propose enriching economic theory. The sociologist denounces this reductionism in order to disqualify economic theory and propose replacing it by another theory, a sociology of real man, one taken in a bundle of links which constitute his sociality and hence his humanity. To paraphrase Galileo facing his judges, we could retort: *eppure calcolano!* (and yet they calculate!). This strategy is therefore no more convincing than that of enrichment. Both carefully avoid the only question worth posing: how can the emergence and formatting of calculative agencies be explained?

Whether we choose to enhance the economic theory of the agent or to denounce it, in both cases we formulate the same critique: *homo economicus* is pure fiction. This introduction as well as the entire book in fact, maintain the contrary. Yes, *homo economicus* really does exist. Of course, he exists in the form of many species and his lineage is multiple and ramified. But if he exists he is obviously not be found in a natural state—this expression has little meaning. He is formatted, framed and equipped with prostheses which help him in his calculations and which are, for the most part, produced by economics. Suddenly new horizons open up to anthropology. It is not a matter of giving a soul back to a dehumanized agent, nor of rejecting the very idea of his existence. The objective may be to explore the diversity of calculative agencies forms and distributions, and hence of organized markets. The market is no longer that cold, implacable and impersonal monster which imposes its laws and procedures while extending them ever further. It is a many-sided, diversified, evolving device which the social sciences as well as the actors themselves contribute to reconfigure.

Michel Callon

Notes

1 Specialists in the history of economic thinking point out, as an exception to this lack of interest, the two chapters by Marshall (Marshall, {1920} 1961) and Robinson (Robinson, {1974} 1979). Coase confirms this: economic theory is interested in the theory of market prices but 'discussion of the marketplace itself has entirely disappeared' (Coase, 1988). The sociology of the market has not received any more attention (the reader is nevertheless referred to: Baker, 1984; White, 1981; White, 1988.

2 It was certainly the French economist Cournot who was the first explicitly to formulate the (abstract) market: 'economists understand by the term market, not any particular marketplace in which things are brought and sold but the whole region in which buyers and sellers are in such free intercourse with one another that the prices of the same goods tend to equality easily and quickly' (Cournot, {1838} 1927). It was Mill who implicitly introduced the notion of supply and demand. J.-B. Say is credited with the formulation of the term 'the law of the market'.

3 The whole world may be looked upon as a vast general market made up of diverse special markets where social wealth is bought and sold.

4 This assumption is clearly made by Williamson in his discussion of the notion of trust: 'Calculativeness is the general condition that I associate with the economic approach and with the progressive extension of economics into the related social sciences' (Williamson, 1993). In order to emphasize the link with this notion of calculativeness I prefer to qualify agents as calculative rather as calculating.

5 Decentralization, among other things, is a form, itself multiple, of distribution.

6 This essential dimension is often overlooked. It is constantly present in economic or socio-economic theory. Weber stresses it at great length, summarizing his position in the striking, oft-cited phrase: the market is a 'battle of man against man: a peaceful conflict'. This view of the market as a process is obviously at the heart of the neo-Austrian conception (Menger, von Mises, von Hayek). Chamberlin, Schumpeter and later the Evolutionists are part of this tradition. White also emphasizes this point by showing that markets are the juxtaposition of niches that competition causes firms to construct.

7 This point is essential. In an excellent book commented on below (Thomas, N., 1991), Nicholas Thomas expresses it clearly in his comparative analysis of commercial transactions and gifts.

8 This definition of calculation is obviously compatible with what is commonly called rational action or formal (substantive) rationality. It is nevertheless more general, in so far as it defines, in a sense, the conditions in which rational action can emerge. It makes the emergence of calculation analysable rather than taken for granted.

9 H. Simon with his notion of bounded rationality is not entirely spared from this critique: he limits the agent's capacity for mental calculation rather than distributing it.

10 This sums up the revolution introduced in cognitive science by Hutchins (Hutchins, 1995).

11 Such situations of radical uncertainty, which should rather be called situations of ignorance, correspond to cases where the list of possible states of the world is unknown and where no probability can thus be assigned to their occurrence.

52

12 Without wanting to go into a critique of the content of this text, we would like to highlight one of its paradoxes. Since the (revisable) contract must retain the possibility of annulation (so as not to lose its quality of a contract) it is necessary to imagine a super contract, *ab initio*, which contains all the possible development of the contractual relationship. Renegotiation will imply not the rewriting of a new contract, but the application of the initial super-contract. The life of a contract thus retains its classical form of the execution of an established plan—a contradiction with the situation of radical uncertainty in which the contract is signed.

13 And if the solution opted for by the agent, rather than being that of successive renegotiations, was to accept the incomplete stage of the agreement, it would mean, without any ambiguity whatsoever, that s/he was engaging in a long-term interpersonal relationship.

14 'The human economy is embedded and enmeshed in institutions, economic and non-economic' (Polanyi, {1957} 1971).

15 This analysis enables us to requalify the actors who supply money: the Federal Reserve may at best share this ability with important private actors, the most dominant of which are financial institutions, albeit non bank ones.

16 For a sharp analysis of disinterestness see: Karpik, 1995.

17 It is the viewpoint argued by Levi-Strauss in his famous critique of Mauss whom he accuses of being misled by his native informant (Lévi-Strauss, 1960). The analysis of the mechanisms whereby the agent misleads himself is not unrelated to the old Kantian question of duty and the possibility of revealing a secret urge for self-esteem behind the greatest sacrifice, that which we believe we accomplish purely through duty whereas it is only accomplished in conformity with duty. Similarly, an act of generosity can always be analysed as conforming to generosity and at the same time denied as an authentic act of generosity. On this point see Bourdieu, (Bourdieu, 1997) p.303.

18 This solution is usually preferred by economists. It explains, according to Coleman, why in situations of extreme uncertainty it is rational for an agent to delegate his or her own will to a third party (the case of speculation) (Coleman, 1994).

19 In the case of the gift, as analysed by Bourdieu, the absence of framing of the counter-gift allows for the proliferation of entanglement from which the receiver can no longer extricate him/herself: 'The obligation which starts at the moment when the initial act of generosity is accomplished and which can only increase as the recognition of this debt, always liable to be settled, turns into incorporated recognition, into the inscription in bodies—in the form of passion, submission or respect—, of an insolvable debt said to be eternal' (Bourdieu, 1997). In other words, without framing, ie without a minimum of disentanglement, the ties gradually become irreversible insofar as they become incorporated. Instead of two distinct agents we have two agents bound together eternally.

20 In this respect the case of labour laws is illuminating. The respective rights of employers and employees are constantly reconfigured, thus extending the range of imputable and calculable actions. Until recently sexual harassment or racial discrimination were part of the expensive and offensive overflowing which the law did not contain and which, not being framed, was not taken into account in the calculation of decisions and relations.

21 See also: Swetz, 1987.

22 Moreover, we talk of the disciplining of the market.

23 Law, for example competition law as analyzed by Dumez and Jeunemaître in the

case of cement industry, obviously promotes the calculability of decisions by framing authorized actions and relations.

24 In passing, Miller gives an example of these theoretical debates which take place in hybrid forums and which oppose those who are supposed to be theoreticians and those who are supposed to be practitioners. Rowland, for example, referred to discounting techniques as dangerous non sense and sheer insanity because the accountant should not lift the veil concealing the future. That Rowland ends up being wrong is not important. What is striking is that the theoretical reflection encompasses all the actors.

25 What the English word currency denotes so well.

26 See: Mugnaini, 1994. 'We find here the variety of messages transmitted by bank notes and the power of these inscriptions to repersonalize what was a relationship between strangers.' Like a prostitute who admitted: 'That evening I loved you naturally. Not you though; you did it . . . and when you switched on the light again you gave me the usual hundred lire note. I wrote the day and the date on it' (Eduardo de Filippo, *Filumena Marturano (I Capolavoir di Eduardo)*, Turin, Einaudi, 1973, t.1 P 332).

27 For a complete demonstration see: Thomas, 1991.

28 DiMaggio talks of framing rules to account for the different logics: those which calculate and those which do not calculate. He discovers half the solution with his notion of framing, but immediately loses it with the notion of rules. Yes, it is a matter of framing, but of framing heterogeneous arrangements.

29 Or in scientific institutions. For a complete demonstration see: Law, 1994.

30 We recall here the analyses proposed by R. Boyer who distinguishes four types of capitalist economies corresponding to four different modes of state regulation of the economy: market capitalism (eg, the UK), meso-corporatist capitalism (eg, Japan), social-democratic capitalism (eg, Sweden) and latin capitalism (eg, Italy and France).

31 We have seen how the zero degree of calculation—the gift—corresponds tot the total externalization of relations. Everything is entanglement.

32 It is striking to note that hedging, which is the word used by the actors themselves (eg, hedging a bet) is a perfect synonym for framing.

33 As indicated, the movement is circular. By making use of mathematics, economics provides the economy with calculating tools. This, in turn, enables economics to calculate the laws resulting from the composition of calculations made by calculating agencies. On the explanation of the mathematization of economics by economic agents' use of mathematical tools, see Porter (Porter, 1995).

References

Appadurai, A., (1986), *The Social Life of Things: Commodities in Cultural Perspective*. Cambridge: Cambridge University Press.

Appadurai, A., (1996), *Modernity at Large. Cultural Dimension of Globalization*. Minneapolis: University of Minnesota Press.

Baker, W., (1984), 'The Social Structure of a National Securities Market'. *American Journal of Sociology 89* 775–811.

Bensa, A. and Freyss, J., (1994), 'La société kanak est-elle soluble dans l'argent?' *Terrain* 23: 11–26.

Block, F., (1994), 'The Role of the State in Economy'. In *The Handbook of Economic*

Sociology, ed. Neil J. Smelser and Richard Swedberg 691–710. Princeton: Princeton University Press.

Bourdieu, Pierre, (1979), *La distinction*. Paris: Le Seuil.

Bourdieu, Pierre, (1997), *Méditations pascaliennes*. Paris: Le Seuil.

Burt, Ronald S., (1993), 'The Social Structure of Competition'. In *Explorations in Economic Sociology*, ed. Richard Swedberg 65–103. New York: Russel Sage Foundation.

Callon, M., (1986a), 'The Sociology of an Actor-Network'. In *Mapping the Dynamics of Science and Technology*, ed. M. Callon, J. Law, and A. Rip. London: Macmillan.

Callon, Michel, (1986b), 'Some Elements for a Sociology of Translation: Domestication of the Scallops and the Fishermen of St Brieuc Bay'. In *Power, Action and Belief. A New Sociology of Knowledge?*, ed. John Law. 196–229. Sociological Review Monograph. Routledge and Kegan.

Callon, M., (1991), 'Techno-economic Networks and Irreversibility'. In *A. Sociology of Monsters: Essays on Power, Technology and Domination*, ed. J. Law. 132–161. London: Routledge.

Callon, M., (1994), 'Four Models for the Dynamics of Science'. In *Handbook of Science and Technology Studies*, ed. S. Jasanoff, G.E. Markle, J.C. Petersen, and T. Pinch. 29–63. London: Sage.

Callon, M. and Cohendet, P., (1997), 'Between Uniformity and Diversity'. In *Engineering, Innovation and Society*, CAETS, London: The Royal Academy of Engineering.

Chamberlin, E., (1933), *The Theory of Monopolistic Competition*. Cambridge MA: Harvard University Press.

Coase, R.H., (1988), 'The Firm, the Market and the Law'. In *The Firm, the Market and the Law*, ed. R.H. Coase. 1–31. Chicago: Chicago University Press.

Coleman, J.S. (1988), 'Social Capital in the Creation of Human Capital'. *American Journal of Sociology 94*, 95–20.

Coleman, J.S., (1994), 'A Rational Choice Perspective on Economic Sociology'. In *The Handbook of Economic Sociology*, ed. Neil J. Smelser and Richard Swedberg. Princeton: Princeton University Press.

Cournot, A., [1838] (1927), *Researches into the Mathematical Principles of the Theory of Wealth*. New York: Macmillan.

D'Andrade, R., (1995), *The Development of Cognitive Anthropology*. Cambridge University Press, Cambridge.

David, P.A., (1984), 'Clio and the Economics of QWERTY'. *American Economic Review 75* no. 2: 332–337.

Deleuze, G. and Guattari, F., (1972), *L'Anti-Oedipe. Capitalisme et schizophrénie*. Paris: Minuit.

DiMaggio, P., (1994), 'Culture and Economy'. In *The Handbook of Economic Sociology*, ed. Neil J. Smelser and Richard Swedberg. 27–57. Princeton: Princeton University Press.

Dobbin, F., (1994), *Forging Industrial Policy: The United States, Britain and France in the Railway Age*. Cambridge: Cambridge University Press.

Dumez, H., (1985), *L'économiste, la science et le pouvoir: le cas Walras*. Paris: PUF.

Durkheim, E., (1970), *Cours de sciences sociales*. Paris: PUF.

Eymard-Duvernay, F., (1996), 'Les supports de l'action dans l'entreprise: règles, contrats, engagements'. In *L'état des relations professionnelles. Traditions et perspectives de recherche*. Presse de l'Université de Montréal et Octarès.

Fligstein, N., (1990), *The Transformation of Corporate Control*. Cambridge MA: Harvard University Press.

Fligstein, N., (1996), 'Markets as Politics: A Political-Cultural Approach to Market Institutions'. *American Sociological Review 61* (August 1996): 656–673.

Fligstein, N., (forthcoming), *Markets, Politics and Globalization*. Uppsala: University of Uppsala Press.

Fox, R. and Swazey, J., (1992), *Spare Parts: Organ Replacement in American Society*. Oxford: Oxford University Press.

Garcia, M-F., (1986), 'La construction sociale d'un marché parfait: Le marché au cadran de Fontaines-en-Sologne'. *Actes de la Recherche en Science Sociales* no. 65; 2–13.

Granovetter, M., (1973), 'The Strength of Weak Ties'. *American Journal of Sociology 78*. 1360–1380.

Granovetter, M. 'The Strength of Weak Ties.' *American Journal of Sociology 78* (1973): 1360–1380.

Guesnerie, R., (1996), *L'économie de marché*. Dominos, Paris: Flammarion.

Hart, O. and Moore, J., (1988), 'Incomplete Contracts and Renegotiation'. *Econometrica*, July 1988, pp. 755–785.

Hatchuel, A., (1995), 'Les marchés à prescripteurs'. In *L'Inscription sociale du marché*, ed. A. Jacob et H. Vérin, Paris: L'Harmattan.

Hennion, A., (1993), *La passion musicale*, Paris: Métailié.

Hodgson, G.M., (1994), 'The Return of Institutional Economics'. In *The Handbook of Economic Sociology*, ed. Neil J. Smelser and Richard Swedberg. Princeton: Princeton University Press.

Hoyle, L.F., (1995), 'Standardization across Non-Standard Domains: The Case of Organ Procurements', *STHV, Vol 20*, no. 4.

Hutchins, E., (1995), *Cognition in the Wild*. MIT Press, Cambridge University, Mass.

Karpik, L., (1995), *Les avocats. Entre l'Etat, le public et le marché*. Paris: Gallimard (forthcoming: Cambridge University Press).

Latour, B., (1987), *Science in Action. How to Follow Scientists and Engineers through Society*. Cambridge Mass: Harvard University Press.

Law, J., (1984), *Organizing Modernity*, Oxford: Blackwell.

Lebaron, F., (1997), 'Le dénégation du pouvoir: le champ des économistes français au milieu des années 1996'. *Actes de la recherche en sciences sociales* 119: 3–26.

Lévi-Strauss, C., (1960), 'Introduction à l'œuvre de Marcel Mauss'. In *Sociologie et Anthropologie*, ed. Marcel Mauss, Paris: PUF.

Marshall, A., [1920] (1961), 'On Markets'. *In Principle of Economics, ed. Alfred Marshall*. 323–330. 1. London: MacMillan and Co.

Maupassant, Guy de, (1987), *Le condamné à mort, Contes et Nouvelles* La Pléiade, tome I. Paris: Gallimard.

Mauss, M., [1925] (1969), *The Gift: Forms and Functions of Exchange in Archaic Societies*. London: Cohen and West.

McCloskey, D.N., (1985), *The Rhetoric of Economics*. Madison Wisconsin: University of Wisconsin Press.

McCloskey, D.N., (1990), *If You're So Smart: The Narrative of Economic Expertise*. Chicago: University of Chicago Press.

Meyer, M.W., (1994), 'Measuring performance in Economic Organizations'. In *The Handbook of Economic Sociology*, ed. Neil J. Smelser and R. Swedberg. Princeton: Princeton University Press.

Mugnaini, F., (1994), 'Messages sur billets de banque. La monnaie comme mode d'échange et de communication'. *Terrains, 23*: 63–80.

Nee, V., (1996), 'Symposium on Market Transition'. *American Journal of Sociology 101*: 908–1096.

North, D.C., (1990), *Institutions, Institutional Change and Economic Performance.* Cambridge: Cambridge University Press.

North, D.C., (1977), 'Markets and other Allocation Systems in History: The Challenge of Karl Polanyi'. *Journal of European Economic History 6* 703–716.

Polanyi, K., [1957] (1971), 'The Economy as Instituted Process'. In *Trade and Market in the Early Empires: Economic in History and Theory* , ed. Karl Polanyi, Conrad Arensberg, and Harry Pearson. Chicago: Henry Regnery Co.

Porter, T.M., (1995), *Trust in Numbers.* Princeton: Princeton University Press.

Portet, F., (1994), 'L'argent de la moto. Créer une richesse ou accepter la pénurie'. *Terrain* 23: 115–122.

Robinson, J., [1974] (1979), 'Markets'. In *Collected Economic Papers*, ed. Joan Robinson. 146–167. 5. Oxford: Blackwell.

Sahlins, M., (1976), *Culture and Practical Reason.* Chicago: University of Chicago Press.

Simmel, G., [1908] (1955), *Conflicts and the Web of Group Affiliations.* New York: The Free Press.

Smelser, N.J. and R. Swedberg, (1994), 'The Sociological Perspective'. In *The Handbooks of Economics Sociology*, ed. Neil J. Smelser and Richard Swedberg. 3–26. Princeton: Princeton University Press.

Smith, C.W., (1994), 'Auctions: From Walras to the Real World'. In *Explorations in Economic Sociology*, ed. Richard Swedberg. 176–192. New York: Russel Sage Foundation.

Star, S.L. and Griesemer, J., (1989), 'Institutional Ecology, "Translations" and Boundary Objects. Amateurs and Professionals in Berkeley's Museum of Vertebrate Zoology, 1907–39" '. *Social Studies of Science*. *19*: 387–430.

Strathern M., (forthcoming), 'What is intellectual property after?' In J. Law (ed.), *Actor Network Theory and After*, University of Keele.

Swedberg, R., (1994), 'Markets as Social Structure'. In *The Handbook of Economic Sociology*, ed. Neil J. Smelser and Richard Swedberg. 255–282. Princeton: Princeton University Press.

Swetz, F., (1987), *Capitalism and Arithmetic.* Chicago: Chicago University Press.

Thomas, N., (1991), *Entangled Objects. Exchange, Material Culture and Colonialism in the Pacific.* Cambridge, Mass: Harvard University Press.

Traimond, B., (1994), 'La fausse monnaie au village. 'Les Landes aux XVIIème et XIXème siècles'. *Terrain* 23: 27–44.

Walras, L., [1926] (1954), *Elements of Pure Economics.* 4th ed. Homewood Ill.: Richard D. Irwin.

Walzer, M., (1983), *Spheres of Justice: A Defense of Pluralism and Equality.* New York: Basic Books.

Weber, M., [1922] (1978), *Economy and Society: An Outline of Interpretive Sociology.* Guenther Roth Claus Wittich ed., Translated by Ephraim Fischoff *et al.* Berkeley: University of California Press.

Weber, M., [1923] (1981), *General Economic History.* New Brunswick, NJ: Transaction Books.

White, H., (1981), 'Where do Markets Come From?' *American Journal of Sociology* 87: 517–547.

White, H., (1988), 'Varieties of Markets'. In *Social Structures: a Network Approach*, ed. B. Wellman and S.D. Berkowitz. Cambridge: Cambridge University Press.

Williamson, O., (1993), 'Calculativeness, Trust and Economic Organization'. *Journal of Law and Economics XXXVI* April: 453–486.

The proliferation of social currencies[1]

Viviana A. Zelizer

In 1913, the Secretary of Agriculture wrote to some 35,000 farm
women asking them how his department could 'better meet the
needs of farm housewives'. It was not so much the hard work that
bothered them, responded many wives, but rather as one Michigan
woman explained, 'when the hard-earned chicken money saved little
by little goes to buy farm seed, pay the hired men or pay for fertil-
izer, that is what wears her out'. As a New York wife reported, the
members of her church society had agreed that 'the first need of the
rural wife is a stated income (. . .) This would enable her to install
up-to-date labour-saving devices (. . .) and obtain clothes when
needed, thereby saving the humiliation of asking for the money we
have earned but don't get'. If a husband wanted a plough, a
Washington farm wife complained, 'he would not think of asking
his wife if he might buy it, while if his wife wants anything for use in
the house she can ask and very often be told, "I cannot afford it." '
(*Economic Needs of Farm Women*, 1915, pp. 11, 17 16).

Within American farm households, husbands and wives thus differentiated their household monies and contested control over its
various segments. The contest did not simply concern power; it concerned the definition of social relations within the household.

What explains these differentiated and contested domestic monies?
After all, the 19th-century American state had worked vigorously to
eliminate distinctions among currencies by creating a single, standardized national money. Consider for instance the 5,000 or more distinct
varieties of state bank notes circulating in the 19th century. Or the privately issued tradesmen's and political tokens used as substitute currency in everyday transactions during the Civil War. Private gold
coins were produced in California, Georgia, and other states.

The government stepped in to make this private production of
monies illegal. It taxed thousands of state-issued paper currencies

out of existence and suppressed the private issue of tokens, paper notes or coins by stores, businesses, churches, and other organizations. The government moved as well against the personalization of money by individuals; it broadened definitions of counterfeiting and mutilation, pursuing for instance the popular 19th-century *trompe l'oeil* paintings of dollar bills. It even forbade the common practice of inscribing coins with sentimental messages.

Social theorists and critics were convinced that the state had succeeded in enforcing a single, homogeneous national currency. Indeed, it is a powerful ideology of our time that money is a unitary, fungible, absolutely impersonal instrument; the very essence of our rationalizing modern civilization. Money's 'colourlessness' as Georg Simmel, ([1908] 1950, p.414) saw it at the turn of the 20th century, repainted the modern world into an 'evenly flat and gray tone'. All meaningful nuances were stamped out by the new quantitative logic that asked only 'how much' but not 'what and how' (Simmel, [1990] 1978, p.259). Or as Gertrude Stein (1936, p.88) put it more succinctly a few decades later: 'Whether you like it or whether you do not money is money and that is all there is about it'.

Simmel and Stein saw only part of what was going on. The 19th century state was engaged in a losing battle. Although it did achieve a significant degree of standardization and monopolization in the physical form of legal tender, its victory was temporary and partial. People continually disrupted monetary uniformity, furiously differentiating, earmarking, and even inventing new forms of monies. The modern consumer society turned the spending of money not only into a central economic practice, but a dynamic, complex cultural and social activity. What should money buy, when, how often? Did the source of money matter? Who could spend properly and freely, who needed guidelines, supervision, restrictions? New forms of earmarking money proliferated in many different settings, both within households and in public locations. Even prisons, for instance, debated the right kind of money for inmates. In general Americans differentiated their monies by the social relations in which they were involved.

Thus, the forms of monetary earmarking multiplied just as official money became *more* uniform and generalized. This is the irony: while the state and the law worked to obtain a single national currency, people actively created all sorts of monetary distinctions. Outside the world of printing and minting, however, people spent less energy on the adoption of different objects as currencies than on the creation of distinctions among the uses and meanings of existing currencies—that is, on earmarking.

This, I claim, is how money works: in order to make sense of their complex and often chaotic social ties, people constantly innovate and differentiate currencies, bringing different meanings to their various exchanges. To make my argument on the earmarking of monies, I examine changes in the public and private uses of money in the United States between the 1870s and 1930s, focusing on three areas of social life which might seem most vulnerable to the dollar's rationalization: domestic transactions, the bestowing of gifts, and charity. Here of all places we should find the standardizing effects of state money. Yet instead of homogeneity we discover a rich and complex social economy.

Money at home

Let us consider domestic transfers. At the turn of the century, money concerns increasingly permeated the American household. As the consumer economy multiplied the number and attractiveness of goods while at the same time the discretionary income of American households rose, the proper allocation and disposition of family income became an urgent and contested matter.

Within their homes, families worked hard at earmarking their monies. They bought the account ledgers and budget books recommended by experts to register their expenses carefully, or else invented all sorts of strategies to differentiate the household's multiple monies. Take for instance Mrs. M's system as she told it to *Woman's Home Companion* in the early 1920s: 'I collected eight little cans, all the same size, and pasted on them the following words, in big letters: groceries, carfare, gas, laundry, rent, tithe, savings, miscellaneous (. . .) we speak of those cans now, as the grocery can, carfare can, etc.' (Bradley, 1923, p.7). Other families used jars, china pitchers, envelopes, or boxes to distinguish their monies physically, while some stashed the monies in stockings or under mattresses and floorboards. In a parallel way, immigrants religiously marked a portion of their hard-earned wages for transmission to relatives back in their home villages.

Or else families relied on a variety of outside institutions to safe-keep and differentiate their monies, from regular or postal savings banks, school banks, to insurance companies, mutual aid societies, budget clubs, buildings and loans associations, war bonds, and even installment payments. In many cases, this was not just accumulation of homogeneous capital but differentiated savings, most dramatically in the case of the 'summer vacation money' or 'Christmas money' deposited in the popular Christmas clubs or vacation clubs, which served as collective 'piggy banks'.

Observers contended that organized budgeting would neatly rationalize household finances. But the domestic earmarking of monies was hardly a smooth accounting process. There was too much at stake in how the money was divided, for what, and by whom. As families increasingly depended on the cash wages brought in by the husband, it became more urgent and complex to negotiate husbands, wives' and children's claims to that money. To what extent did the husband's wage become a collective possession? Once his money entered the household who had the right to control it? Should husbands hand over all their salary to their wives, or how much could they keep for themselves? How much money should a wife receive and for which expenses? Was that money a gift from her husband or was a wife entitled to a particular share of the income? What about children: should they be given their own money to spend or was it their duty to earn it through household chores? How should children spend their money?

This new 'tightened competition for the family income', as Robert Lynd (1932, p.90) described it, prompted a general revision of economic transfers within households, a search for appropriate domestic currencies for wives, husbands and children. But it was the housewife's money which became the most paradoxical, contested, and uncertain currency—precisely because relations between wives and other household members were in transition and at issue. As the tasks of shopping for household needs expanded, women took over most of them. Yet this increased financial role came without a salary and most often without even a fixed and dependable income. Indeed, turn-of-the-century wives, even those married to wealthy men, often found themselves without a dollar of their own.

Worse still, women had lost most claims to the economic resources of the family. While the labour contributions of colonial wives were recognized, the 19th-century domestication of housewives placed married women outside the productive economy (eg, see Folbre, 1991). No matter how hard they worked or how much their families depended on their labours, women's housework was defined—and valued—as a task of affect but hardly of material import. Thus when it came to the household's economic welfare, it was the husband's wage-work not the wife's housework that mattered. His money became hers only as his gift, not as her earned share of the income. Tellingly, her money even had a special vocabulary that set it apart from ordinary cash: allowance, pin money, 'egg money', 'butter money', spending money, pocket money, or 'dole'.

Women's stratagems to extract some cash from their unforth-coming husbands fed jokes and vaudeville routines. But the domestic fiscal problem turned serious, forcing a difficult and controversial reevaluation of women's household money as well as of their earned income. To better understand what was at issue, we need to distinguish among three possible ways of organizing monetary transfers of any kind; as compensation (direct exchange), as entitlement (the right to a share) and as gift (one person's voluntary bestowal on another). Each implies a different quality of social relations among the parties. With compensation, the parties are involved in an equal exchange of values, while money as an entitlement suggests legitimate claims to power and autonomy by the recipient. Money as a gift denotes intimacy but also the possibility of subordination and arbitrariness. For a long time women and advocates of women rights wrestled over which was supposed to be women's proper share of the family income. Until recently, these distinctions had attracted little attention from historians and economists of the family. Largely due to the predominant model of what Amartya Sen (1983) calls the 'glued-together family', questions about how money is divided among family members are seldom even asked.

Family members thus struggled to redefine the relevant social relations, creating distinctive currencies for that purpose and employing a series of ingenious techniques for distinguishing currencies from each other. Implicitly they faced three issues: What were they distinguishing? On what grounds were they distinguishing? How did they make the distinctions?

What were they distinguishing? Basically, they distinguished significantly different stocks and flows of money: stocks in the form of separate funds, inflows from different sources of income, outflows to different kinds of expenditure. On what grounds were they distinguishing stocks and flows? Basically, they distinguished meaningfully different social relations: relations to various providers of income, relations within households, relations to various recipients of payments or beneficiaries of those payments. How did they make the distinctions? They separated stocks and flows in two different ways: by *methods of allocation* and by *objects of expenditures*. Methods included social routines within households that gave different family members the power to offer, receive, store, conceal, transfer, or expend household funds, while objects of expenditure established the range of acceptable uses for domestic funds.

As to *methods of allocation*, in the hierarchically structured family, husbands gave wives part of their income. Upper and middle-class wives received an irregular dole, or more rarely, a regular allowance from their husbands for housekeeping expenses, including household goods and clothing. Working-class wives, on the other hand, were given their husbands' paychecks and were expected to administer and distribute the family money. The amount of money wives received was not determined by the efficiency or even the quantity of their domestic contributions but by prevalent beliefs of what was a proper amount. Therefore, a larger paycheck for the husband need not translate into a rise in the housekeeping allowance. On the basis of gender economics, it might in fact simply increase a husband's personal money.

Legally, domestic money was a husband's property. Even if a woman managed to save some money from her housekeeping expenses the law ultimately considered that money as her husband's property. For instance, in 1914, when Charles Montgomery sued his wife, Emma, for the $618.12 she had saved from household expenses during their 25 years of marriage, Justice Blackman of Brooklyn's Supreme Court ruled for the husband, arguing that 'not matter how careful and prudent has been the wife, if the money (. . .) belonged to the husband it is still his property' (*New York Times*, Dec. 16, 1914, p.22). Thus a wife's channels to additional cash were limited to a variety of persuasion techniques: asking, cajoling, downright begging, or even practicing sexual blackmail. If these techniques failed, there was also a repertoire of underground financial strategies, ranging from home pocket picking to padding bills.

Changes in gender relations influenced the method of allocation of married women's money. As women's consumer role expanded at the beginning of the 20th century, the traditional 'dole' or asking method became not only inefficient but also inappropriate in increasingly egalitarian marriages. Yet monetary compensation of a housewife's domestic labour was an unacceptable alternative. Late 19th- and early 20th-century earnings statutes which first granted women rights to their own labour, also opened up the legal possibility of wages for housework. Did women's right to their earnings include money earned from housekeeping? Some feminists were saying yes, but the courts responded with an emphatic no: the law awarded wives' a right to income from their 'personal labour' for third parties, but not for household labour performed for spouse or family. Courts, Reva Siegel (1994A: 2181) tells us in a pathbreaking account of legal resistance to monetizing domestic work, 'were uniform in their conviction that the statutes, not matter how phrased, could not be construed to allow interspousal contracts regarding a wife's household labour'. Monetary compensation for domestic work, courts feared, would 'transform the marriage relationship into a market relationship', and the wife into a servant or worse still, a prostitute (Siegel, 1994A: 2140, 2191, see also Siegel, 1994B).[2]

The weekly or monthly allowance—an entitlement to a portion of the domestic income—was praised by social commentators as a more equitable method of allocation for wives' income than a gift or compensation. Yet allowances were in turn later condemned by the home-efficiency experts of the 1920s and 30s as an unsatisfactory payment for modern wives. The joint account emerged as the new cultural ideal. As social relations between husbands and wives changed, so did the forms of domestic payment.

A wife's money was further earmarked by its *objects of expenditure*. Wives' money meant housekeeping money, a necessary allotment restricted to family expenses and excluding personal spending money. Pocket money was a budgetary expectation for husbands and children, but not for wives. Gender marked the uses of women's money even when their income was earned. Women's income was still earmarked as separate and treated differently. Among farm families, for instance, women's egg money and butter money were distinguished from husbands' wheat money or corn money, and used for different purposes. In the 1920s and 30s, as more married women entered the labour force, their earnings, regardless of the sums involved, were treated as 'pin money' categorized as supplementary income, used for the family's extra expenses, or earmarked by more affluent couples as discretionary 'fun' money. A wife's pin money, regardless of its quantity, remained a more frivolous, less serious earning than her husband's wages.

The same sort of earmarking appeared elsewhere in household social relations, indeed in the relations between households and the world outside. Ties to third parties—employers, relatives, authorities, and, of course, children—strongly affected the ways that household members organized their uses of money.

Families thus constructed distinct forms of monies shaped by a powerful domestic culture and by changing social relations between husbands and wives, parents and children. As a matter of fact, similar changes in currencies appeared outside the family, for instance in gift exchanges and charitable donations, as individuals and organizations invented an extensive array of currencies, ranging from money gifts, gift certificates, remittances, to tips, penny provident savings, mother's pensions, and food stamps. People sorted ostensibly homogeneous legal tender into distinct categories, and they created other currencies that lacked backing from the state.

Future currencies

As we reach the turn of the 21st century, the transformation of money persists. To be sure the forms of legal tender have changed and the uses of money multiplied. Yet there is no sign that people are relinquishing the earmarking of their multiple monies. In the case of contemporary households, a wide range of evidence indicates that monetary differentiations areas prevalent as ever. For example, cognitive anthropologist Jean Lave (1988, pp.132–3) tells us how Orange County, California residents segregate their monies for special uses by keeping a variety of household 'cash stashes': 'generally one in the billfold of each adult, children's allowances and piggy banks, a "petty cash" fund in a teapot-equivalent'—or with 'banked stashes of money', including Christmas club savings and accounts designated for special expenditures such as property or other taxes, vacations, home and car insurance payments.

True, with new internationalized and electronic currencies, the scope of earmarking may increase and techniques for earmarking will vary, but differentiation persists. Agencies far outside of the range of government—banks, universities, transportation companies, commercial firms, utilities, and even Club Med—are creating their own forms of electronically mediated money. From the viewpoint of the creators of money, important distinctions are emerging among four types of electronic currency: first, Internet currencies such as Digicash and Cybercash which transfer value from one financial agency to another; second, cards that establish a debt on the part of the user, such as the standard credit cards; third, cards that transfer a given person's money from one category to another for example from a bank account into cash, such as automated teller cards and what are coming to be known as debit cards; and fourth, those stored-value cards that users purchase for special purposes, such as cards for telephones or public transportation. Agencies such as universities, to be sure, are producing a combination of these categories as in the cards that students now use to pay for a wide variety of services—access to the library, computer facilities, vending machines, meals, and including tuition—as well as to receive scholarship money and other income. (For information on recent electronic banking innovations, see Mayer, 1997.)

Indeed, with the explosion of personal computers people's capacity to create and segregate new currencies is expanding even faster than any standardization of international money. From the view point of users, however, the major distinctions still concern the category of social relation involved with the payment and its meaning; for example, the distinction between remittances of currencies by migrants to their relatives back home and their payment of a home mortgage to a bank.

If my analysis is correct, people and organizations will take advantage of the new forms not to make all monetary transactions uniform but to innovate earmarking strategies. Significantly, even the bills of Europe's projected European Currency Unit (ECU), carefully designed to avoid 'national bias'—they will feature no people or words, only images of non-existent, anonymous bridges and monuments—will still retain a small space for each country to print its own national symbol (Andrews, 1996:35–6).

The vision of a fully commoditized society is no more than a mirage. Money has not become the free, neutral, and dangerous destroyer of social relations. As the world becomes more complex, some things do of course standardize and globalize, but as long-distance connections proliferate, for individuals everywhere life and its choices become more, rather than less intricate. As the case of domestic money illustrates, earmarking currencies is one of the ways in which people make sense of their complicated social ties, bringing different meanings to their varied exchanges. That is why we can expect new forms of earmarking to multiply with social change. To the extent that money does become more prominent in social life, people will segregate, differentiate, label, decorate, and particularize it to meet their complex social needs.

Notes

1 This is a revised version of 'The Creation of Domestic Currencies', *American Economic Review Papers and Proceedings* 84 (May 1994): 138–142. For more extensive documentation concerning the multiple uses of money, see my *The Social Meaning of Money* (Basic Books, 1994); 'Payments and Social Ties', (1996); and 'How Do We Know Whether a Monetary Transaction is a Gift, an Entitlement, or Compensation?' (1998). For some recent treatments of the relationship between money and social processes see: Bloch, 1994; Dodd, 1994; Guyer, 1995; Helleiner, 1996; Mizruchi and Stearns, 1994; Radin, 1996; Shell, 1995; Thirft and Leyshon,

1994; Wuthnow, 1994. On the domestic economy, Lundberg and Pollak, 1996; Schwartz, 1994; Singh, 1996, 1998. For related work on categorical distinctions and symbolic boundaries, see Bourdieu, 1984; Zerubavel, 1991; Lamont, 1992; Tilly, 1998.

2 For a provocative critical overview of the persistent and widespread legal resistance to monetary compensation of wives' domestic labour, see Silbaugh, 1996. See also Williams (1994) on how courts' 'commodification anxiety' affects current divorce settlements.

References

Andrews, E.L., (1996), 'Europeans Report Breakthrough in Monetary Union Effort', The New York Times, December 14: 35–36.

Bloch, M. (ed.), (1994), 'Les usages de l'argent', *Terrain* 23.

Bourdieu, P., (1984), *Distinction*, Cambridge: Harvard University Press.

Bradley, A., (1923), 'Fifty Family Budgets', New York: *Woman's Home Companion*.

Dodd, N., (1994), *The Sociology of Money*, New York: Continuum.

'Economic Needs of Farm Women', (1915) Report No. 106. Washington: Government Printing Office.

Guyer, J.I. (ed.), (1995), *Money Matters*, Portsmouth, NH: Heinemann.

Folbre, N. (1991), 'The Unproductive Housewife: Her Evolution in Nineteenth-Century Economic Thought', *Signs*, Spring, 16, pp. 463–484.

Helleiner, E., (1996), 'Money And The Nation-State in North America'. Unpublished paper, Department of Political Science, York University, Canada.

Lamont, M., (1992), *Money, Morals, and Manners*, Chicago: University of Chicago Press.

Lave, J., (1988), *Cognition In Practice*, New York: Cambridge University Press.

Lundberg, S. and Pollak, R.A., (1996), 'Bargaining and Distribution in Marriage', *Journal of Economic Perspectives* 10:139–158.

Lynd, R.S., (1932), 'Family Members as Consumers', Annals of the American Academy of Political and Social Science, 160, pp. 86–93.

Mayer, M., (1997), *The Bankers: The Next Generation*, New York: Truman Talley Books/Dutton.

Mizruchi, M.S. and Brewster Stearns, L., (1994), 'Money, Banking, and Financial Markets'. In N. Smelser and R. Swedberg (eds), *The Handbook of Economic Sociology*: 313–341. Princeton, NJ: Princeton University Press and New York: Russell Sage Foundation.

Radin, M.J., (1996), *Contested Commodities*, Cambridge: Harvard University Press.

Schwartz, P., (1994), *Peer Marriage*, New York: Free Press.

Sen, A., (1983), 'Economics and the Family', *Asian Development Review* I, pp. 14–26.

Shell, M., (1995), *Art & Money*, Chicago: University of Chicago Press.

Silbaugh, K., (1996), 'Turning Labour Into Love: Housework And The Law', 91 *Northwestern University Law Review* 1.

Siegel, R.B., (1994A), 'The Modernization of Marital Status Law: Adjudicating Wives' Rights to Earnings, 1860–1930', 82 *Georgetown Law Journal* 2127.

Siegel, R.B., (1994B), 'Home as Work: The First Woman's Rights Claims Concerning Wives' Household Labour, 1850–1880', 103 *Yale Law Journal* 1073.

Singh, S., (1996), 'The Use of Electronic Money in the Home', Policy Research Paper

No. 41, Melbourne: Centre for International Research on Communication and Information Technologies.

Singh, S., (1998), *Marriage money*, Sydney: Allen & Unwin.

Simmel, G., ([1908] 1950), *The Sociology of George Simmel*, edited by Kurt H. Wolf. Glencoe, Ill.: Free Press.

Simmel, G., ([1900] 1978), *The Philosophy of Money*, Trans. Tom Bottomore and D. Frisby. London: Routledge & Kegan Paul.

Stein, G., (1936), 'Money'. *Saturday Evening Post*, July 13, 208, p. 88

Thrift, N. and Leyshon, A., (1994), 'A phantom state? The de-traditionalization of money, the international financial system and international financial centres', *Political Geography* 15 (July): 299–327.

Tilly, C., (1998), *Durable Inequality*, Berkeley: University of California Press.

Williams, J., (1994), 'Is Coverture Dead? Beyond a New Theory of Alimony', 82 *Georgetown Law Journal* 2227.

Wuthnow, R., (1994), *God and Mammon in America*, New York: Free Press.

Zelizer, V., (1994), *The Social Meaning of Money*, New York: Basic Books.

Zelizer, V., (1996), 'Payments and Social Ties', *Sociological Forum* 11:481–495.

Zelizer, V., (1998), 'How Do We Know Whether a Monetary Transaction is a Gift, an Entitlement or Compensation?' In Avner Ben-Ner and L. Butterman (eds), *Economics, Values, and Organization*, New York: Cambridge University Press.

Zerubavel, E., (1991), *The Fine Line*, New York: Free Press.

Markets as cultures: an ethnographic approach

Mitchel Y. Abolafia

The microeconomics textbook that I used as an undergraduate defined a market as 'a group of firms or individuals that are in touch with each other in order to buy or sell some good' (Mansfield, 1972). The book went on to explain the abstract magic of the pricing mechanism under conditions of perfect and imperfect competition. Looking back, it's the 'in touch with each other' that catches my eye. Although my textbook was encyclopedic on the forces of supply and demand, it was rather vague in its description of the process of economic exchange. But when people are 'in touch with each other' they are socially embedded in a network of important social relations and culturally embedded in a meaning system of norms, rules and cognitive scripts. The transaction is not a simple dyadic exchange. Its outcome is a reflection of the social and cultural as well as economic, forces shaping it. These forces determine who may transact with whom, how bids and offers will be coordinated, when and where they may transact, how the commodity is defined and a variety of other conditions of transaction that affect buyers and sellers.

In this chapter I will focus on markets as cultures.[1] The phrase 'markets as cultures' is meant to denote that as *loci* of repeated interaction/transaction, markets exhibit their own distinct set of mutual understandings. These understandings are both enabling and restraining; ie, market participants use them both to pursue their interests and to limit the range of alternatives available to each other. These understandings emerge in interaction but become institutionalized. As such, they tend toward persistence and become resources in market participant's capacity to act. Nevertheless, market culture is not fixed. It is because market culture must be continually reproduced through exchange relations that it is vulnerable to change. We will examine some of the forces precipitating change in market culture.

The markets as cultures approach focuses on three areas of research: constitutive rules and roles, local rationality, and the dynamics of power and change. I will explore each of these in the next three sections of the chapter. In a fourth section I will discuss methodological issues involved in studying markets as cultures using an ethnographic approach. Throughout the chapter I will use examples from my own ethnographic studies in the stock, bond, and futures markets on Wall Street (see Abolafia, 1996a).

Constitutive rules and roles

The greatest advantage in conceiving markets as cultures is that it enables one to overcome the atomized view of markets in which masses of individuals engage in frictionless[2] transaction. It allows the analyst to explore the consequence of repeated transaction, ie, the construction of institutionalized relationships and systems of meaning. Through repeated interaction market participants develop expectations about appropriate behaviour and scripts for the performance of roles. It is through these rules and roles that participants constitute the market.

In this view markets are not created at the moment of interaction, nor are existing rules and roles the only ones that could have developed in efficient markets. Rather, these constitutive rules and roles are produced by the repeated interaction of powerful interests competing for control. The market is a reflection of this ongoing competition. Shifts in the balance of power within a market determine who may design or redesign the rules and role relationships. Going further, this competition is shaped by the political, economic and regulatory environments of the market. Thus, although market participants may all be self-interested rational maximizers, they enact differing market cultures depending on internal and external pressures.

Constitutive rules

The cultural analyst of markets will find that market makers, those actors who buy and sell in a market on a continuous and frequent basis, are guided by numerous informal and formal rules. Many of these rules are *regulative* rules designed to govern the pursuit of self-interest.[3] For example, on the trading floor of the New York

Stock Exchange (NYSE) I found that traders operate under the 'rule of agency' ie, that the customer's order always get executed before the market maker's at any given price. It is a straightforward prescription involving monitoring and sanctions. It is a rule that is strictly enforced because incentive to violate is high. In fact, this enforcement was externally imposed by the Securities and Exchange Commission in the 1960s because of widespread earlier violations.

On the other hand, the NYSE traders frequently talked about price integrity. This is a *constitutive* rule that says that price must be determined by open competition in which all bids and offers are exposed to the market. This rule explains how a market *should be* constructed. Its consequence is that market makers maintain a system in which all bids and offers in a particular stock are sent to a centralized spot where they can be matched. The traders' assumption that this is the only appropriate (*fair*) way to constitute a market is reflected in the following quotes from market makers on the floor. 'Fair pricing is exposing all bids and offers to the market. The method of price discovery, which is what we do for a living, has created a price that has more integrity than those prices created anywhere else in the world.' Another said, 'The value that the Stock Exchange brings is to have all the fairness of execution, where all the orders are competing with each other. The best price.' The normative, proud, and righteous tone is unmistakable. 'You have an actual two-legged buyer meeting an actual two-legged legitimate seller. And that has to be fair by the nature of the beast.' Traders are often indignant that this constitutive rule is not shared by traders in competing over-the-counter markets.

Although many constitutive rules, like the rule of price integrity, are based on norms and values about what is appropriate, there is a second, more tacit kind of constitutive rule that is based on institutionalized scripts that are taken for granted. Traders on the floor of the New York Stock Exchange take for granted that all trading occurs on 'the floor', that all bids and offers not at the current price will be placed in 'the book',[4] and that transactions go 'on the tape'[5] as soon as humanly possible. These rules are part of the orthodoxy of the Exchange community. New recruits learn them by imitating what is already common practice. These are the scripts by which the market is reproduced on a daily basis. To members of the culture, these assumptions are beyond question. There is little fear of rule violation because everyone agrees that this is how the market is made.

Mitchel Y. Abolafia

Constitutive roles

In addition to the rules that constitute the market, the cultural analyst will find that market makers have constructed rich social identities that have come to define the behaviour and interaction of role incumbents. Rather than the calculative unit actor described by economists, we see an astute participant suing a toolkit of strategies that is culturally available in the market. These strategies are learned by recruits for successful role performance. As new recruits are socialized by veterans, the scripts begin to define what is valued and to have a taken-for-granted character. Like police, physicians, and gangsters, market-makers employ these identity tools to reduce uncertainty and risk in their environment and to maximize survival.

In my research in the bond market between 1987 and 1989, I studied traders at four of the ten largest investment banks on Wall Street. Very early in my fieldwork I was struck by the repeated use among traders of the words 'entrepreneur' and 'entrepreneurial' to describe themselves. My first reaction was that I was standing in a room with two or three hundred traders and salesmen employed by a large, publicly traded corporation. In what sense were these people entrepreneurs? Over the ensuing weeks I came to understand that 'entrepreneur' was an identity through which they constituted their role performance. It defined how traders related to each other in their transactions and how they thought of themselves. The identity consists of strategies that are a caricature of the spirit of capitalism described by Weber. These strategies include self-reliance, emotional control, risk taking, heightened materialism and opportunism.

Traders are very clear that they are expected to be self-reliant. 'It's a very entrepreneurial business. No one is going to help you make money. They're too busy helping themselves.' Traders sit in a room full of other traders transacting with the market through the telephone and computer networks. Said another trader, 'I don't really feel like I can rely on anybody here. *That's the way this business is.* You've got to rely on yourself.' Such statements define both actors and action. They describe an impersonal environment in which trust and co-operation are nearly absent. This is in noted contrast to traders at the New York Stock Exchange where traders transact face to face and talk about trust and building relationships with customers.

A second component of the bond trader's toolkit is emotional control. The bond traders' ideal is the trader who is disciplined,

72

cool-headed, and focused. Traders engage in a continuous stream of fateful decisions involving millions of dollars. They characterize their work as exciting, risky and stressful. 'There's definitely a high degree of excitement. The pace is very fast. The stakes are high.' The culturally approved response to these conditions is an unflappable demeanour. As one explained, 'I have a first rule of survival: not to become too personally involved in the market. Otherwise you can get caught up in fighting this thing and you can't win.' Such expressions of emotional distance are made to confirm the trader's own sense of control as well as reflect it to whomever may be watching.

Risk-seeking is a third major component of the trader identity. The risk-seeking identity is a complex one to manage. At the same time that traders see themselves as disciplined and cool-headed, they see themselves as game for action. It suggests that market-making combines elements of both nerve and fear. 'You've got to keep your position balanced. You've got to be in a situation so that no one trade can take you out. You've got to be viable to play tomorrow.' Market makers in different industries are bound to enact different levels of risk-seeking. In the traders' identity, risk seeking is what Goffman (1967) called 'a practical gamble'.

A fourth component in the identity is the strategic use of guile. Traders referred to this kind of behaviour as 'aggressive'. It connotes action in which the trader uses his advantage to deceive a trading partner. My informants told stories about 'laying off bonds' on customers and 'showing a bid in the street' when you had no intention of buying at that price. These and other strategies were scripts learned by the role incumbents that reproduced the kind of opportunistic bond markets that were prevalent in the 1980s.

The purpose of these strategies is the pursuit of unabashed materialism as a status indicator. Bond traders are very clear about what constitutes a skilled role performance. '*Money is everything in this business*. Whatever money you make is what you're worth.' Unlike high tech markets where market makers tie their identity to innovation, or service industries, such as restaurants, where it is tied to customer satisfaction, bond traders sanctify heightened materialism. Money, and what it can be used to acquire, provide an identity that prevails over charisma, physical attractiveness, or sociability as the arbiter of success and power on the bond trading floor. But it is not the money itself that is important, rather it is the status and approval it brings among peers that is at the heart of the identity. As a result, the unfettered pursuit of wealth is deemed appropriate and scruples which might deter market makers in other industries are unnecessary.

73

Constitutive rules and roles will vary from market to market. There will be different rules for auction markets, wholesale markets, and retail markets. The roles of brokers and dealers, buyers and sellers will differ. We expect that in some markets participants will be more self-reliant, in others more co-operative. Some will be highly opportunistic, others more trusting. Using the markets as cultures approach, the analyst discovers the different rules and roles by which participants construct their market and the conditions underlying these differences.

Local rationality

Economists, and in particular financial economists, treat rationality as a cultural universal. As such it is explained as part of human nature. The markets-as-cultures perspective treats rationality as a community-based, context-dependent cultural form. Rationality on the trading floor is different from the rationality of cattle dealers or auto dealers. A cultural approach endeavours to identify context specific cognitive limits and socially constructed local forms of rationality. The ethnographer explores the market participants' construction of the decision making process and the individual as well as social means of establishing value in the marketplace.

Market makers in financial markets might seem to fit the economist's ideal type of decision-maker, using an extraordinarily rich flow of information in the unbridled pursuit of gain. Bond, stock, and futures traders come closer than expected to the self-interested, perfectly informed, rational maximizer portrayed in the finance literature on market makers; nevertheless they are cognitive and social beings, and as a result, imperfect information processors who are susceptible to habit, custom, and the institutionalized myths of trading. Observation and interviews reveal that market makers in stock, bond, and futures markets construct local forms of rationality out of the resources and conditions in which they are embedded. Even in the highly rationalized world of financial markets, conditions of uncertainty, ambiguity, and institutionalization elicit adaptations.

Local rationality in a market culture can be understood by exploring the decision tools used by the market makers. Decision tools are the scripts created by decision makers for coping with the uncertainty and ambiguity in their environment (see Abolafia, 1996b, for a more detailed discussion). These tools become institutionalized so that they are available to all participants in a particular market context. Individuals learn to depend on these tools when faced with market decisions of consequence. In my study of bond traders, decision tools were manifest as habits or ritualized customs that are tacitly but continuously invoked throughout the trading day. The most important decision tools in the bond market involve stylized versions of *vigilance* and *intuitive judgment*.

Vigilance involves the ability to search and assimilate a broad range of information that one expects may be useful in decision making. In bond trading, vigilance consists of several related elements: sorting, networking, and establishing value. The first step in vigilance is *sorting*. The volume of information available is so overwhelming that a subsidiary industry has grown up to supply information and analysis of market trends to traders. Every trader must sort through both the numbers and their multiple interpretations. Traders often favour a particular brand or fashion in interpretation and become 'chartists',[6] 'fundamentalists'[7] or followers of some other interpretation. Most develop a routinized sorting procedure to cover their favoured sources of information. This procedure is enacted daily prior to the start of trading and continues throughout the day.

Once information has been gathered and sorted, traders employ a *networking* routine to see how others are perceiving the same or different information. They are in contact with a network of brokers, traders, salespeople, economists, and informants in government agencies. Traders are generally aware that it is not the correctness of the interpretation that counts, but rather the degree to which others will read the same information the same way. *Establishing value* is the final step in the script for vigilance. It is the local term for making an estimate of where a bond 'ought to be' in terms of price. As Smith (1989) notes, in this kind of highly liquid market, recent transactions are among the most important sources of information for establishing value. There are also norms and myths about appropriate price movement over time and the influence of movement in one instrument on another that shape process of establishing value.

The scripts for vigilance reflect the analytic inclinations of market makers. Sorting, networking, and establishing value are common strategies which each market maker can describe in some detail because of their habitual repetition. In practice, these tools orient the traders toward each other creating competing or shared interpretations of where the market has been and where it is going. On the basis of their understanding of these interpretations, individual traders decide when and how to transact in the market. Sometimes this leads to herd-like behaviour or a contrarian reaction to the herd, but more often the data are equivocal and the interpretations' predictive ability uncertain. As a result, analytic routines do not complete the repertoire of decision tools used by market makers. As my subjects were quick to tell me, '(trading) is not a science, it's an art'. No prescription exists. Rather it is learned, usually during a lengthy apprenticeship. As another subject said, 'Traders cannot put into words what they've done . . . They have a knack'. That knack is *intuitive judgment*. The market-maker develops an abstract sense of how the market reacts under various conditions. These abstractions or images are developed through watching others transact by transacting and by reliance on market folklore.

Intuitive judgment is most likely to be found under conditions of high uncertainty. In the end, indicators, reports, and networking cannot predict the direction of prices with certainty. Final decisions are ultimately based on intuitive judgment about a particular transaction. The environment in which market-makers operate is both uncertain and ambiguous. The uncertainty comes from both the cognitive limits of the individual and the time constraints set by the flow of transactions in the market. The flow of information about the market cannot be fully assimilated. Recruits learn that they must develop 'the knack' or fail. Although researchers, unless they are participants, may never fully understand intuitive judgment, they can map market-makers' images and the conditions shaping them. In this way, the craft of market making can be made less mysterious. The economists' assumption of rational maximizing can be replaced by the empirical description of local rationality.

Decision tools are moulded from the context in which the market-makers work. Different forms of vigilance and intuitive judgment, as well as different decision tools, are too be expected in other markets. The manner in which different industries organize information, even what they deem to be *useful* information, is highly variable. The age of an industry, its technology, the education level of its market-makers and its degree of competitiveness all help to shape the decision tools it uses. Computerization and globalization are important forces for change here, but because market-making is a craft, historic methods of establishing value are likely to persist.

Dynamics of power and change

Constitutive rules and local rationalities are created by market-makers and, in turn, come to shape their behaviour. In the process, stable and orderly markets are enacted. But rules, roles, and even rationalities are not immutable. Existing market culture reflects the efforts of powerful market actors to shape and control their environment even as it is shaping and controlling them. These efforts do not go unopposed. Groups within the market, based on such factors as market segment, region, or the buy or sell side of the market, compete for the ability to define the culture. Those groups with the most power will have the greatest influence in reconfiguring of rules, roles, and rationalities. The probability that any group's strategic change effort will succeed is strongly influenced by the action or inaction of control agents in the environment such as industry organizations and government regulatory agencies.

The dynamics of power and change in market cultures occur in the context of institutional pressures. At the lowest level is the individual trader. As we have seen, although individual traders are driven by self-interest, they are also culturally embedded in a system of rules and roles that is the product of their interaction. The toolkit from which these rules and roles are drawn defines the range of culturally sanctioned behaviours in the market. Competition and conflict amongst groups in the market may create pressure for change in rules and roles.

Just above this level is the kind of informal and formal self-regulation imposed by membership in the market's reputational networks and its industry and trade groups. In many markets, participants have organized to interact regularly over standards, lobbying, and other collective goods. Finally, governments have a role in culture change. As we can see in the events surrounding the tobacco industry in the last years of the 20th century, government can have a strong influence on changes in the rules, roles, and local rationalities of a market.

But none of these levels of institutional pressure can be perfectly predictive of when and how culture will change. Market-makers are likely to resist outside efforts and the market power of the resistor will be an important determinant of the success of the resistance. Cultural change may result from internal power dynamics or as an adaptation to environmental change. One type of culture change involves the redefinition of opportunism, those gray areas at the boundaries of acceptable behaviour. My research in stock, bond, and futures markets suggest that these markets go through cycles of opportunism, periods when the definition of how much guile will be tolerated rises and falls. The cycles are tied to changing economic and political conditions, but these changes are not perfectly predictive. At times, powerful coalitions have successfully resisted culture change despite strong environmental pressures.

A rather dramatic example of culture change comes from the market makers at the New York Stock Exchange. We will divide our story into two periods: pre- and post-change. The pre-change period runs from the 1930s to the 1960s. During this period, specialists, ie, market-makers on the floor of the New York Stock Exchange, continued the floor culture that had existed prior to the crash of 1929. Even after the establishment of the Securities and Exchange Commission (SEC) in 1934, specialists still frequently traded ahead of their customers and used the information available to them for personal advantage. When the chair of the SEC, William O. Douglas, declared that specialists could no longer be both brokers and dealers the Exchange threatened to close and the SEC backed off. Specialists enjoyed unchallenged power on the floor from the 1930s to the 1950s and the culture reflected their unimpeded self-interest.

The post-change period begins with a major market decline. The decline in 1962 was not as substantial as the crash of 1929, but the controversy over specialists' power was rekindled. The SEC found that specialists had not performed their market-stabilizing function. As a result, explicit rules for specialists were developed. Over the course of the 1960s and 1970s the specialists power at the Exchange eroded as institutional investors came to dominate trading. As specialists lost their power at the transactional level, they were no longer able to fight rules and regulation. Securities firms and the institutional investors who were their customers demanded better service from the market makers. By the early 1990s, when I was on the floor, the market culture had dramatically shifted to rule reverence and customer service.

Ethnography in market settings

Gaining access

Ethnographic research on the production and reproduction of market culture is inherently difficult. In most sectors of advanced capitalist economies, market-making is the province of corporate elites. They make the highly consequential buy and sell decisions that determine the success of their organizations. They generally have power and status that derive from their position in these organizations. Like other elites, they are insulated from observation and protective of their time. The researcher must often pass through several levels of gate-keepers to gain access and may be rebuffed at any level.[8] Market-makers can let you in or keep you out and once you're in, you can still be asked to leave at any time. It is easy to see why elites are rarely the target of ethnography. Most ethnography is done among the poor, the powerless, the deviant, and in the less developed societies.

My three studies in stock, bond and futures markets reflect three different modes of access and the three different types of data that these mode of access yield. My initial interest in and access to the futures market was through a childhood friend who happened to be a lawyer at the Commodity Futures Trading Commission in Washington. As a result, this study was initially limited to the analysis of legal documents from court and regulatory proceedings and interviews with the regulators and defense lawyers involved in the cases. The thousands of pages of documents opened up a world of descriptive information about the arcane business of futures trading. I soon learned that regulatory agency libraries and court filings were treasure troves of untapped documentary evidence on the behaviour of economic actors. When I approached the futures exchanges at which the events in these cases had transpired, hoping for access to the floor, I was rebuffed. At this point, in 1979, futures markets were hypersensitive from negative publicity and newly enhanced regulation. Several years later, after I began publishing in the area of futures markets, one of the exchanges became more hospitable. I was given access to the floor and interviews were arranged with a broad cross section of traders.[9]

Access for my study of bond markets proved significantly easier. In 1983 I moved to the business school at Cornell University. By 1987 the bond market was the fastest growing market on Wall Street and masters of business administration (MBA) students were clamouring to get jobs at the investment banks where bonds were traded. I was able to use contacts with my current and former students to gain entrance to bond trading floors at four major banks. In each case a managing director approved my project after a short interview. Only one firm refused me access, although they kept calling for a copy of my findings. At each bank the understanding was that I would arrange 15 to 20 interviews with traders of my own choice. The traders could, of course, decline to participate. The traders were chosen in consultation with my former students based on criteria of age, tenure, years trading, and area of specialization. Interviews were generally done on the trading floor after hours and during slow periods in the trading day. Less formal conversations continued in restaurants and bars.

Mitchel Y. Abolafia

It was only at the New York Stock Exchange that I gained the kind of unlimited access for which ethnographers yearn and that extended observation requires. The initial contact was provided by an *alumni* that I met at a business school cocktail party. He was introduced as a specialist (market-maker) at the New York Stock Exchange. After learning about my previous research, he graciously invited me to the floor of NYSE. After a morning on the floor with him and his staff, he introduced me to the man who would become my key informant and supporter. This man believed that the culture of the floor was changing and wanted someone to document it. He had been at the Exchange for over 20 years, served on many governance committees, and was able to introduce me to a cross-section of the floor community. I was his guest on the floor for several months, observing from his post, until a trader who served on the Board of Trustees became aware of my presence, objected to it, and brought it to the attention of the Board. They voted to allow me to stay providing a permanent floor pass and a large office in the economic research department on the seventeenth floor. I was 'in' or as one anthropologist described it, the natives had built me a hut. With this degree of access my fieldnotes soon supplanted interviews as the major source of data.

For me, the key to success in gaining access to market-makers has been in making and aggressively using connections. Market-makers wanted to know that I was credible and trustworthy. They needed assurance that I wasn't there to steal proprietary information or to write a sensationalistic account that would reflect poorly on them, their occupation, or their market. My university affiliation was not sufficient. A personal connection was needed to open the door. My MBA students, *alumni*, and a personal friend served this function. Informants often questioned me about these connections on first meeting and made reference to them thereafter. I was often described as being a friend or professor of 'X'. My list of previous contacts signalled that I was connected. At NYSE everyone knew who my key informant was and it was his credibility that took me a long way until the Exchange approved my presence.

Establishing rapport

Although the researcher may have gained access, a successful project is not assured. As mentioned above, market-makers possess a wealth of information that they deem proprietary. They and their organizations have spent considerable resources to gather market data, formulate a strategy, and implement it. They are likely to be highly protective of that information and somewhat suspicious of your motives. The researcher must convince the market-maker that his or her motives are innocent (scientific rather than commercial or muck-raking), that the project is important enough to be worth their time, and ultimately that the researcher is capable of 'getting it right'. The quality of the ethnography is contingent on the extent to which rapport is established.

I found that people on the trading floor generally knew about me before I met them. I discovered that my prospective informant usually knew my institutional affiliation, who my connection was, and the theme of my study. It was extremely important then that the theme of the study, as they understood it, was something they found interesting and worthy of their time. In presenting the study I always looked for a broad frame that would be considered useful or important. Within that frame I was able to pursue a wide variety of questions. Since market-makers feel grossly misunderstood, it was not that hard to convince them a serious study was a good thing. More difficult was getting them to trust that I could get it right. A significant number of my informants initially expressed doubt that I could. 'I've seen too many journalists come down here looking for a story and getting it all wrong.' Accounts in the press frequently misinterpret their job and its functions. A popular book written in the 70s, *Wall Street Jungle* was premised on a misinterpretation of their function and its consequences for the market. My response to this was both direct and indirect. I told them that I planned to make repeated visits to the floor over several years and to interview widely. I also showed through my questions that I had taken the time to learn technical aspects of their work and that I was familiar with current issues in their occupational community.

I went to great lengths to give a convincing performance that would build trust. I began by taking a course to become a futures trader. At the end of the course I took a national exam and received certification. I also sat in on courses in finance from my colleagues, scoured the financial press every morning for stories about the market I was studying, and spent time with key informants off the floor. At the beginning of each study I started by working with a small group of market-makers that generally included my students and their friends until I became confident and conversant enough to go out on my own. This cautious approach also had the benefit of introducing me to behavioural and linguistic norms in a relatively

81

safe environment. It also made me a more welcome figure on the trading floor and improved the quality of the data I gathered.

Getting good data

In the process of gaining access and establishing rapport with business elites the researcher feels cautious and at a certain disadvantage. Elites can refuse or revoke access. Moreover, market-makers typically have greater power, wealth, and prestige than social science researchers. They are used to deference. But once the researcher begins to gather data, that imbalance begins to adjust. I found that market-makers had tremendous verbal facility and were used to controlling the definition of the situation they were in. Yet, playing the scientist gives one interpretive power. My informants were quite sensitive to this. While it made a small portion of my informants initially defensive, most easily assumed the role of a research subject. They showed real concern that their own performance was useful to me and interviews often went well over the time we had scheduled to talk. After an initial warm-up period, the more that I directed the interview and pursued questions I cared about, the more responsive my informants became.

Nevertheless, the ethnographic interview is a subtle form of strategic interaction. The market-makers in my study often had a well-developed perspective on the sociology and psychology of the trading floor. As an ethnographer I endeavoured to cast the broadest possible net searching for detailed descriptions of everyday life. To fill this net I asked market-makers to describe their day, to describe their career, to tell stories about key incidents and to explain a wide variety of social institutions associated with trading. I allowed them to talk about their pet issues, but I often had to direct them back to the issues that were emerging in my data. The market-makers communicated a combination of behaviours, emotions, opinions, and ideologies, all of them data to be analysed.

Perhaps the hardest thing about gathering data in this setting for me was subverting my critical stance. In all my research I start with a critical stance, questioning the norms, procedures, structures, and values of my subjects. These are things a student of markets should never take for granted. But the market-makers themselves are suspicious of such a stance. They want you to share their assumption that their world is as it should or must be. They want you to believe in the importance and rationality of what they do from the start and not to question it. A critical stance would present me as an outsider not to be trusted. This puts the researcher in a difficult position. I decided that my stance would be that I was open to anything. That was hard to do because some of the things I heard from bond traders were shocking. But I learned to keep a dispassionate 'straight' face, shaking my head and taking it in. The subtle threat here is the temptation to go native, ie, to buy into their interpretation of the world or simply to join that world.[10] It's very easy to get caught up in their interpretation of their world because it's a powerful one. The economic ideology that dominates Wall Street is a clear and comprehensive system for understanding everything from individual behaviour to the government's role in the market. Everything that happens on a daily basis is sifted through this ideology. It may be easy to maintain your ethnographic distance when your subjects are illiterate, impoverished or stigmatized. If the belief system is one that is part of your own society, it is harder. But here your method protects you. In the field you are open to recording anything, but at home, with the data, the critical facility must return. All the norms, procedures, and values of market-makers become culturally embedded social institutions to be understood.

Getting the native view of market culture can be a daunting challenge. Gaining access may require connections to someone at the site, although persistence may substitute for connections in some cases. Establishing rapport calls for a presentation of self that is knowledgeable and trustworthy from the native's viewpoint and a project rationale that is deemed both legitimate and non-threatening. Finally, getting good data requires a subtle balance of deference and being directive. The power and wealth of market-makers creates unique challenges for the ethnographer, but the value of gathering data that reflect the market makers' understanding of their world makes it worth the effort.

Conclusion

What, then, are the advantages and disadvantage of the markets-as-cultures approach? First, by treating markets as cultures we don't take rationality for granted. It is because most neoclassical economic studies treat rationality as undifferentiated that we need to explore decision-making in natural settings. The kind of decision tools discussed here and the biases and heuristics identified by Kahneman and Tversky (1982) and their colleagues are best discovered by inductive research. Second, the markets-as-cultures approach does not fall into the functionalist fallacy, common to agency theory and transaction costs theory, that market rules and roles are reflections of the efficiency demands of the market. Rather, these are social arrangements that reflect power, status, and historical contingency (path dependence) in the market. This approach allows us to see how market culture is socially constructed.

A third advantage of this approach is that its focus on the subjective experience of market makers as they enact their rules and roles draws attention to the fact that these rules and roles are not static. Informants reveal institutional history. When augmented by archival material, the ethnographer may explore the dynamics involved in cultural change. Even with these strengths, the markets-as-cultures approach has one clear disadvantage. It requires ethnographic field-work. As discussed above, access is often difficult, gaining informants' trust takes time. Good data sets are unwieldy and costly to analyse. Nevertheless, the markets-as-cultures approach challenges the taken-for-granted understanding of what goes on in markets that is so much a part of Western culture. It offers empirical access to the diversity of economic behaviour and its forces us to examine our assumptions about existing arrangements.

Notes

1 Earlier sociological work focused on financial markets as networks (Baker, 1984), Markets as Politics (Fligstein, 1996). and financial markets as cognitive structures (Smith, 1981).
2 See Granovetter (1985) for a discussion of the frictionless imagery in economic thinking.
3 See Scott (1995) for a discussion of the distinction between regulative and cognitive (constitutive) rules. My use of the term differs from Scott's in that the mechanism of compliance in constitutive rule sis not just cognitive, but may also be normative.
4 The 'book' is a record of all bids and offers that have come to the floor but have not yet been matched.
5 The 'tape' is a real time record of all transaction on the floor. It makes market information public to the world.
6 Chartists are traders who map the price fluctuations of the market and predict future movements based on the past.
7 Fundamentalists base their trading on information about a firm and its market position.
8 Jackall (1988 and Thomas (1993) discuss the frustration, expense and lost time involved in gaining access to business elites.
9 If this hospitality was meant to be co-optive, they certainly never made any demands. Nevertheless, I was aware of the threat and made an extra effort not to pull my punches.

10 I did receive one job offer during my year of research. When I declined, my prospective employer asked me why. I told him that I was going to write a doctoral dissertation. He asked if I would get paid for that. I told him how much my assistantship was worth. He responded, 'Maybe I misjudged you'.

References

Abolafia, M.M., (1996a), *Making Markets: Opportunism and Restraint on Wall Street*. Cambridge: Harvard University Press.

Abolafia, M.Y., (1996b), 'Hyper-rational Gaming'. *Journal of Contemporary Ethnography*, Vol. 25 No. 2, pp. 226–250, July.

Baker, W., (1984), 'The Social Structure of a National Securities Market' *American Journal of Sociology* Vol. 89, pp. 775–811.

Fligstein, N., (1996), 'Markets as Politics: A Political–Cultural Approach to Market Institutions.' *American Sociological Review*, Vol. 61, pp. 656–673.

Goffman, E., (1967), *Interaction Ritual*, Garden City, New York: Anchor.

Granovetter, m., (1985), 'Economic Action and Social Structure: The Problem of Embeddedness'. *American Journal of Sociology*, Vol. 91, pp. 481–510.

Jackall, R., (1988), *Moral Mazes*, New York: Oxford University Press.

Kahneman, D., Slovic, P. and Tversky, A., (1982), *Judgment Under Uncertainty: Heuristics and Biases*, Cambridge: Cambridge University Press.

Mansfield, E., (1972), *Principles of Microeconomics*, New York: W.W. Norton.

Scott, W.R., (1995), *Institutions and Organizations*, Thousand Oaks, Calif.: Sage Publications.

Smith, C., (1981), *The Mind of the Market*, Totowa, New Jersey: Rowman and Littlefield.

Smith, C., (1989), *Auctions: The Social Construction of Value*, Berkeley: University of California Press.

Thomas, R., (1993), 'Interviewing Important People in Big Companies', *Journal of Contemporary Ethnography*, Vol. 22 No. 1, pp. 80–96.

Efficiency, culture, and politics: the transformation of Japanese management in 1946–66

Bai Gao

What determines the outcome of institutional transformation of economic governance? Social scientists have posited three distinctive perspectives. The economic perspective emphasizes efficiency. It argues that property-right structures are very important in promoting efficiency. While some economists recognize that the market does not always work and firms have to solve the problems of co-operation, they limit their discussion within the scope of transaction cost (North, 1990; Williamson, 1985). The cultural perspective asserts either the regulatory effect of culture on the economy, tracing economic governance to an inherited pattern of behaviour and value systems, or the constitutive effect of culture on the economy, demonstrating how different environments shape the strategy of economic actors (DiMaggio, 1994; Zelizer, 1988). The political perspective focuses on power and domination. One version of this perspective highlights the joint forces of interests in constituting the foundation of economic institutions. It asserts that economic institutions play an important role in balancing the competing interests for economic welfare (Hirschman, 1970, Olson, 1982; and Sabel, 1994).

In this chapter, I assess the relative efficacy of each of these perspectives in explaining the transformation of Japanese management during 1946–1966. Rather than rejecting any particular perspective, I explore the validity and limit of each perspective. I argue that the search for efficiency often serves to discredit the present governance mechanisms and initiates change, but it contributes more to providing stimulus for change than shaping the outcome of this change. I argue that the transformation of economic governance is determined more by how economic actors perceive what is rational, how they define their interest, and the political process in which they reach agreement on how to distribute economic welfare in the new institution. First, I describe the transformation of Japanese management in the years from 1946 to 1966. Then, I employ each of these three perspectives, illustrating how each of them can enrich our understanding of the transformation of economic governance. Finally, I critique and discuss the explanatory power of each perspective and specify its limits.

The transformation of Japanese management

Japanese management in this chapter refers to the practices of lifetime employment, a seniority-based wage system and company-based labour unions. Lifetime employment means that an individual, once employed, can work for the same firm until retirement. The seniority-based wage system refers to the practice of determining an employee's status and wage in the firm according to his years of service and his age. This practice supplements lifetime employment. Many studies have pointed out that the term lifetime employment needs further clarification. First, it is practised mainly in big firms, not in all firms; only about one-third of the Japanese labour force is covered by this practice. Second, lifetime employment does not mean employment until death or even until the end of one's likely participation in the labour force; in this system, employees retire from the firm at age 55. Third, this practice applies primarily to male full-time permanent employees, including managers, white-collar personnel, and highly skilled blue-collar workers, but not to all employees in the firm (Brinton, 1992; Cole, 1972; Lincoln and McBride, 1987). The primary concern of this study is neither whether or how Japanese management differs rom its Western counterparts, nor to what extent Japanese management can be characterized by the practice of lifetime employment, a seniority-based wage system, and company-based labour unions, but how these practices, defined within the scope established by previous studies, were institutionalized, and what factors contributed to this process.

Although the origins of Japanese management can be traced back to early this century when the development of heavy industries necessitated the retention of highly-skilled workers by firms, the system was not widely institutionalized until the 1960s. Japanese management was first patterned during World War II. As part of the war mobilization, the state tightly controlled the relationship between management and labour. After the China War broke out in 1937, both layoffs and strikes were prohibited, all workers began to receive a fixed annual increase in salary, and they were all organized into company-based labour unions (Gao, 1997).

In the early postwar period (1946–1949), the occupation authority regarded the support and labour unions as an effective measure for eliminating the social foundation of Japanese militarism. The increasing strength of labour unions in national politics and the dissolution of *zaibatsu* considerably weakened the power of Japanese managers. After the end of wartime thought control, Marxism revived and became the leading ideology of labour movements; class struggle was the most appropriate concept for interpreting Japanese labour relations in those days (Masamura, 1985). As the United States changed its policy toward Japan in the late 1940s, the power relations between managers and workers changed dramatically: firms returned to the offensive, while labour unions had to take a defensive position (Ōuchi, 1949). In 1948 the Japan Federation of Employers Associations announced that in order to reduce production costs, Japanese firms had to conduct large-scale layoffs. The Federation demanded that the government help Japanese firms to re-establish management's power (Nikeiren, 1948). This confrontational strategy toward labour taken by Japanese firms and supported by state policy in the 1949–1955 period represented a U-turn in the political struggle for power between the two sides, and labour relations were characterized by constant confrontations.

In the mid 1950s, progressive business leaders who formed the Japan Committee of Economic Development initiated the productivity movement with the support of the state, aimed at including labour unions in their programme of promoting exports. In order to pursue comparative advantage in production technology, some big firms made a historical tradeoff. They started giving up allocative efficiency, as measured in short-term cost-benefit analysis, which had been their primary concern in the 1950s. In exchange they wanted labour's co-operation in technological innovation and quality control; to do this, they were required by the labour unions to provide job security and to increase salaries. This solution to the labour conflicts, however, was not widely accepted by both sides until the 1960s. In 1960, management and labour were involved in a major confrontation at the national level (Gao, 1997).

In the 1960s the attitudes of management and labour toward each other changed dramatically. A document issued at the national meeting of the Japan Federation of Employers Associations in 1963 argued that:

... in the past 18 years of the postwar era, management and labour have experienced together how much turmoil the class confrontation between management and labour, the political struggle, and the prejudice toward labour unions could bring to labour relations and social order ... In order to pursue the mission of promoting stability and social welfare, we must re-examine frankly the mistakes we have made ... We should co-operate with each other to pursue peace between management and labour, the prosperity of the firm, and the development of the national economy in order to meet the demands of the era (Nikeiren, [1963] 1966a:461).

As a result, the practices of lifetime employment, the seniority-based wage and the firm-based labour union became widely institu-tionalized in big companies, and Japanese labour relations entered an era of corporatism. This system attracted global attention after Japanese companies effectively coped with two oil crises in the 1970s. Given more than a decade's conflicts and tensions in the period 1945–1960, why did Japanese managers and workers change from confrontation to co-operation? What was the driving force behind the institutional transformation of Japanese management? Below, I test the validity of three competing theories.

The economic explanations

The economic perspective emphasizes efficiency. Douglass North (1981:24) points out that a major role played by the state is to spec-ify the fundamental rules of competition and co-operation which will provide a structure of property rights for maximizing the rents accruing to the ruler, to reduce transaction costs in order to foster maximum output of the society and, therefore, to increase tax revenues accruing to the state. Although the economic perspective generally assumes that the market is the most efficient form of gov-ernance, it also holds that when the market fails to maintain order, nonmarket governance structures may develop. Nevertheless, as Williamson (1985, 1990) asserts, corporate hierarchies emerge to co-ordinate economic transactions when the costs of such exchanges through the market are perceived by economic actors as too high. In other words, when economic actors can no longer efficiently con-summate transactions through existing mechanisms, they will develop other, more efficient, governance mechanisms. He acknow-ledges the diversity of governance mechanisms but believes that they are derived for promoting efficiency and reducing transaction cost. According to the economic perspective, the structure of economic governance is a calculated expression of economically rational persons pursuing profit.

The economic perspective in studies on Japanese management focuses on the x-efficiency, which is characterized by effort and the pursuit of rationality, and individuals' determination of how much of each to give to their job. It also holds that the Japanese employment system is driven by internal labour markets in which employees are recruited with lifetime commitment, receive on-the-job training, and compete with one another for promotion into higher positions, which sharply contrasts to the external labour markets in the Western countries where employees often pursue promotions by changing the company they work for. The internal labour market, it is argued, induces commitment by increasing employees' chances for tenure and promotion (Hatvany and Pucik, 1981); skills that employees learn are company-specific and cannot be realized at full value outside the company (Koike, 1984); the seniority benefits and the lack of alternative employment opportunities at comparable wage levels for workers with previous experience, as well as the insufficiency of public welfare, combine to make an employee both unwilling and unable to move (Hatvany and Pucik, 1981; Tachibanaki, 1984); the articulated and unique philosophies held by Japanese firms foster team spirit and co-operation, which reconcile the firm's objectives of pursuing profits and of perpetuating the firm as a group; even the intensive socialization functions to immerse employees in the firm (Hatvany and Pucik, 1981).

The search for efficiency under structural changes was certainly the driving force that triggered the transformation of Japanese management in the late 1940s after the Japanese economy reengaged in the international competition.

During the war, the Japanese economy had been sustained by cheap materials and labour, and by huge captive markets in its colonies and occupied areas, including China, Manchuria, Korea, Taiwan and the Southeast Asian countries. After defeat, Japanese firms no longer had access to these countries. Also, Japan was virtually prohibited from international trade until 1948. As a result, Japan's position, as measured by the amount of exports, declined from fifth in the world in 1934 to thirty-third in 1947. If the average level of Japanese exports between 1930 and 1934 was 100, it was only 8.8 in 1946, 11.7 in 1947, and 16.2 in 1948 (Tsusan Daijin Kanbō Chōsaka, 1954:93). The low quality of Japanese products was a major problem to Japanese firms. Japanese products had been well known for low price but poor quality. Among 634 claims received by MITI from foreign consumers between the end of World War II and April 1950, 327 concerned the poor quality of products, and 366 of these came from the United States, Japan's largest trading partner (Gao 1997:179).

The operation of the Japanese economy during 1946–1949 relied on 'two stilts': the financing of Japanese firms was heavily subsidized by the government, which adopted an easy money policy, while the budget of the Japanese government depended, to a considerable degree, on financial aid from the United States. During that period, 40 per cent of the capital of Japanese firms was provided by the government (Arisawa, 1960). Meanwhile, the Japanese government received about $5 million annually from the U.S. government (Economic Planning Agency, 1991). In order to allocate the limited domestic resources effectively so as to survive the economic hard times and initiate the postwar reconstruction, the Japanese government launched the 'priority production program' in 1946. At that time policy makers believed that the market would not be able by itself to achieve an equilibrium between supply and demand; thus the state had to intervene (Arisawa, 1976:281). This managed economy was similar in many respects to a planned economy, in which the function of the market in resource allocation was largely replaced by the state. In the priority production program, the state controlled the distribution of production materials and products for daily life according to quotas that it set up; these quotas favoured several strategic industries including coal, iron and steel, and fertilizers (Gao, 1994; 1997). State policy focused on the supply effectiveness of the economy at the macro level rather than on the production efficiency of individual firms at the micro level (Ōkita, 1949). In this managed economy, the operation of firms was sustained by a huge amount of government loans through the Reconstruction Finance Bank (Arisawa, 1960:65–66).

Against this background, the change in the U.S. policy toward Japan and the implementation of the Doge plan in the late 1940s was the most important structural factor that forced the Japanese to face the issue of efficiency. Because the Communists were to take over China, the U.S. government in 1948 changed its policy toward Japan from ensuring that 'Japan will not again become a menace to the United States or to the peace and security of the world' (SWNCC-150/3, [1945] 1982), to sustaining Japan as 'a self-sufficient democracy, strong enough and stable enough to support

Bai Gao

itself and at the same time to serve as deterrent against any other totalitarian war threats which might hereafter arise in the Far East', and to 'cease to be a financial burden to the United States' (Royall, [1948] 1982). At the end of 1948, Joseph M. Doge, the president of the Bank of Detroit, travelled to Japan as the envoy of the U.S. government. He presented a systematic policy package to the Japanese government, which later became widely known as the Dodge Plan. Dodge informed the Japanese that the U.S. government would end its financial aid to Japan in the near future; the Japanese government must 'achieve a true balance in the consolidated budget', 'assure rigorous limitation in the extension of credit', and 'pursue maximum expansion in total government revenues' in an effort to eliminate inflation immediately. At the same time, the Dodge Plan established a fixed exchange rate of 1 dollar to 360 yen, which enabled Japan to regain access to the international market. The Dodge Plan had two major goals: first, Japan must achieve its economic independence by participating in the international division of labour and promoting exports rather than by depending on the United States; second, Japanese firms must survive by themselves through market competition, rather than relying on government subsidies.

At the time, efficiency was socially constructed as a real challenge. Because Japan had few natural resources, it was argued, 'imports and exports could be the two pillars to support Japan's industrialization and huge population', and to 'solve economic problems of one country at the global level' (Nakayama, 1949:3–6). At that time, Japanese managers held that 'The reconstruction and independence of the Japanese economy rely upon the promotion of exports. The promotion of exports is impossible without the rationalization of firms . . . the goal of the rationalization of firms is to produce, as much as possible, low-priced products with good quality . . . the rationalization of firms in the managed economy was controlled by the policy and administration of the state. As a result, irrationality and inefficiency were the biggest obstacles to the rationalization of firms. In order to make Japanese firms competitive internationally, we need to eliminate bureaucratic control and its major problems, such as unrealistic equality, and introduce the principles of free competition and efficiency (Nikeiren, [1949] 1966:183). Both government officials and business leaders believed that 'the best medicine for the Japanese economy would be to open it up to the world economy and the discipline of international competition' (see Johnson, 1982:189). To promote efficiency, the rationalization

92   © The Editorial Board of The Sociological Review 1998

movement was launched in the early 1950s and allocative efficiency, as measured by production cost and short-term profits, was perceived as the top issue by management.

At the time, cheap labour policy and downsizing were two major strategies adopted by Japanese firms to promote efficiency. In May 1949 the average hourly wage in Japanese industries was 62.74 yen; wages in Britain and the United States were 221.20 yen and 494.28 yen respectively, or 3.5 and 7.9 times higher than in Japan. Cheap labour was concentrated particularly in the textile industry, whose proportion of total Japanese exports was 75.5 per cent in 1947 and 61.1 per cent in 1948. The hourly wage in Japanese textile industry was only 21.55 yen in 1949, in comparison with 183.49 yen in Britain and 428.15 yen in the United States. In the spinning industry, the Japanese hourly wage was only 13.50 yen, in comparison with 156.24 yen in Britain and 387.36 yen in the United States (Ekonomisuto, 1950). Japanese firms also conducted massive layoffs. From February 1949 to May 1950, 10,375 private firms leg go 400,000 employees, while government and public agencies laid off 419,000 persons (Rekishigaku Kenkyūkai, 1990:137). Meanwhile most firms froze new recruitment and began the intensive use of temporary and nonskilled workers, who earned much lower salaries than regular workers (Takajima, 1953). As late in 1954, Japanese steel, coal, and chemical firms still used layoffs and increased working hours as the major means of rationalizing production, which resulted in a record high of 840,000 unemployed in March of that year (Ekonomisuto, 1955, July 9). Between 1947 and 1956, manufacturing production increased by 650 per cent, while employment increased by only 12 per cent. In the mineral industry, production increased by nearly 200 per cent while employment decreased by 30 per cent (Satō, 1958).

This efficiency-oriented strategy adopted by Japanese firms in the early 1950s indicates that there was nothing in Japanese culture to preclude Western individualistic economics and that Japanese firms could adopt the same strategies as their Western counterparts. The cheap labour policy and downsizing driven by efficiency consideration, however, contradict sharply with the characteristics of Japanese management described earlier. Thus, while the economic perspective rings true about the stimulus in the early stage of change, it cannot explain the final outcome of the transformation of Japanese management because, as I discuss below, this efficiency-oriented strategy did not work well after the Korea War ended and was rejected by Japanese companies.

The cultural explanation

The cultural perspective holds that 'economic processes have an irreducible "cultural" component' (DiMaggio, 1994:27). It can be divided into two different views: one emphasizes culture's regulatory impact on the economy. It treats economic behaviour as analytically distinct from culture and stresses the ways in which norms and conventions constrain the individual's unrestrained pursuit of self-interest. The regulatory view of cultural perspective is very influential in studies on Japanese management. It traces the contemporary Japanese practices of lifetime employment, a seniority-based wage system, and company-based labour unions to Japan's indigenous value of harmony. It maintains that the operation of Japanese industrial organizations conforms to the Confucian ethics embodied in pre-modern organizations, the *ie* (household) or the *mura* (village) (Abegglen, 1958; Ōuchi, 1981; Rohlen, 1974). At the core of Japanese economic relations lies 'good will'—'the sentiments of friendship and the sense of diffuse personal obligation which accrue between individuals engaged in recurring contractual economic exchange' (Dore, [1983] 1992:160).

The other view, in contrast, focuses on culture's constitutive impact on economic institutions. It views culture and economic behaviour as mutually generative and holds that culture provides the categories and understandings that enable us to engage in economic action (DiMaggio, 1994:24). A new practice is often institutionalized as a response to structural changes. Since actors urgently seek new solutions when the established practice is discredited and the new solutions must be legitimated before they can be institutionalized (Dobbin, 1993; Hall, 1992; Krasner, 1984; Weir and Skocpol, 1985), ideas often stand out as a major source in the explanations of institutional change (North, 1990). In particular, 'the availability of the ideas that provide the rationale' is an important condition for institutional innovation (Weir, 1989:54). The constitutive view of the cultural perspective does not exclude itself from efficiency or interest. Rather, it argues the institutionalized beliefs on how the economy works and how efficiency and competitiveness are promoted strongly influence how economic actors perceive the situation, define their interests, formulate their strategy, fight for legitimacy and determine what kind of economic institution eventually will be established (Gao, 1997).

On the one hand, these ideas and ideologies are 'subjective' rather than 'correct', 'true', or 'valid' (Weber, 1968). They are neither simply a collection of analytic abstractions and transcriptions on an already given reality nor a set of principles for purely utilitarian calculations. Rather, they serve as a symbolic instrument, a 'cultural tool', and a 'construction of the world' of economic actors for discovering, elaborating, and expressing the meanings about what is a rational way to define their relationship in modern economic activities, in an effort to create an order for this temporal world (Block, 1990; Gudeman, 1986; Swidler, 1986). On the other hand, they have not yet been institutionalized, and do not have much ritual power. In comparison with their later state as 'highly rationalized myth', they (institutionalized rules in their infant state) are real and concrete in the sense that economic actors regard them as the source for searching for the most effective way to handle their relationship in economic reality. They reflect the economic actors' realistic reasoning rather than ceremonial conformity to any existing rituals of culture. After they have been accepted by all parties concerned, rational meanings become institutionalized rules (Gao, 1997).

Cultural effects, both regulatory and constitutive, played a very important role in demonstrating the new direction of institutional transformation after the strategy of cheap labour policy and downsizing failed in Japan by reinterpreting what is comparative advantage and what needs to be done to acquire such a comparative advantage. Below I examine successively the applications of these two views in the Japanese case. I strongly reject the pervasive interpretation of the Japanese style of management as simply a natural inheritance of indigenous values.

The strategies of cheap labour policy and downsizing were shaken in the mid-1950s by two structural reasons. One is that while Japanese firms made massive layoffs in the late 1940s and the early 1950s, their access to the international market was sustained primarily not by efficiency but by a huge amount of special procurement from the U.S. government during the Korean War, which soared as high as $1.6 billion between June 1950 and May 1955 (Masamura, 1991:611). In the early 1950s, the conservative politicians and business leaders assured Japanese companies' access to the international market by connecting the Japanese economy with the cold war system. They regarded international tension as an opportunity for Japan and argued that Japan should achieve its economic independence by depending on the United States politically and militarily in exchange for economic advantages. Meanwhile, Japan should hold its defence expenditures to a minimum in order to concentrate all its resources on the economy (Keidanren, 1953; Yoshida, 1957; also see Gao, 1997; Pyle, 1992; Samuels, 1994). In this sense the Korean War presented Japanese companies with a great opportunity to make profits without genuine competition in the international market. Nevertheless, this situation did not last long. When the war ended, ensuring a share of Japanese products in the international market once again became a major issue. Facing competition from developing countries, low price alone could not help much and without labour's co-operation, quality control programmes could not be well supported.

The other structural reason is that the strategy of cheap labour policy and downsizing caused strong reactions from labour unions in the early 1950s. The 'collective struggle', which involved labour unions' participation in both single and multiple industries, became a popular form of labour strategy (Ōta, 1953). Stopping layoffs and reducing the intensification of work were the two major goals of labour movements at the time. In August 1953 the Association of Labour Unions (the national organization of Japanese labour unions) adopted the slogan 'fighting against the layoff of even one person, the wage reduction of even one cent, and the intensification of work by even one piece.' To protect labour's interests, the Association asserted that Japanese workers should organize industry-based and regionally based collective strikes to fight the capitalists (Takajima, 1953). In its outline of action, opposition to low wages and layoffs was the most important issue. According to statistics, job security was the major reason for labour disputes in the first half of the 1950s and the massive layoffs even resulted in violence.

After the mid 1950s, some Japanese managers began to promote harmony, aiming to regulate the behaviours of manager and workers by traditional values. This so-called cultural effect, however, was not naturally inherited from Japan's past; it was stimulated by cross-national learning and was promoted for strategic reasons. In 1953 a group of Japanese managers, who were the core members of the Japan Committee of Economic Development (Nihon Keizai Dōyūkai), visited West Germany. They discovered that German management depended heavily on the concept of a 'blood tie' between managers and workers, which came from the idea of 'race' or 'nationality'. This 'blood tie' not only made German managers and workers co-operate voluntarily for the sake of the nation during the postwar reconstruction; it also made the German workers believe that their living standard could not be improved without an increase in productivity, and made the German managers strongly appreciate the active participation of German labour unions in the reconstruction of the late 1940s—the most difficult period in modern German history. Kōshi Kōhei, one of these Japanese managers, asserted that this 'blood tie' between management and labour could be a medium of continuous communication, which could constitute the foundation of healthy labour relations in Japan (see Nihon Seisansei Honbu, 1985, pp.30–32). Soon after his trip to West Germany, Kōhei founded the Headquarters of Productivity, and put his belief into practice. As Granovetter (1985:486) points out, 'culture is not a once-for-all influence but an ongoing process, continuously constructed and reconstructed during interaction. It not only shapes its members but also is shaped by them, in part for their own strategic reasons'.

Although these Japanese managers intended to rely upon the regulatory effect of culture on the economy to induce labour's co-operation, this strategy did not generate enough support from the labour unions because, without addressing the issues of unemployment and low salaries (the two issues that concerned workers most deeply), a cultural declaration of harmony did not appeal to the Japanese labour unions. Providing more economic benefits to labour, however, was in conflict with the leading economy theory at the time, that stressed the allocative efficiency. Thus, the question of whether these Japanese managers could find legitimacy for their cultural perspective became critical for the further development of the Japanese management system.

The constitutive effect of culture on the economy, measured by the institutionalized beliefs of how the economy works and how efficiency is promoted, played a very important role in shaping the direction of further transformation of Japanese management. The diffusion of Joseph Schumpeter's theory of innovation changed not only the Japanese definition of comparative advantage in international competition, but also the managers' perception of their self-interests. This new theory completely discredited the strategy of cheap labour policy and downsizing, demonstrating an alternative way of promoting competitiveness.

Schumpeter has been influential in Japan since the prewar period, and he played an important role in shaping the development of Japan's non-Marxist economics. He trained several Japanese students, at both Bonn University in Germany and Harvard University in the United States, who became prominent economists in postwar Japan. One of these students, as I discuss later in this paper, is

Nakayama Ichirō who was the vice-president of the Headquarters of Productivity and played a decisive role in shaping the direction of Japanese labour relations. After Schumpeter died in 1950, all of his major works were translated into Japanese (for details, see, Gao, 1997:207).

Drawing directly on Schumpeter's theory of innovation, the 1956 White Paper on the Economy published by the Japanese government, argued that the global economy had developed through three waves of industrial revolution: the first took place between 1788 and 1815 and was represented by the invention of the steam engine; the second occurred between 1843 and 1873 and was sustained by the spread of railroads; the third appeared between 1897 and 1920 and was caused by the emergence of the electronics, chemical, automobile, and airplane industries; and now the fourth industrial revolution was under way; this was stimulated by the use of atomic power and automation. More important, each industrial revolution had generated long-term growth in the global economy. Even if a short-term recession occurred, it would simply be a minor episode between waves of economic growth (Keizai Kikakuchō, 1956, pp. 33–35). The comparative advantage in international trade in such a new era, according to the White Paper, would be based on production technology. Innovation would be a powerful instrument for promoting production technology, production relationships, patterns of consumption, the structure of trade, and a position in the division of labour among industries, professions, and nations (Gotō, 1956). In the era of the new industrial revolution, the winners and losers in market competition would be determined by their strength in production technology. On the basis of this understanding, the White Paper argued that 'it is no longer the postwar era. The growth sustained by economic recovery has ended. Further economic growth must be based on modernization' (Keizei Kikakuchō, 1956).

Under this new definition of comparative advantage based on production technology, labour was bestowed with new significance. Because innovation referred to 'a more effective combination of production elements', labour was a matter of great importance in production. Criticising the strategy of cheap labour for its exclusive attention to wage and production costs and its general neglect of the human element, economists began to argue that labour relations deserved ample attention because the conflicts and confrontations between the firms and labour would be the greatest obstacle to innovation and the promotion of increased productivity. Unless the problems in wage and employment were solved, productivity could not be promoted (Nakayama, [1956] 1972). According to this new perception, labour was no longer considered simply as one type of production material, but rather as human capital, important for absorbing the new production technology and improving the quality of products. In the words of a group of progressive managers who gathered at the Headquarters of Productivity, 'the promotion of productivity cannot be done effectively without the co-operation of managers and workers, who conduct the production, and a deeper understanding from the general public' (Nihon Seisansei Honbu, [1955] 1966:305). It is clear that only after Schumpeter's theory of innovation changed the managers' perception of labour, that the value of x-efficiency to the promotion of productivity caught their attention.

The new definition of comparative advantage based on production technology also changed the way Japanese firms perceived their interests. It was clear to Japanese firms that without an institutional framework to generate and sustain mutual trust, workers would always be sceptical about managers' intentions. Resistance by organized labour forced Japanese managers to re-examine their managerial philosophy. Some managers came to believe that before Japan could achieve economic independence, managers must learn that the interest of the firm was not in short-term profits but in long-term international competitiveness. Even if the firm could win the struggle with labour, what the firm could gain was still too little in comparison with what it could gain from the international market. In these circumstances, they should 'get rid of the arbitrariness of the old capitalism that follows the instinct of pursuing profits' (Nihon Seisansei Honbu, 1985:35). According to the new wisdom, managers needed to establish freedom from shareholders; the 'arbitrariness of capital' should be restricted and revised; the social function, mission, and responsibility of the firm should be stressed; management should transcend a self-centred approach and should recognize labour as one of the most important components of the firm; 'the esteem of human beings' must be recognized during the process of economic growth and technological progress. These managers argued that 'scientific management' in the Japanese context was different from Taylorism in the United States because any business strategy that neglected human relations in management was not 'scientific' in the first place. Instead of asking workers to sacrifice their own interests for firms, managers should co-operate with workers on equal terms in order to promote production technology and enhance the competitiveness of the firm (Nihon Seisansei Honbu, 1985:39–40).

Influenced by Schumpeter's idea of innovation, many Japanese firms shifted their strategy regarding labour from confrontation to co-operation. With the help of the U.S. and Japanese governments, the Headquarters of Productivity was established. It gathered representatives from management, labour unions, state bureaucracies and academia to seek better labour relations. The Headquarters of Productivity sent delegations overseas, invited many experts to Japan to give lectures, conducted studies and investigations on management issues, and disseminated technologies regarding production, marketing, and personnel management through training and consulting. The Headquarters systematically introduced the latest developments in managerial science from the West, especially the United States (Nihon Seisansei Honbu, 1985).

Organized labour, however, gave a divided response to the call for co-operation from management. The General Council of Trade Unions (Sōhyō) refused to co-operate with management, as it regarded the proposal as new way for management to exercise its control; the General Federation of Labour (Sōdōmei), in contrast, decided to gain its interests by making a conditional promise to co-operate (see Sōdōmei, [1955] 1966; Sōhyō, [1955] 1966). Through the 1950s, the majority of both management and labour still remained very sceptical about each other and the transformation of Japanese management was not accomplished until the 1960s after a major confrontation at the national level.

Cultural effects indeed played an important role in identifying the new direction of development and they changed the framework by which Japanese managers perceived what was rational and what was in their interest. However, they cannot explain why these new ideas still faced strong resistance from both management and labour.

The political explanation

The political perspective emphasizes interest, power, and control. It argues that 'actors in key institutions realize considerable gains from the maintenance of those institutions' (DiMaggio, 1992; Fligstein, 1992), and goal-oriented élites intervene at each critical point in the institutional evolution in order to define their interest in the new governance mechanisms (Brint and Karabel, 1992; DiMaggio, 1992; Galaskiewicz, 1992). Drawing on the Weberian tradition, Hamilton and Biggard (1988:75) argue that 'all organizations, no matter what their purpose or historical setting (although related to both), have an internal pattern of command and compliance'. Organizations only exist insofar as there is a probability that certain persons will act in such a way as to carry out the order governing the organization. Lindberg, Campbell and Hollingsworth (1991:10) argue that if the arrangement of governance mechanisms systematically restricts the actor's control over the terms of exchange under which he attempts to obtain resources and information, they may press for governance transformation. Perrow (1981, 1986) further argues that firms are profitable not merely because they are efficient but because they are successful instruments of domination.

Another stream of research stresses the nature of a productive institution as an equilibrium of political forces. Different from the view that emphasizes the importance of a dominant actor in the governance arrangement, this view highlights the correlation between fair distribution of economic welfare and efficiency and productivity. According to this view, control and domination are only means of organization. The goal of a business organization is to promote and sustain competitiveness. To achieve this goal, management must establish an incentive structure for labour to co-operate. When the voice, in this case the demand for a fair distribution of economic welfare, is not taken seriously, Albert Hirschman (1970) maintains that actors may choose to 'exit', and refuse to engage in co-operation. This will make business enterprises vulnerable in market competition. Charles Sable (1994:137) argues that the central dilemma of economic growth is to achieve a balance between 'learning—acquiring the knowledge to make things valued in the markets', and 'monitoring—the determination by the transacting parties that the gains from learning be distributed according to the standards agreed to between them, as interpreted by each'. When organizations encompass a substantial portion of the societies of which they are a part, Mancur Olson (1982) points out, they have more incentive to make the society more prosperous. According to this version, the political struggle among economic actors for a fair distribution of economic welfare often results in the transformation of economic governance.

The political perspective illustrates well the dynamics behind the institutionalization of Japanese management. DiMaggio (1988:13) points out that 'Institutionalization is a product of the political efforts of actors to accomplish their ends and . . . the success of an institutionalization project and the form that the resulting institution takes depend on the relative power of the actors who support, oppose, or otherwise strive to influence.' Facing a proposal from management for the productivity movement, the labour unions' major concern was the negative impact of this movement on employment and on wages. Marxists argued that even if science and technology could transcend class struggle, they would have to be applied in a capitalist society: 'Automation itself may provide some benefits and happiness; its capitalist application, however, will cause many negative effects and much unhappiness to human society' (Kanbayashi, 1958:53). Automation, they believed, would not only exert an even greater threat to workers' job security, which already was a major concern because of the pressure of overpopulation in the 1950s, it would also cause a wage decrease for male workers because it would simplify the working process so that firms could depend more heavily on female and young workers (Arisawa, 1956; Ōkōchi 1957). Besides, technological innovation through automation would further increase the workload, creating more alienation among workers. As a whole, said the Marxists, technological innovation would only strengthen the power of capital and weaken the power of labour in the class struggle (Horie, 1955; Kanbayashi, 1958).

To establish an 'agreed pattern of monitoring', economist Nakayama Ichirō, then vice-president of the Headquarters of Productivity, proposed the famous three principles for the productivity movement. First, the ultimate purpose of promoting productivity was to increase employment. Government and business must make every effort at preventing unemployment. Second, management must consult with labour on how to promote productivity according to actual conditions at each firm. Third, the benefits created by the promotion of productivity must be distributed fairly between the firm and labour (Nakayama, [1956] 1972). In accordance with these three principles, some Japanese companies began to address the issue of fair distribution of economic welfare by making efforts of maintaining job security. New technologies were introduced during the productivity movement, primarily in the frontier industries, so as not to cause large-scale layoffs. Even when the reduction of the labour force became inevitable in a sunset industry, many firms transferred workers to other fields rather than letting them go. According to a survey conducted at the end of the 1950s, among the 91 per cent of 409 firms that made technological innovations, only two firms actually laid off workers; 71 per cent of these firms avoided layoffs through job transfers (Nihon Seisansei Honbu, 1960).

The agreed pattern of monitoring, however, came only after actors knew the limits of their political strength and the importance of compromise. Although the productivity movement began to address the issue of fair distribution of economic welfare, the majority of both management and labour still remained highly sceptical toward each other's intentions, influenced by the memories of confrontations in the recent past. In such an atmosphere, both sides clashed on the issue of how to retain workers in the sunset industries. In response to the structural change from coal-based to oil-based energy, the Mitsui Company intended to lay off 6,000 workers at the Miike coal mine. This was the first step in a series of large-scale layoffs, estimated at 110,000 industry-wide. This initiative was backed by the government and business leaders. Labour unions showed strong resistance, however, and engaged in violent conflicts with the police in 1960. The strike lasted for 313 days.

The process of transformation of Japanese management in 1946–1966 indicates that only when a balance of power among actors was achieved, did the new institution begin to be stabilized. Although the Mitsui confrontation ended with labour's failure, it forced the state, management, and labour unions to re-examine the confrontational strategy they had adopted. In the past, the state had adopted a pro-business policy, treating labour disputes as an issue of public security. It had helped the private companies to strengthen their power in labour relations; made the establishment of new labour unions more difficult; outlawed strikes against layoffs; and withdrew the labour unions' right to negotiate (Sanbetsu Kaigi, 1949).In 1951 the Japanese government even conducted the 'red purge', arresting many leaders of labour unions. After the Miike strike, however, the Liberal Democratic Party began to perceive labour relation as an issue of social policy. It changed from a pro-business labour policy to a preference for stable labour relations. In 1963 the chairman of the National Organizational Committee of the LDP argued that the party should 'take a neutral position on the issues concerning labour relations and represent the interest of the nation by mediating competing interests' (Rekishigaku Kenkyūkai, 1990:13–14; Gao, 1997).

Management also recognized the huge cost of a confrontational strategy. When the Minister of Labour negotiated the resolution with the president of Mitsui, all the major business leaders who were invited to be present showed their concern about labour relations. Besides in 1963 demand outperformed supply in the Japanese labour market for the first time in history. Beginning at that time, the shortage of labour became a major problem to Japanese firms; starting salaries for young workers increased at an annual average of more than 13 per cent in the early 1960s, in comparison with less than 5 per cent in 1954–1958. In such circumstances, the introduction of lifetime employment and the seniority-based wage system in large Japanese firms was no longer simply a way to balance economic welfare between the firm and labour, but also a necessary strategy for preserving a skilled labour force. In the meantime, labour unions also realized that national-level and industry-level confrontations could not effectively protect their interests and decided to participate fully in the productivity movement. Even the Communist Party and the Socialist Party began to shift their platforms in national politics from 'revolution' to 'structural reform' within the framework of capitalist institutions (Gao, 1997).

In 1963, the deputy director of the Japan Federation of Employers Associations spoke at the national meeting about lifetime employment and the seniority-based wage. He argued that there were only two ways to bring about peace between management and labour. One was a long-term, stable wage policy; the other was continuous communication between management and labour within the firm. He also pointed out that 'We have had the practice of lifetime employment in Japan and the seniority-based wage which supports it . . . They were born and nurtured in the Japanese culture. This is an advantage. We should make good use of this Japanese tradition. Japan's lifetime employment is completely opposite to the short-term contracts practiced in Europe and North America . . . Speaking of Japanese management, we must devise a Japanese style of wage system and employment system' (Nikeiren, [1963] 1966b:462). In the 1960s, the practices of lifetime employment, the seniority-based wage, and the firm-based labour union, were widely institutionalized, at least among big companies, in the productivity movement. Starting at the end of the 1940s with efficiency oriented downsizing and cheap labour policy, this movement experienced several twists, and eventually achieved a distinctive pattern of economic governance. The productivity movement had the power to penetrate the daily operation of the firm and to induce mass participation in innovation. The major reason for this success, according to a MITI official, is that the introduction of lifetime employment and seniority-based wage demonstrated a great vision:

it concerned not only the interests of the firm, but also the interests of labour (see Nihon Seisansei Honbu, 1985:124).

It is clear that this political perspective is powerful in explaining the mechanism in which the confrontational labour relations were eventually settled in postwar Japan. Nevertheless, it also has its limits. The political perspective alone can hardly explain why economic actors decide to break the existing agreed-pattern of monitoring. It also has difficulties in explaining why economic actors agreed in any particular way on the pattern of monitoring and what kind of symbolic instruments economic actors used in constructing a new order for themselves.

Discussion

This study shows that efficiency, measured by low production cost, was indeed the primary concern at the end of the 1940s and the beginning of the 1950s and Japanese firms indeed intended to promote efficiency by cheap labour policy and downsizing. This is very important to our understanding of the pressure of structural changes on the existing governance structure and the source of the dynamics of change. Promoting efficiency by layoffs and low salaries was later regarded as the major barrier to the goal of building comparative advantage in production technology. Moreover, Japanese firms made a historical tradeoff: they shifted from allocative efficiency to x-efficiency by giving up short-term profits in exchange for labour's co-operation in technological innovation. Here, efficiency, though a different type, still mattered. The economic perspective, however, cannot explain why Japanese firms decided to shift their focus in managerial practice from allocative efficiency to x-efficiency. In this sense, the economic perspective contributes more to revealing the stimulus of change, rather than interpreting the particular pattern of outcome in the transformation of economic governance.

The regulatory view of the cultural perspective is supported by this study to some extent. The indigenous value of harmony indeed played an important role in reorienting the direction of Japanese managers in the mid 1950s. It also served to sustain the emergence of corporatism in the 1960s. After Japanese management was institutionalized, it contributed even more greatly to institutional reproduction. Nevertheless, this view in studies of Japanese management often assumes implicitly that the economic actors in Japanese society internalize indigenous values unconsciously and obey the norms of institutional settings voluntarily. In other words, Japanese culture shapes Japanese behaviour in economic activities mechanically by insinuating itself into the minds and bodies of individual Japanese. As a result, economic actors are overwhelmed by societal forces and have no 'engine of action' (Coleman 1988, 1990; Granovetter, 1985; Wrong, 1960). But current Japanese management did not acquire its present pattern until the 1960s and the institutionalization of this system was full of interruptive, nonlinear changes (Gao, 1997; Garon, 1986; Gordon, 1985; Masamura, 1985). Indigenous value matters only when economic actors assert it strategically. The regulatory view of culture in studies of Japanese management has largely failed to explain under what conditions and through what processes orientations toward harmony and co-operation were eventually institutionalized in Japanese firms.

In the existing literature on Japanese management, both the economic perspective and the regulatory view of the cultural perspective tend to disregard the time-space contingency of economic institution. As a result, 'theory is not historicized, and history, particularly its "time-conditionedness" and temporal contingencies, is not theorized' (Isaac and Griffin, 1989:875). As Berger and Luckmann (1966:54–55) point out, 'institutions always have a history, of which they are products. It is impossible to understand an institution adequately without an understanding of the historical process in which it was produced'.

In this study, I found the constitutive view of the cultural perspective on the economy and the political perspective that highlights the concurrence of political interests illuminating because they allow us to investigate the historical contingencies that shaped the outcome of the transformation of economic governance. In this historical process, the constitutive view of the cultural perspective emphasizes the intellectual environment, linking the alternatives of new patterns of economic governance to the availability of specific economic ideas. It also shows that both economic laws and cultural traditions are never fixed. They are the changing outcome of a many-sided process in which the identities, interests, modalities of calculation are constantly redefined and renegotiated. In this sense, unless economic actors believe that efficiency or harmony serve their strategic purposes, neither factor can influence the pattern of the transformation of economic institutions. This view is powerful in explaining why Japanese firms shifted their focus from allocative efficiency to x-efficiency and changed their strategy toward labour from confrontation to co-operation.

The political perspective that highlights power and domination is indeed suggestive when we analyze the process of transformation of Japanese management in the 1950s. Labour unions fought hard to establish their power in the firm in the 1940s while management made a comeback in reinstalling their control over production in the 1950s. What happened in the 1960s, however, indicates that this power view of the political perspective may have caught only one side of the story. Japanese management was institutionalized by the concurrence of political forces under which actors reached an agreed pattern of monitoring. Both lifetime employment and the seniority-based wage are business customs, not legal contracts (Cole, 1972). They are what North (1990) calls 'self-imposed codes of conduct' in Japanese firms, enforced by the potential retaliation of labour. Their nature as an institution is to set rules for behaviour by providing different incentives to each party. Not until after the Miike strike of 1960 in which both management and labour recognized the limits on the strength of their political power, did most large Japanese firms introduce the system of lifetime employment and the seniority-based wage as a way of delivering economic welfare to workers. Only then did most of the Japanese labour unions begin to co-operate fully with management in an effort to promote production technology.

This study demonstrates that each of the three leading perspectives in studies of the institutional transformation of economic governance has certain merits and they are complementary to each other. The economic perspective helps us understand the importance of structural changes in the economy as the driving force in initiating institutional transformation. The political perspective teaches us that an institutional transformation is a political process and its accomplishment is sustained by a mechanism which balances the competing interests among the major players. The cultural perspective shows us the strategies adopted by economic actors in the institutional transformation are never predetermined and are strongly influenced by their intellectual environments.

References

Abegglen, J.C., (1958), *The Japanese Factory*, Glencoe: The Free Press.
Aoki, M., (1984), 'Shareholders' Non-Unanimity on Investment Financing: Banks vs. Individual Investors'. In *The Economic Analysis of the Japanese Firm*, edited by Masahiko Aoki. Amsterdam: Elsevier Science Publishers B.V., pp.193–224.

Arisawa, H., (1956), 'Nihon shihonshugi to koyō' (The Japanese Capitalism and Employment). *Sekai* January:23–34.

Arisawa, H., (1957), 'Keizai kakudai wa koyō mondai o kaiketsu shiuru ka' (It is Possible to Solve the Problem of Employment by Economic Expansion). *Sekai* 135 (March):34–44.

Arisawa, H., (1960), *Gendai nihon sangyō kōza* (Lectures on Modern Japanese Industry). Tokyo: Iwanami Shoten, Vol. 8.

Arisawa, H. (ed.), (1976), *Shōwa keizaishi* (The History of the Shōwa Economy). Tokyo: Nihon Keizai Shinbunsha.

Arisawa, H. and Hidezō, I., (1966), *Shiryō sengo nijunenshi* (Literature on Twenty Years' Postwar History). Tōkyō: Nihon Hyōronsha, Vol. 2.

Berger, P.L. and Luckmann, T., (1966), *The Social Construction of Reality*. New York: Anchor Books.

Blaine, M., (1993), 'Profitability and Competitiveness: Lessons from Japanese and American Firms in the 1980s'. *California Management Review* Fall:48–74.

Block, F., (1990), *Postindustrial Possibilities*, Berkeley: University of California Press.

Block, F., (1994), 'The Roles of the State in the Economy'. In *The Handbook of Economic Sociology*, edited by Neil J. Smelser and Richard Swedberg. Princeton: Princeton University Press, pp.691–710.

Brint, S. and Karabel, J., (1991), 'Institutional Origins and Transformations: The Case of American Community Colleges'. In *The New Institutionalism in Organizational Analysis*, edited by Paul J. DiMaggio and Walter W. Powell. Chicago: The University of Chicago Press, pp.337–360.

Brinton, M., (1992), *Women and the Economic Miracle: Gender and Work in Postwar Japan*. Berkeley: University of California Press.

Butler, S., Knight, R., Guttman, M. and Williams, M., (1994), 'Sinking Deeper in the Drowning Pool', *U.S. News and World Report* May 16:56–57.

Campbell, J.L., Hollingsworth, R. and Lindberg, L.N. (eds), (1990), *Governance of the American Economy*. Cambridge: Cambridge University Press, pp.319–355.

Cohen, J.B., (1949), *Japan's Economy in War and Reconstruction*. Minneapolis: University of Minnesota Press.

Cole, R.E., (1972), 'Permanent Employment in Japan: Facts and Fantasies'. *Industrial and Labor Relations Review*, 26:615–630.

Coleman, J., (1988), 'Social Capital in the Creation of Human Capital', *American Journal of Sociology*, 94:95–120.

Coleman, J., (1990), *Foundation of Social Theory*, Cambridge: Harvard University Press.

DiMaggio, P., (1988), 'Interest and Agency in Institutional Theory'. In *Institutional Patterns and Organizations*, edited by Lynn G. Zucker. Cambridge: Balligner Publishing Company, pp.3–21.

DiMaggio, P., (1994), 'Culture and Economy'. In Neil J. Smelser and Richard Swedberg, eds, *The Handbook of Economic Sociology*, Princeton: Princeton University Press, pp.27–57.

DiMaggio, P.J. and Powell, W.W., (1991), 'Introduction'. In *The New Institutionalism in Organizational Analysis*, edited by Paul J. DiMaggio and Walter W. Powell. Chicago: The University of Chicago Press, pp.1–38.

Dobbin, F., (1993), 'The Social Construction of the Great Depression', *Theory and Society* 22:1–56.

Dore, R., (1973), *British Factory: Japanese Factory: The Origins of National Diversity in Industrial Relations*, Berkeley: University of California Press.

Dore, R., (1987), *Taking Japan Seriously*, London: The Athlone Press.

Dore, R., (1992 [1983]), 'Goodwill and the Spirit of Market Capitalism'. In *The Sociology of Economic Life*. Boulder: Westview Press, pp.159–180.

Economic Planning Agency, (1990), *The Japanese Economy, 1955–65*.

Ekonomisuto, (1950), 'Nihon teichingin to kokusai hikaku' (Japan's Low Wage and International Comparison). June 21:31–32.

Ekonomisuto, (1955), 'Seisansei undō no teikō to kyōryoku (The Resistance and Co-operation in Productivity Movements)'. July 9:50–52.

Ekonomisuto, (1994a), 'Hado na koyō chōsei no kanōsei mo (A Possibility of Tough Adjustment in Employment)'. May 9:54–55.

Ekonomisuto, (1994b), 'Zuhyō de miru seizōgyō no kūdōka (An Illustration of the Deindustrialization of Manufacturing Industries)'. July 5:32–34.

Ekonomisuto, (1994c), 'Genzai no nihon kara wa dasshutsu suru igaini michi wa nai (There is no Alternative but Escaping from Japan)'. August 2:38–44.

Engardio, P., Barnathan, J. and Glasgall, W., (1993), 'Asia's Wealth'. *Business Week* November 29:100–108.

Fligstein, N., (1991), 'The Structural Transformation of American Industry: An Institutional Account of the Causes of Diversification in the Largest Firms, 1919–1979'. In *The New Institutionalism in Organizational Analysis*, edited by Paul J. DiMaggio and Walter W. Powell. Chicago: The University of Chicago Press, pp.311–336.

Friedland, R. and Alford, R.R., (1991), 'Bringing Society Back In: Symbols, Practices, and Institutional Contradictions'. In *The New Institutionalism in Organizational Analysis*, edited by Paul J. DiMaggio and Walter W. Powell. Chicago: The University of Chicago Press, pp.232–263.

Friedman, D., (1988), *The Misunderstood Miracle*, Ithaca: Cornell University Press.

Futoda, K., (1953), 'Gōrika tōsō o ikani tatakau ka (How to Fight with Rationalization)'. *Shakaishugi* 27 (September):2–5.

Gaiko Forum, (1994), 'Kuroji endaka kūdōka keizai no saizensen kara (From the Economic Frontier: Trade Surplus, the Appreciation of Yen and Deindustrialization'. June:18–27.

Galaskiewicz, J., (1991), 'Making Corporate Actors Accountable: Institution-Building in Minneapolis-St. Paul'. In *The New Institutionalism in Organizational Analysis*, edited by Paul J. DiMaggio and Walter W. Powell. Chicago: The University of Chicago Press, pp.293–310.

Gao, B., (1997), *Economic Ideology and Japanese Industrial Policy: Developmentalism from 1931 to 1965*. New York: Cambridge University Press.

Garon, S., (1987), *The State and Labor in Modern Japan*. Berkeley: University of California Press.

Gordon, A., (1985), *The Evolution of Labor Relations in Japan: Heavy Industry, 1853–1955*. Cambridge: Council on East Asian Studies, Harvard University.

Gotō, Y., (1956), 'Kijutsu kakushin to wa nani zo ya (What is Technological Innovation?)'. *Ekonomisuto*. Betsusatsu (separate volume), Autumn:9–24.

Granovetter, M., (1985), 'Economic Action and Social Structure: The Problem of Embeddedness'. *American Journal of Sociology* 91:481–510.

Gross, N. and Rebello, K., (1993), 'A Tsunami of Gizmos'. *Business Week* September 27: 56–57.

Gudeman, S., (1986), *Economics as Culture: Models and Metaphors of Livelihood*. London: Routledge & Kegan Paul.

Hachiyo, M., (1994), 'Nihon ni mitomerareru aratana koyō kikai no sōshutsu (The

Creation of New Employment Opportunities Demanded by Japan)'. *Ekonomisuto* July 12:64–67.

Hall, P.A., (1989), *The Political Power of Economic Ideas: Keynesianism Across Nations*. Princeton: Princeton University Press.

Hamilton, G. and Biggart, N.W., (1988) 'Market, Culture, and Authority: A Comparative Analysis of Management and Organization in the Far East. *American Journal of Sociology* pp. 52–94.

Hatvany, N. and Puckik, V., (1981), 'An Integrated Management System: Lessons from the Japanese Experience'. *Academy of Management Review* 6(3):469–480.

Hirschman, A.O., (1970), *Exit, Voice, and Loyalty*. Cambridge: Harvard University Press.

Holyoke, L., (1993), 'What? Everyday Bargains? This can't be Japan'. *Business Week* September 6:41.

Holyoke, L., (1994), 'Psst! Wanna Buy A Used Steel Plant?' *Business Week* August 22:48.

Horie, M., (1955), 'Sensansei kōjō undō hihan (Criticism on the Movement of Promoting Productivity)'. *Chūō Kōron* October:144–155.

Imai, K., (1993), 'Nihon sangyō, saikōchiku shiron (On the Reconstruction of Japanese Industries)'. *Ekonomisuto* November 16:40–49.

Isaac, L.W. and Griffin, L.J., 'Ahistoricism in Time-Series Analyses of Historical Process'. *American Sociological Review* 54(6):873–890.

Johnson, C., (1982), *MITI and the Japanese Miracle*. Stanford: Stanford University Press.

Kamiyo, W., (1994), 'Nihonteki koyō kankō no meritto to demeritto (The Merit and Demerit of the Japanese Employment Custom)'. *Rōdōjipō* June:20–23.

Kanbayashi, T., (1958), 'Kijutsu kakushin no hyōka (The Evaluation of Technological Innovation)'. *Ekonomisuto* January 25:50–54.

Keidanren, J., (1953), 'Shintokuju no igi to keizai kyōryoku no kōsō ni tsuite (On the Significance of New Special Procurements and the Proposal of Economic Cooperation)'. *Keizai Rengō*.

Keizai, K. (ed.), (1956), *Keizai hakusho: nihon keizai no seichō to kindaika* (The Economic White Paper: Japan's Economic Growth and Modernization). Tokyo: Shiseidō.

Kinzley, W.D., (1991), *Industrial Harmony in Modern Japan: the Invention of a Tradition*. London: Routledge.

Koike, K., (1984), 'Skill Formation Systems in the U.S. and Japan: A Comparative Study'. Pp.47–75 in *The Economic Analysis of the Japanese Firm*, edited by Masahiko Aoki. Amsterdam: Elsevier Science Publishers B.V.

Kojima, A., (1994), 'Kakaku "daikyōsō jidai" no bakuaki (The Beginning of an Era of Intensive Competition)'. *Chūō Kōron* September:52–65.

Kono, M., (1994), 'Kyūrokunen made seizōgyō no shisan atsushuku wa tsuzuku (The Continuance of the Reduction in the Capital of Manufacturing Industries)'. *Ekonomisuto* May 24:38–41.

Krasner, S.D., (1984), 'Approaches to the State: Alternative Conceptions and Historical Dynamics'. *Comparative Politics* January:223–246.

Kumamoto, Y., (1994), 'Seisansei jōshō de ima nani ga okiteiruka (What is Happening after the Promotion of Productivity)'. *Ekonomisuto* July 12:60–63.

Kurokawa, T. and Gosaku, S., (1970), *Nihon seisansei honbu: so no jittai to yakuwari* (The Headquarter of Productivity: its Entity and Function). Tokyo: Aomi Shoten.

Kuwahara, Y., (1994), 'Gurōbaruka ga umu shigyō no kyōi (The Threat of Unemployment Caused by Globalization)'. *Ekonomisuto* July 12:54–59.

Efficiency, culture and politics

Lazonick, W., (1991), *Business Organization and the Myth of the Market Place.* Cambridge: Cambridge University Press.

Leibenstein, H., (1984), 'The Japanese management System: An X-Efficiency-Game Theory Analysis'. In *The Economic Analysis of the Japanese Firm*, edited by Masahiko Aoki. Amsterdam: Elsevier Science Publishers B.V., pp.331–357.

Lincoln, J.R. and McBride, Kerry, (1987), 'Japanese Industrial Organization in Comparative Perspective'. *Annual Review of Sociology*, 289–312.

Lindberg, L.N. and Campbell, J.L. (1991), 'The State and the Organization of Economic Activity'. In John L. Campbell, J. Rogers Hollingsworth and Leon N. Lindberg, eds, *Governance of the American Economy*. Cambridge: Cambridge University Press, pp.356–90.

Mandel, M.J. and Gross, N. (1993), 'For Japanese Companies, A Double Whammy}. *Business Week* November 15:154.

Masamura, K., (1985), *Sengoshi* (Postwar History). Tokyo: Tsukuma Shobō.

Masamura, K., (1991), 'Chōsen tokuju (The Korean Special Procurement)'. In *Encyclopedia of Postwar Japan 1945–1990*. Tokyo: Sansentō, p.611.

Meyer, J.W. and Rowan, B., (1977), 'Institutionalized Organizations: Formal Structure as Myth and Ceremony'. *American Journal of Sociology* 83: 340–363.

Miyao, T., (1994), ' "Shinsangyō taibōron" wa maboroshi (The Wait-and-See Attitutde Towards New Industries is an Illusion)'. *Bungei Shunju* May:164–173.

Murakami, Y., (1987), 'The Japanese Model of Political Economy'. In *The Political Economy of Japan: Vol. 1 The Domestic Transformation*, edited by Kozo Yamamura and Yasukichi Yasuba. Stanford: Stanford University Press.

Nakano, T., (1993), 'aisha ga abunaku nareba jinin seiri wa tōzen da (If the Company Gets into Trouble, the Employment Adjustment is Inevitable)'. *Shūkan Tōyō Keizai* April 24:12.

Nakayama, I., (1949), 'Nihon keizai no kao (The Look of Japanese Economy'. *Hyōron* December:3–6.

Nakayama, I., (1959), 'Chingin nibai o teishō (Doubling the salary)'. *Yomiuri Shibun* Jan.3.

Nakayama, I., (1972), 'Sensansei no riron to jissai (The Theory of Productivity and Reality)'. In *Seisansei kōjō shirizu* (Series on the Promotion of Productivity). Tokyo: Seisansei Honbu, pp.331–344.

Neff, R., (1993), 'Well, It's a Start: Japan Talks Deregulation at Last and More Changes may be Coming'. *Business Week* September 13:48–49.

Neff, R. and Gross, N., (1993), 'Japan: How Bad?' *Business Week* December 13:56–59.

Neff, R., Ullmann, O. and Glasgall, W., (1993), 'How Badly will Yen Shock Hurt?' *Business Week* August 30: 52–53.

Nihon, S.H., ([1955] 1966), 'Nihon seisansei honbu seitsuritsu kyokuisho (The Purpose for Establishing the Japan Headquarters of Productivity)'. In Ōkochi Kazuo, ed., *Shiryō: sengo nijūnen shi*. Tokyo: Nihon Hyōronsha, p.305.

Nihon, S.H., (1960), *Kijutsu kakushin to nihon keizai* (Technological Innovation and the Japanese Economy).

Nihon, S.H., ([1960] 1966), 'Sōritsu gōshūnen sengen'. In Ōkochi Kazuo, ed., *Shiryō: sengo nijūnen shi*. Tokyo: Nihon Hyōronsha, p.305.

Nihon, S.H., (1985), *Sensansei undō 30 nen shi* (A Thirty Year History of the Movement of Productivity). Tokyo: Nihon Seisansei Honbu.

Nikeiren, ([1948] 1966), 'Keieken kakuhō ni kan suru ikensho (A Statement Regarding the Protection of the Management Authority)'. In Ōkochi Kazuo, ed., *Shiryō: sengo nijūnen shi*. Tokyo: Nihon Hyōronsha, pp.102–104.

Bai Gao

Nikeiren, ([1949] 1966), 'Kigyō gōrika ni kansuru kenkai (Our Position on the Rationalization of Enterprises)'. In *Shiryō: sengo nijūnen shi: keizai* (materials on the Twenty Year History of the Postwar Japan: the Economy), edited by Arisawa Hiromi and Inaba Hidezō. Tokyo: Nihon Hyōronsha, p.305.

Nikeiren, (1966 [1963]a), 'Kongo no rōshi kankei to keieisha no kenkai (Labour Relation From Now on and the Managers' Perspective)'. In *Shiryō: sengo nijūnen shi: rōdō* (Materials on the Twenty Year History of the Postwar Japan: Labour), edited by Ōkōchi Kazuo. Tokyo: Nihon Hyōronsha, p.461.

Nikeiren, (1966 [1963]b), 'Maeda senmu riji rōdō jōsei hōkoku "nihon-teki rōmu kanri o sodateyō" (The Deputy Director Maeda's Keynote Report "Let's Foster Japan's Labour Management)'. In *Shiryō: sengo nijūnen shi* (Materials on the Twenty Year History of the Postwar Japan), edited by Ōkōchi Kazuo. Tokyo: Nihon Hyōron-sha, pp.461–462.

North, D.C., (1981), *Structure and Change in Economic History*. New York: W.W. Norton & Company.

North, D.C., (1990), *Institutions, Institutional Change and Economic Performance*. Cambridge: Cambridge University Press.

Ōkita, S., (1949), 'Kawase reito settei igo (After Fixing the Exchange Rate)'. *Asahi Hyōron* April:64–69.

Ōkōchi, K., (1957), 'Gijutsu kakushin to rōdō kaikyū (Technological Innovation and the Working Class)'. *Sekai* 136(March):86–92.

Okumura, T. and Dore, T., (1993), 'Nihon no "hōjin shugi" wa hokorobi hajimeta (Has Japan's Corporate Capitalism Started Breaking Down?)'. *Ekonomisuto* May 25:28–33.

Olson, M., (1982), *The Rise and Decline of Nations: Economic Growth, Stagflation, and Social Rigidities*. New Haven: Yale University Press.

Ōta, K., (1953), 'Gōrika tōsō o ikani kakatau ka (How to Fight the Battle of Rationalization)'. *Shakaishugi*, 27(Sept.):2–5.

Ouchi, W., (1981), *Theory Z*. Reding, Mass: Addison-Wesley.

Ouchi, W., (1984), *The M-form Society*. Reading, Mass: Addison-Wesley.

Ouchi, H., (1949), 'Dojji rain wa antei o motarasu ka (Does the Dodge Line Bring About Stability?)'. *Hyōron* June:2–13.

Perrow, C., (1981), 'Markets, Hierarchies and Hegemony'. In Andrew Van de Ven and William Joyce, eds, *Perspectives on Organization, Design, and Behavior*. New York: Wiley, pp.371–386.

Powell, B., (1993a), 'Japan Inc. R.I.P.' *Newsweek* December 13:48–50.

Powell, B., (1993b), 'Losing Their Lead'. *Newsweek* December 13:51–54.

Powell, B. and Takayama, H., (1993), 'The End of the Miracle Era'. *Newsweek* August 30:46.

Pyle, K.B., (1992), *The Japanese Question*. Washington, DC.: AEI Press.

Rekishigaku, K., *Nihon Dojidai-shi: Enryo Seisaku no Tenkan to Kowa*. (The Contemporary History of Japan: The Transition of Occupation Policy and the Conclusion of Peace Treaty) 1990:137.

Rōdōjipō, (1994), 'Wa ga kuni no chingin seido no kongo no kōkō (The Future Direction of the Japanese Wage System)'. June:12–19.

Rōdōjipō, (1994), 'Heisei gonen jōki koyo dōkō chōsa (A Survey on the Trend of Employment in the First Half of 1994)'. 2:40–42.

Rohlen, T.P., (1974), *For Harmony and Strength*. Berkeley: University of California Press.

Rostow, W., (1979 [1960]), *The Stages of Economic Growth*. New York: Cambridge

University Press.

Royall, K.C., (1982), 'Royall's Speech on American Policy Towards Japan' in *Shōwa zaisei-shi: shūsen kara kōwa made* (The History of Finance of the Showa Period: From the End of the War to the Conclusion of the Peace Treaty), edited by Ōkurashō Zaiseishishitsu. Tokyo: Tōyō Keizai Shinpōsha, Vol. 20.

Sabel, C., (1994), 'Learning by mOnitoring: The Institutions of Economic Development'. In *The Handbook of Economic Sociology*, edited by Neil J. Smelser and Richard Swedberg. Princeton: Princeton University Press, pp.137–165.

Saeki, K., (1994), 'Sekai o oou "keizai no seijika" to heisei fukyō (The Global Spread of "the Politicalization of Economy" and the Depression of Heisei)'. *Ekonomisuto* May 13:44–50.

Samuelson, R.J., (1994), 'Here's Some Good News, America', *Newsweek* January 31:51.

Samuels, R.J., (1994), *Rich Nation, Strong Army*. Ithaca: Cornell University Press.

Sanbetsu, K., (1949), 'Dantai nado kiseiryō igi to yakuwari (The Significance and the Function of the Revision of Organizations)'. In *Shiryō: sengo nijūnen shi: keizai* (Materials on the Twenty Year History of the Postwar Japan: Labour), edited by Ōkōchi, Kazuo. Tokyo: Nihon Hyōronsha, pp.120–124.

Sato, N., (1958), 'Seisansei kōjō to chingin, koyō (The Promotion of Productivity and Salary and Employment)'. *Ekonomisuto* February 22:50–55.

Sawa, T., (1984), *Kōdo seichō: rinen to seisaku no dōjidaishi* (The High Growth: Histories of Both Theory and Policy). Tokyo: Nihon Hōsō Shuppankai.

Scott, W.R., (1991), 'Unpacking Institutional Arguments'. In *The New Institutionalism in Organizational Analysis*, edited by W. Powell and Paul J. DiMaggio. Chicago: The University of Chicago Press, pp.164–182.

Shimada, H., (1983), 'Japanese Industrial Relations—A New General Model? A Survey of the English-Language Literature'. In *Contemporary Industrial Relations in Japan*, edited by T. Shirai. Madison: University of Wisconsin Press.

Shimada, H., (1993), 'Senshinkoku gata koyō ni shifuto o isoge (Accelerating the Shift Towards the Employment Pattern of Advanced Countries)'. *Shūkan Tōyō Keizai* April 24:22–24.

Shimada, H., (1994a), ' "Shinsangyō, koyō sōshutsu kigaku" o isoge (Making Plans Quickly for the Creation of Employment: New Industries)'. *Chūō Kōron* January:48–62.

Shimada, H., (1994b), 'Kisei kawa de shinkoyō no sōshutsu o (Creating New Employment by Deregulation)'. *Shūkan Tōyō Keizai* (August):13–20.

Shimomura, O., (1958), *Keizai seichō jitsuken no tame ni* (For the Realization of Economic Growth). Tokyo: Kōchikai.

Shimomura, O., (1959a), 'Nihon keizai no kichō to sono seichōryoku (The Basic Condition of the Japanese Economy and its Growth Power).' In *Shimomura riron to sono hihan*, edited by Kin'yū Zaisei Jijō Kenkyūkai, pp.3–30.

Shimomura, O., (1959b), 'Nihon keizai no seichōryoku to seichō riron (The Growth Power of the Japanese Economy and the Growth Theory)'. In *Shimomura riron to sono hihan*, edited by Kin'yū Zaisei Jijō Kenkyūkai, pp.187–272.

Shimomura, O., (1962), *Nihon keizai seichō-ron* (On the Japanese Economic Growth). Tokyo: Kin'yū Zaisei Jijō Kenkyūkai.

Shimura, Y., (1994), 'Consumer Technology Gone Astray'. *Japan Echo*. Vol. XXI (Special Issue).

Shiozawa, Y., (1993), 'Sa-, yūgana botsuraku o junbi shiyō (Let's Prepare An Elegant Decline)'. *Ekonomisuto* December 7:68–73.

Bai Gao

Shukan Tōyō Keizai, (1994), 'Keiki handan krea kisei kanwa made j¯u no pointo (Ten Points: From the Prediction of Economic Situation to Deregulation)'. August:13–20.

Sōhyō, ([1855] 1966), 'Seisansei zōkyō ni taisuru kihonteki taido (The Basic Position on the Promotion of Productivity)'. In Ōkochi Kazuo, ed., *Shiryō sengo nijūnenshi: Vol. 4 rōdō*. Tokyo: pp.306–308.

Sōdōmei, 'Dainikai chūō iinkai kettei: seisansei kōjō undō ni taisuru sōdōmei no taido (The Decision by the Second Meeting of Central Committee: Sōdōmei's Attitude Toward the Productivity Movement)'. In Ōkochi Kazuo, ed., *Shiryō sengo nijūnenshi: Vol. 4 rōdō*. Tokyo: p.308.

Sugita, H., (1989), *Shōwa no ekonomisuto* (Showa Economists). Tokyo: Chūō Keizai-sha.

Swedberg, R. and Granovetter, M., (1992), 'Introduction'. Pp. 1–26 in *The Sociology of Economic Life*, edited by Mark Granovetter and Richard Swedberg. Boulder: Westview Press.

Swidler, A., (1986), 'Culture in Actions: Symbols and Strategies', *American Sociological Review* 51:273–286.

SWNCC-150/3, (1982 [1945]), 'United States Initial Post-Defeat Policy Relating to Japan: SWNCC 150/3'. In *Shōwa zaisei-shi: shūsen kara kōwa made* (The History of Finance of the Showa Period: From the End of the War to the Conclusion of the Peace Treaty), edited by Ōkurashō Zaiseishishitsu. Tokyo: Tōyō Keizai Shinpōsha, Vol. 20, pp.63–67.

Tachibanaki, T., (1984), 'Labor Mobility and Job Tenure'. In *The Economic Analysis of the Japanese Firm*, edited by Mashiko Aoki. Amsterdam: Elsevier Science Publishers B.V., pp.77–102.

Takajima, K., (1953), 'Mujun no shōchōteki hyōgen-gōrika (The Profound Reflection of Contradiction-Rationalization)'. *Keizai Hyōron* August:50–57.

Tominaga, K., (1993), 'Fukyō ga kasoku suru nihonteki shisutemu no shukushōka (The Decline of the Japanese System Accelerated by the Recession)'. *Ekonomisuto* May 25:18–23.

Tsuruda, S., (1994), 'Hikanteki sugiru sangyō kūdōkaron (The Over-Pessimistic Theory of Deindustrialization)}. *Ekomoisuto* July 5:40–43.

Tsūsan, D.K.C., (1954), *Sengo keizai jūnenshi* (A Ten Year History of the Postwar Economy).

Tsūsanshō, (ed.), (1957), *Sangyō gōrika hakusho* (The White Paper of Industrial Rationalization). Tokyo: Nikkan Kōgyō Shinbunsha.

Uchihashi, K., (1993), ' "Nihon gata koyō chōsei" no ugami o tadase (Correcting the Distortion of the Japanese Style Adjustment of Employment)'. *Shūkan Tōyō Keizai* April 24:18–20.

Uchihashi, K. and Taizō, Y., (1993), 'Mono zukuri ni shimei to hokoru o torimodose (Taking Back the Mission and the Pride in Making Things)'. *Economisuto* November 16:34–38.

Ueda, N., (1994), 'Endaka, kisei, shōkankō ga kūdōka o kasoku suru (The Appreciation of Yen, the Government Regulation and the Business Custom are Accelerating the Deindustrialization). *Ekonomisuto* July 5:30–31.

Weber, M., (1968), *Economy and Society*. New York: Bedminster Press, Vol. 1.

Weir, M., (1989), 'Ideas and Politics: The Acceptance of Keynesianism in Britain and the United States'. In *The Political Power of Economic Ideas: Keynesianism Across Nations*, edited by Peter A. Hall. Princeton: Princeton University Press, pp. 53–85.

Weir, M. and Skocpol, T., (1985), 'State Structures and the Possibilities for "Keynesian" Responses to the Great Depression in Sweden, Britain, and the United States'. In *Bringing the State Back In*, edited by Peter B. Evans, Dietrich Rueschemeyer and Theda Skocpol. Cambridge: Cambridge University Press, pp.103–167.

Williamson, O.E., (1975), *Markets and Hierarchies: Analysis and Antitrust Implication*. New York: The Free Press.

Williamson, O.E., (1985), *The Economic Institutions of Capitalism*. New York: The Free Press.

Williamson, O.E., (1987), 'The Economies of Organization: The Transaction Cost Approach'. *American Journal of Sociology*, 87(3).

Wrong, D., (1961), 'The Oversocialized Conception of Man in Modern Sociology'. *American Sociological Review* 26:183–193.

Yamakishi, A., (1993), 'Nijū seiki wa ōberyū no rōshi kankei ni tenkan (The Transformation Towards the Euro-American Style of Labor Relations)'. *Shūkan Tōyō Keizai* April 24:13.

Yoshida, S., (1957), *Kaisō jūnen* (Ten Years' Recollection). Tōkyō: Shinchōsha. Vols. 1, 2, 3, 4.

Zelizer, V.A., (1988), 'Beyond the Polemics on the Market: Establishing a Theoretical and Empirical Agenda'. *Sociological Forum*, 3(4):614–634.

Zukin, S. and DiMaggio, P., (1990), 'Introduction'. In *Structures of Capital: Social Organization of the Economy*, edited by Sharon Zukin and Paul DiMaggio. New York: Cambridge University Press, pp.1–36.

Recombinant property in East European capitalism

David Stark

Introduction: The science of the not yet

Sociology began as a science of transition, founded at our century's turn on studies of the epochal shifts from tradition to modernity, rural to urban society, Gemeinschaft to Gesellschaft, feudalism to capitalism, and mechanical to organic solidarity. For the founders of sociology, the crisis besetting European societies at the end of the 19th century was diagnosed as a normative and institutional vacuum. The old order, regulated by tradition, had passed but a new moral order had not yet been established.

During our own *fin de siécle*, not the crumbling of traditional structures but the collapse of communism gives new life to the transition problematic (see Alexander, 1994, for an extended critical discussion). As the science of the not yet, transitology studies the present as an approximation of a designated future (Blanchard, Froot and Sachs, 1994), risking an underlying teleology in which concepts are driven by hypostasized end-states.[1] In that framework, the transitional present is a period of dislocation as society undergoes the passage through a liminal state suspended between one social order and another (Bunce and Csanadi, 1992), each conceived as a stable equilibrium organized around a coherent and more or less unitary logic.

But is ours still the century of transition? And is that model of social change, so formative in the launching of sociology, still adequate for understanding the momentous changes in contemporary Eastern Europe?

Difficult to assimilate within the transition problematic are the numerous studies from Eastern Europe documenting parallel and contradictory logics in which ordinary citizens were already experiencing, for a decade prior to 1989, a social world in which various domains were not integrated coherently (Gábor, 1979, 1986;

Szelenyi, 1988; Stark, 1986, 1989).[2] Through survey research and ethnographic studies, researchers have identified a multiplicity of social relations that did not conform to officially prescribed hierarchical patterns. These relations of reciprocity and marketlike transactions were widespread inside the socialist sector as well as in the 'second economy' and stemmed from the contradictions of attempting to 'scientifically manage' an entire national economy. At the shop-floor level, shortages and supply bottlenecks led to bargaining between supervisors and informal groups; at the managerial level, the task of meeting plan targets required a dense network of informal ties that cut across enterprises and local organizations; and the allocative distortions of central planning produced the conditions for the predominantly part-time entrepreneurship of the second economies that differed in scope, density of network connections, and conditions of legality across the region (Gábor, 1979; Kornai, 1980; Sabel and Stark, 1982; Szelenyi, 1988).

The existence of parallel structures (however contradictory and fragmentary) in these informal and interfirm networks that 'got the job done' means that the collapse of the formal structures of the socialist regime does not result in an institutional vacuum. Instead, we find the persistence of routines and practices, organizational forms and social ties, that can become assets, resources, and the basis for credible commitments and co-ordinated actions in the post-socialist period (Nelson and Winter, 1982). In short, in place of disorientation, we find the metamorphosis of *sub-rose* organizational forms and the activation of preexisting networks of affiliation.

If, by the 1980s, the societies of Eastern Europe were decidedly not systems organized around a single logic, they are not likely in the post-socialist epoch to become, any more or less than our own, societies with a single system identity. Change, even fundamental change, of the social world is not the passage from one order to another but rearrangements in the patterns of how multiple orders are interwoven. Organizational innovation in this view is not replacement but recombination (Schumpeter, 1934).

Thus, we examine how actors in the post-socialist context are rebuilding organizations and institutions not *on the ruins* but *with the ruins* of communism as they redeploy available resources in response to their immediate practical dilemmas. With such a conception of path dependence we explain not the persistence of the past but how multiple futures are being contested in the present. Instead of paralysis and disorientation or of condemnation to repetition or retrogression,[3] we see ongoing processes of organizational innovation—for it is through adjusting to new uncertainties by improvising on practiced routines that new organizational forms emerge (Nelson and Winter, 1982; White, 1993; Kogut and Zander, 1992; Sabel and Zeitlin, 1996). The analysis that follows emphasizes the organizational reflexivity that is possible when actors manoeuvre across a multiplicity of legitimating principles and strategically exploit ambiguities in the polyphony of accounts of work, value, and justice that compose modern society (Boltanski and Thevenot, 1991; White, 1992; Stark, 1990; Padgett and Ansell, 1993).

A new type of mixed economy?

This chapter examines the recombinatory logic of organizational innovation in the restructuring of property relations in Hungary. It asks, 'Are recombinant processes resulting in a new type of mixed economy as a distinctively East European capitalism?'

For more than 30 years' policy analysts in Eastern Europe debated the 'correct mix of plan and market' (Stark and Nee, 1989). By the mid-1980s in Hungary, the debate had shifted to the correct mix of 'public and private property' as the earlier sacrosanct status of collective property eroded with the growth of the second economy. It was thus, in the waning years of state socialism, that Gábor (1986) and Szelenyi (1988) coined the term 'socialist mixed economy' to designate the new economic configuration.[4] Meanwhile, Stark (1989, p. 168), amplifying Gábor's call to acknowledge a mixed economy 'as a viable hybrid form and not as inherently unstable and necessarily transitional', wondered nonetheless whether the concept of mixed economy was adequate to grasp the emergent phenomena of late socialism. On the basis of field research on 'intrapreneurial' subcontracting units in Hungarian firms, he argued that aspects of emergent private property were not respecting the boundaries of the second economy but were being fused with public ownership *inside* the socialist firm, resulting in a 'diversification of property forms'. Identifying 'hybrid mixtures of public ownership and private initiative', Stark (1989, pp. 167–8) argued that, instead of a mixed economy with well-bounded public and private sectors, analysis should begin to address the growing plurality of 'mixed property forms' that transgressed and blurred traditional property boundaries.

Scholars of economic reforms in China subsequently developed related concepts to analyse the fiscal reforms reshaping incentives among local governments that gives rise to 'township and village enterprises'. Oi's (1992) concept of 'local corporatism', Nee's (1992) 'hybrid property', and Cui's (in press) notion of 'moebius-strip ownership' each illuminated a particular facet of Chinese property reforms that supported the general conclusion that China's is not a simple mixed economy but a kaleidoscope of mixed public and private property forms.

Of special relevance to my concerns is Walder's (1994) insight that property reform should not be equated with privatization. Walder argues that 'clarification of property rights' in the Chinese fiscal reforms can yield performance enhancing incentives even while maintaining 'public ownership' without privatization. Our analysis of the Hungarian case also demonstrates that property transformation can occur without conventional privatization.[5] The difference, however, is that property transformation in Hungary does not necessarily clarify property rights. As we shall see, the emerging new property forms in Hungary blur (1) the boundaries of public and private, (2) the organizational boundaries of enterprises, and (3) the boundedness of justificatory principles. To denote these processes of triple boundary blurring I adopt the term *recombinant property*.

Recombinant property is a form of organizational hedging, or portfolio management, in which actors respond to uncertainty in the organizational environment by diversifying their assets, redefining and recombining resources. It is an attempt to hold resources that can be justified or assessed by more than one standard of measure.

The distinctive variant of organizational hedging that is recombinant property in Hungary is produced in two simultaneous processes: Parallel to the *decentralized reorganization of assets* is the *centralized management of liabilities*. On the one hand, decentralized reorganization produces the crisscrossing lines of inter-enterprise ownership networks; on the other, debt consolidation transforms private debt into public liability. Although these two dimensions are discussed separately, their simultaneity gives distinctive shape to Hungarian property. The clash of competing ordering principles produces organizational diversity that can form a basis for greater adaptability but, at the same time, creates acute problems of accountability.

Data

My arguments are based on data collected during an 11-month stay in Budapest in 1993–94. That research includes (1) field research in

David Stark

six Hungarian enterprise,[6] (2) compilation of a data set on the ownership structure of Hungary's 200 largest corporations and top 25 banks,[7] and (3) interviews with leading actors in banks, property agencies, political parties, and government ministries.[8]

The decentralized reorganization of assets

Although they fail to correspond to the policy prescriptions of either big bang or evolutionary economics, significant property transformations are taking place in Hungary. Since 1989, there has been an explosion of new economic units. In Table 1 we see that:

- the number of state enterprises declined by about 60 percent from the end of 1988 to the middle of 1994;
- the number of incorporated shareholding companies (*részvénytársaság*, or RT) increased by more than twenty-fold (from 116 to 2,679); and
- the number of limited liability companies (*korlátolt felelősségű társaság*, or KFT) increased most dramatically from only 450 units in 1988 to over 79,000 by the middle of 1994.

Table 1: Main enterprise forms in Hungary, 1988–94

Organization Form	1988	1989	1990	1991	1992	1993	1994
State enterprises	2,378	2,400	2,363	2,233	1,733	1,130	892
Shareholding companies (RTs)	116	307	646	1,072	1,712	2,375	2,679
Limited liability companies (KFTs)	450	4,464	18,317	41,206	57,262	72,897	79,395

Source: National Bank of Hungary, *Monthly Report* 1994/2, and Hungarian Central Statistical Office, *Monthly Bulletin of Statistics*, 1995/5
Note: The data represent the number of firms counted in December of each year, except for 1994, which uses the count from May

Table 1 clearly indicates the sudden proliferation of new units in the Hungarian economy. But does the table provide a reliable map of property relations in contemporary Hungary? No, at least not if the data are forced into the dichotomous public/private categories that structure the discussion about property transformation in the post-socialist countries. As we shall see, actors within the large formerly state firms are transforming property relations at the enter-

120 © Copyright held by The American Journal of Sociology

prise level. The results, however, are not well-defined rights of private property, yet neither are they a continuation or reproduction of old forms of state ownership.

New forms of state ownership

Take first the shareholding companies (RTs) on line two of the table. Some of these corporations are private ventures newly established after the 'system change'. But many are the legal successors of the state-owned enterprises that would have been enumerated in the previous year on line one of the table. Through a mandatory process of 'corporatization', the former state-owned enterprise transforms its legal organizational form into a shareholding company. The question, of course, is who is holding the shares? In most of these corporatized firms the majority of shares are held by the State Property Agency or the newly created State Holding Corporation (ÁV-Rt). That is, as 'public' and 'private' actors co-participate in the new recombinant property forms, the nature and instruments of the 'public' dimension change: Whereas 'state ownership' in socialism meant unmediated and indivisible ownership by a state ministry (e.g., Ministry of Industry), corporatization in post-communism entails share ownership by one or another government agency responsible for state property.

Such corporatization mandated by a privatization agency in the current context has some distinctive features of renationalization. In the 1980s, managers in Hungary (and workers in Poland) exercised *de facto* property rights. Although they enjoyed no rights over disposal of property, they did exercise rights of residual control as well as rights over residual income streams. In the 1990s, corporatization paradoxically involves efforts by the state to reclaim the actual exercise of the property rights that had devolved to enterprise-level actors. Ironically, the agencies responsible for privatization are acting as agents of *étatization* (Voszka, 1992).

The 'trap of centralization' (Bruszt, 1988), already well known in the region, stands as a warning, however, that the effective exercise of such centralized control varies inversely with the scope and the degree of direct intervention. One encounters, therefore, proposals for privatizing the asset management function. In such programmes, the state retains the right to dispose of property but delegates its rights as shareholder to private consulting firms and portfolio management teams who oversee daily operations and strategic decisions on a subcontracting or commission basis.

David Stark

Inter-enterprise ownership

The state is seldom, however, the sole shareholder of the corporatized firms. Who are the other shareholders of the RTs enumerated on line two of Table 1? To answer this question, I compiled a data set on the ownership structure of the largest 200 Hungarian corporations (ranked by sales).[9] These firms compose the 'Top 200' of the 1993 listing of *Figyelő*, a leading Hungarian business weekly. Like their *Fortune* 500 counterparts in the United States, the *Figyelő* 200 firms are major players in the Hungarian economy employing an estimated 21 percent of the labour force and accounting for 37 percent of total net sales and 42 percent of export revenues (*Figyelő*, 1993). The data also include the top 25 Hungarian banks (ranked by assets). Ownership data were obtained directly from the Hungarian Courts of Registry where corporate files contain not only information on the company's officers and board of directors but also a complete list of the company's owners as of the 1993 annual shareholders' meeting. The data analysed here are limited to the top twenty shareholders of each corporation.[10] In the Budapest Court of Registry and the 19 County Registries we were able to locate ownership files for 195 of the 200 corporations and for all of the 25 banks, referred to below as the 'Top 220' firms.

Who holds the shares of these 220 largest enterprises and banks? I found some form of state ownership—with shares held by the ÁV-Rt (the State Holding Corporation), the SPA (the State Property Agency), or the institutions of local government (who had typically exchanged their real estate holdings for enterprise shares)—present in the overwhelming majority (71 percent) of these enterprises and banks. More surprisingly, given the relatively short time since the 'system change' in 1989–90, we found 36 companies (i.e., more than 16 percent of this population) in majority foreign ownership. Hungarian private individuals (summed down the top 20 owners) hold at least 25 percent of the shares of only 12 of these largest enterprises and banks.

Most interesting from the perspective of this paper is the finding of 87 cases in which another Hungarian company is among the 20 largest shareholders. In 42 of these cases the other Hungarian companies together hold a clear majority (50 percent plus one share). Thus, by the most restrictive definition, almost 20 percent of our Top 220 companies are unambiguous cases of inter-enterprise ownership; and we find some degree of inter-enterprise ownership in almost 40 percent of these large companies.

122   © Copyright held by The American Journal of Sociology

Figure 1 presents two discrete networks formed through such inter-enterprise ownership. (Numbers refer to specific firms; lines indicate the direct ownership ties among them.) Weak ties (shareholdings with other firms that do not have at least one other tie, whether as owner or owned, to any other firm in the network) are not displayed.[11] The relations depicted in the figure, we emphasize, are the direct horizontal ties among the very largest enterprises— the superhighways, so to speak, of Hungarian corporate networks. The diagrams presented in Figure 1 indicate a different way of mapping the social space of property transformation than that suggested in Table 1. Whereas Table 1 grouped entities according to their legal corporate status, here we trace not the distribution of attributes but the patterns of social ties.

In analysing the relational dynamics of recombinant property, we now shift our focus from the corporate thoroughfares linking the large enterprises to examine the local byways linking spin-off properties within the gravitational field of large enterprises.

Corporate satellites

We turn thus to the form with the most dramatic growth during the post-socialist period, the newly established limited liability company (KFT), enumerated on line three of Table 1. Some of these KFTs are genuinely private entrepreneurial ventures. But many of these limited liability companies are not entirely distinct from the transformed shareholding companies examined above. In fact, the formerly socialist enterprises have been active founders and continue as current owners of the newly incorporated units.

The basic process of this property transformation is one of decentralized reorganization: Under the pressure of enormous debt, declining sales, and threats of bankruptcy (or, in cases of more prosperous enterprises, to forestall takeovers as well as to increase autonomy from state ministries) directors of many large enterprises are breaking up their firms (along divisional, factory, departmental, or even workshop lines) into numerous joint stock and limited liability companies. It is not uncommon to find virtually all of the activities of a large public enterprise distributed among 15–20 such satellites orbiting around the corporate headquarters.

As newly incorporated entities with legal identities, these new units are nominally independent—registered separately, with their own directors and separate balance sheets. But on closer inspection, their status in practice is semi-autonomous. An examination of the

123

David Stark

Network I

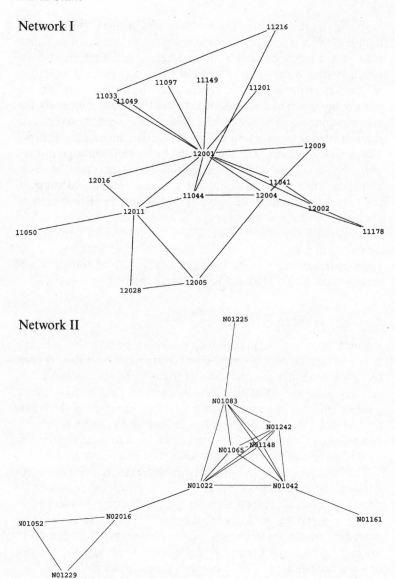

Figure 1 *Two inter-enterprise ownership networks in Hungary*

computerized records of the Budapest Court of Registry indicates, for example, that the controlling shares of these corporate satellites are typically held by the public enterprises themselves. This pattern is exemplified by the case of one of Hungary's largest metallurgy firms represented in Figure 2. As we see in that figure, 'Heavy Metal', an enormous shareholding company in the portfolio of the State Holding Corporation, is the majority shareholder of 26 of its 40 corporate satellites.

Like Saturn's rings, Heavy Metal's satellites revolve around the giant corporate planet in concentric orbits. Near the centre are the core metallurgy units, hot-rolling mills, energy, maintenance, and strategic planning units held in a kind of geo-synchronous orbit by 100 percent ownership. In the next ring, where the corporate head-quarters holds roughly 50–99 percent of the shares, are the cold-rolling mills, wire and cable production, oxygen facility, galvanizing and other finishing treatments, specialized castings, quality control and marketing units. As this listing suggests, these satellites are

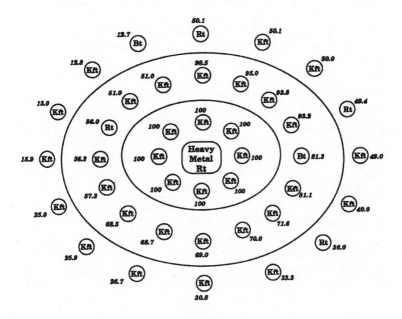

Rt = **Shareholding Company**
Kft = **Limited Liability Company**
Bt = **Partnerships**
Numerals in italics indicate Heavy Metal's ownership stake in a given satellite.

Figure 2 *Corporate satellites at Heavy Metal (based on data from internal company documents)*

David Stark

linked to each other and to the core units by ties of technological dependence. Relations between the middle-ring satellites and the company centre are marked by the centre's recurrent efforts to introduce stricter accounting procedures and tighter financial controls. These attempts are countered by the units' efforts to increase their autonomy—co-ordinated through personal ties and formalized in the bi-weekly meetings of the 'Club of KFT Managing Directors'.

The satellites of the outer ring are even more heterogenous in their production profiles (construction, industrial services, computing, ceramics, machining) and are usually of lower levels of capitalization. Units of this outer ring are less fixed in Heavy Metal's gravitational field: some have recently entered and some seem about to leave. Among the new entrants are some of Heavy Metal's domestic customers. Unable to collect receivables, Heavy Metal exchanged inter-enterprise debt for equity in its clients, preferring that these meteors be swept into an orbit rather than be lost in liquidation. Among these satellites launched from the old state enterprise are some for which Heavy Metal augments its less than majority ownership with leasing arrangements to keep centrifugal forces in check.

The corporate satellites among the limited liability companies enumerated on line 3 of Table 1 are, thus, far from unambiguously 'private' ventures; yet neither are they unmistakably 'statist' residues of the socialist past. Property shares in most corporate satellites are not limited to the founding enterprise. Top- and mid-level managers, professionals, and other staff can be found on the lists of founding partners and current owners. Such private persons rarely acquire complete ownership of the corporate satellite, preferring to use their insider knowledge to exploit the ambiguities of institutional co-ownership. The corporate satellites are thus partially a result of the hedging and risk-sharing strategies of individual managers. We might ask why a given manger would not want to acquire 100 percent ownership in order to obtain 100 percent of the profit, but from the perspective of a given manager the calculus instead is 'Why acquire 100 percent of the risk if some can be shared with the corporate centre?' With ambiguous interests and divided loyalties, these risk-sharing (or risk-shedding) owner/managers are organizationally hedging (Sabel, 1990).[12]

Not uncommonly, these individuals are joined in mixed ownership by joint stock companies and limited liability companies—sometimes by independent companies, often by other KFTs in a similar orbit around the *same* enterprise, and frequently by shareholding companies or KFTs spinning around some *other* enterprise

126   © Copyright held by The American Journal of Sociology

with lines of purchase or supply to the corporate unit (Voszka, 1991). Banks also participate in this form of recombinant property. In many cases, the establishment of KFTs and other new corporate forms is triggered by enterprise debt. In the reorganization of the insolvent firms, the commercial banks (whose shares as joint stock companies are still predominantly stated owned) become shareholders of the corporate satellites by exchanging debt for equity.

We have used the term 'corporate satellite' to designate this instance of recombinant property. An exact (but cumbersome) terminology reflects the complex, intertwined character of property relations in Hungary: a limited liability company owned by private persons, by private ventures, and by other limited liability companies owned by joint stock companies, banks, and large public enterprises owned by the state. The new property forms thus find horizontal ties of cross-ownership intertwined with vertical ties of nested holdings.

Recombinets

The recombinant character of Hungarian property is a function not only of the direct (horizontal) ownership ties among the largest firms and of their direct (vertical) ties to their corporate satellites but also of the network properties of the full ensemble of direct and indirect ties linking entities, irrespective of their attributes (large, small, or of various legal forms) in a given configuration. The available data do not allow us to present a comprehensive map of these complex relations. Records in the Courts of Registry include documents on the owners of a particular firm, but enterprises are not required to report the companies in which they hold a stake. However, on the basis of enterprise level field research, examination of public records at the State Property Agency, and interviews with bankers and executives of consulting firms we have been able to reconstruct at least partial networks represented in Figure 3.

For orientation in this graphic space, we position Figure 3 in relation to Figures 1 and 2. Figure 1 presented inter-enterprise ownership networks formed through horizontal ties directly linking large enterprises. Figure 2 zoomed in on the corporate satellites of a single large enterprise. With Figure 3 we pull back to examine a fragment of a broader inter-enterprise ownership network bringing into focus the ties that link corporate satellites to each other and that form the indirect ties among heterogenous units in a more loosely coupled network.

David Stark

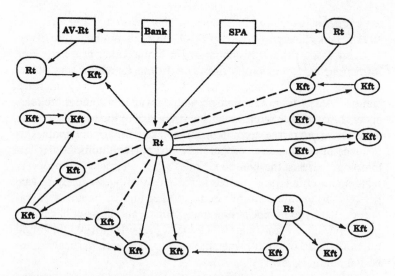

Figure 3 *A metamorphic network (based on data from Heavy Metal internal documents, SPA files, corporate files, and the Budapest Court of Registry)*

We label this emergent form a *recombinet*, a term designating a *network of recombinant property*. Here we see that the limited liability companies that began as corporate spin-offs are oriented through ownership ties either to more than one shareholding company and/or to other limited liability companies. In the recombinet, actors recognize the network properties of their interdependent assets and regroup them across formal organizational boundaries. These creative regroupings fail to respect the organizational boundaries between enterprises as well as the boundaries between public and private.

With few exceptions (Sabel and Prokop, 1994), the literature on post-socialist property transformation (most of it confined to 'privatization') assumes that the *economic unit to be restructured is the individual enterprise*. But the identification of interfirm networks suggests that policies and practices aimed at restructuring should target not the isolated firm but *networks of firms*. Such an alternative strategy of restructuring recognizes that assets and liabilities have distinctive network properties (Stark and Bruszt, 1998).

The industrial structure of the socialist economy commonly grouped, within a single enterprise, assets that were incompatible (except within the logic of central planning). Merely separating or simply regrouping such assets within existing enterprises alone (on firm-by-firm basis) cannot equal the more fruitful recombinations of complementary assets across a set of firms. Restructuring via the recombinet thus opens the possibilities of increasing the value of existing assets through their recombination. This regrouping does not necessarily imply bringing interdependent assets under the common ownership umbrella of a hierarchically organized enterprise. As such, Hungarian recombinant property provides examples of intercorporate networks as alternatives to a dichotomously forced choice between markets and hierarchies.

The centralized management of liabilities

In the previous section, we examined the decentralized reorganization of assets. Property transformation, however, involves not only assets and rights but also liabilities and obligations. In this section, we analyse what happens in a post-socialist economy when actors are called to account for enterprise debt.

Taking the last small steps

The liabilities management story begins in 1991 when the Hungarian government fundamentally modified three important laws regulating the accounting of assets and liabilities in an attempt to maintain its lead in regional competition for foreign investments and international credits. Hungary's comparative advantage, it appeared, was its gradualism, which, across the decades of the 1970s and 1980s, had yielded a full range of market-like institutions. Admittedly, these were not the institutions of a market economy, but they were close; and so, the government reasoned, why not take the last small steps? As the pioneer attempt to bring post-socialist practice in full conformity with Western accounting and banking standards, the new measures could be cast as a bold move when appealing to international lending agencies. But because they were not big steps, the new measures could gain external legitimation without creating a domestic shock. Thus, the new Accounting Law of 1991 (which took effect on January 1, 1992) required enterprises to switch to Western-style accounting principles. A simultaneously enacted, tough new Western-style Bankruptcy Act similarly contained stiff personal penalties for directors of enterprises that failed to file for bankruptcy after the accountants (using the new accounting principles) sounded

129

the alarm. At the same time, the new Act on Financial Institutions introduced in December 1991 was designed to put Hungary's commercial banks on a Western footing. In particular, the reserve requirements for measuring capital-adequacy ratios were modified and the securities and other financial instruments for provisioning against qualified loans were respecified.

The last small steps proved to be a leap into the abyss. Already reeling from the collapse of the CMEA markets, enterprise directors now learned from their accountants that the new accountant practices were colouring the companies' books even redder than expected. By the end of 1992, over 10,000 bankruptcies and liquidation proceedings had been initiated—a figure ten times higher than during the previous year when enterprises had experienced the worst shock of the collapsed Eastern markets (Bokros, 1994). With one-third to one-half of enterprises in the red, the loss-making firms began to stop payment on their bank credits. By the end of 1992, the overdue loan stock of the banking system was 127 billion forints (Ft), (1.5 billion in U.S. dollars) up 90 percent from the previous year (National Bank of Hungary, 1992, p. 109).

With thousands of firms filing for bankruptcy, the banks were forced by the new banking law to reclassify loans. The subsequent dramatic increase in the new legally-required provisionings against poorly performing loans cut deeply into bank profits, slashed dividends and tax revenues from the banking sector to the state treasury, and turned the banks' capital-adequacy ratios from positive to negative. The banking system was in crisis—first announced, no less, in *The Financial Times* (Denton, 1993).

From small steps to big bailouts

The same government that had launched an unintended financial shock now initiated a bold plan to save the banks. In its 1992 loan consolidation programme the government bought 104.9 billion forints (about $1 billion) of qualified debt (almost all in the 'bad' debt classification) involving 14 banks and 1,885 companies. In a related move in early 1993, the government also purchased the bank debt of 11 giant enterprises (the so-called dirty dozen) for roughly $300 million. But the loan consolidation and enterprise recapitalization programmes did not restore stability in the banking sector. By September 1993, only nine months later, financial experts were estimating that loans in arrears had once again soared to 20 percent of

130

total loan portfolios. And the 10 largest banks were again hovering at or below the zero percent capital-adequacy ratio (a condition of technical insolvency).

For the government, the new banking rules did not exclude bailing out banks and enterprises again and again. But the big bailout of 1993 had a new twist. Instead of buying the debt from the banks, this time the government adopted a two-stage strategy of first recapitalizing the banks and then using the banks to work out the enterprise debt. By injecting enormous sums of fresh capital into the banks, the Ministry of Finance became the dominant shareholder of the large commercial banks. The first stage of the strategy, then, could be summarized in a phrase: Don't acquire the debt; acquire the banks.

The second stage of the strategy was designed to harness the expertise of the banks to the service of the state. Because it was the banks, and not the state, that would be left holding the qualified debt, the banks would have an incentive to collect that debt, or at least the part they had not already written off their books. And they would do so, this time, not with the state as their sometime partner but with the state as their majority owner. But efforts to exercise control through direct ownership do not equal more effective state capacity. The conservative-nationalist government seemed determined to learn the lesson of the 'trap of centralization' from its own experience. Banks have shown almost no willingness to use the consolidation funds for actively restructuring firms; and despite the assumption that the Ministry of Finance's ownership would yield control of the banks, the government has been almost entirely ineffective in monitoring how the banks use the recapitalization funds.

The massive bailout programmes were not, of course, without effects: At 300 billion forints ($3 billion)—amounting to 10 percent of Hungarian GDP and 18.3 percent of the 1994 national budget[13]—the bailouts created a long queue of banks and firms with their hands out, reaching for the state's pocketbook.

Thus, at the same time that the corporate networks were engaged in the decentralized reorganization of assets, the Hungarian state attempted the centralized management of liabilities. That centralization has not left the decentralized processes untouched. From the perspective of the enterprises, 'debt consolidation' triggers the organizational separation of debts from assets. The Hungarian government's attempt at the centralized management of liabilities stimulates the networks to complement their strategies of risk spreading with new strategies of risk shedding. Two types of strategies can be

131

identified, each based on the organizational separation of assets and liabilities. In one type, assets are distributed to the satellites and debts are centralized, increasing the enterprises' chances of inclusion in the government-funded debt consolidation. In the other, assets are closely held by the enterprise centre and liabilities are distributed to the satellites where network ties and political connections manipulate proceedings in a Hungarian version of 'bankruptcy for profit' (Akerlof and Romer [1993] coin the term in their study of state-managed liabilities in the U.S. savings and loan bailout).

We thus see a new paternalism in Hungary: Whereas in the state socialist economy paternalism was based on the state's attempts to centrally manage assets (Kornai, 1993a), in the first years of the post-socialist economy paternalism is based on the state's attempts to centrally manage liabilities. Centralized management of liabilities will not continue indefinitely, but the organizational dynamics of enterprises formed under the new paternalistic conditions are likely to have strong path dependent effects.

The multiple accounts of recombinant property

In the highly uncertain organizational environment that is the post-socialist economy, relatively few actors (apart from institutional designers) set out with the aim to create a market economy. Many, indeed, would welcome such an outcome. But their immediate goals are more pragmatic: at best to thrive, at least to survive. And so they strive to use whatever resources are available. That task is not so simple because one must first identify the relevant system of accounting in which something can exist as a resource. At the extreme, it is sometimes even difficult to distinguish a liability from an asset. If the liabilities of your organization (enterprise or bank) are big enough, perhaps they can be translated into qualifications for more resources. And what could be more worthless than a bankrupted limited liability company—except, of course, if you have shed the risk to the banks (and then to the state) and put the assets in another form. Assets and liabilities have value not in themselves but in relation to legitimating principles.

To examine how economic actors in the post-socialist setting manoeuvre not only through an ecology of organizations but also through a complex ecology of ordering principles we need to understand the doubly associative character of assets. There are no free floating resources. To exist as an asset a potential resource must be mobilizable through ties of association among persons (Granovetter, 1985). And to be of *value* a potential resource must also have relative worth according to a standard of measure. To be able to circulate through the ties that bind (and thus contribute to that binding) an asset must be justified within a relatively stabilized *network of categories* that make up a legitimating principle (Thévenot, 1985; Boltanski and Thévenot, 1991; Latour, 1988; White, 1992).[14] Regrouping assets thus involves making new associations—not only by rearranging social ties among persons and things but also by drawing on diverse repertoires of justificatory principles.

To emphasize the patterned and the performative aspects of this process, I exploit a notion of *accounts*. Etymologically rich, the term simultaneously connotes bookkeeping and narration. Both dimensions entail evaluative judgments, and each implies the other: Accountants prepare story lines according to established formulae, and in the accountings of a good storyteller we know what counts. In everyday life, we are all bookkeepers and storytellers. We keep accounts and we give accounts, and most importantly, we can all be called to account for our actions. When we make such an accounting, we draw on and reproduce social orders. We can competently produce justifications only in terms of established and recognized ordering principles, standards, and measures of evaluation Because we do not simply give reasons but also have reasons for doing things, accounts are not simply retrospective; the imperative of justification (Boltanski and Thévenot, 1991) structures what we do and not simply how we explain. We can never simply 'calculate' because we must do so with units and instruments of measurement that are deeply structured by accounts of what can be of value. We reproduce these units of measurement and we recalibrate the measuring instruments when we assert our worthiness, when we defer to the 'more worthy', or when we denounce their status according to some other standard of evaluation. When we give an account, we affirm or challenge the ordering criteria according to which our actions (and/or those of others) have been or will be evaluated. And it is always within accounts that we 'size up the situation', for not every form of worth can be made to apply and not every asset is in a form mobilizable for the situation. We *evaluate* the situation by manoeuvering to use scales that measure some types of worth and not others thereby acting to validate some accounts and discredit others.

133

The multiple accounts of recombinant property respond to and exploit the fundamental, though diffused uncertainty about the organizational environment. In transformative economies, firms have to worry not simply about whether there is demand for their products, or about the rate of return on their investment, or about the level of profitability but also about the very principle of selection itself. Thus, the question is not only 'Will I survive the *market test*?'—but also, under what conditions is proof of worth on market principles neither sufficient nor necessary to survive? Because there are multiply operative, mutually coexistent principles of justification according to which you can be called on to give accounts of your actions, you cannot be sure what counts. By what proof and according to which principles of justification are you worthy to steward such and such resources? Because of this uncertainty, actors will seek to diversify their assets, to hold resources in multiple accounts.

This ability to glide among principles and to produce multiple accountings is an organizational hedging. It differs, however, from the kind of hedging to minimize risk exposure that we would find within a purely market logic—as, for example, when the shopkeeper who sells swimwear and sun lotion also devotes some floor space to umbrellas. Instead of acting within a single regime of evaluation, this is organizational hedging that crosses and combines disparate evaluative principles. Recombinant property is a particular kind of portfolio management. It is an attempt to have a resource that can be justified or assessed by more than one standard of measure (as, for example, the rabbit breeder whose roadside stand advertises 'Pets and Meat' in the documentary film, *Roger and Me*). In managing one's portfolio of justifications, one starts from the dictum: diversify your accounts. The adroit recombinant agent in the transformative economies of East Central Europe diversifies holdings in response to fundamental uncertainties about what can constitute a resource. Under conditions not simply of market uncertainty but of organizational uncertainty, there can be multiple (and intertwined) strategies for survival—based in some cases on *profitability* but in others on *eligibility*. Where your success is judged, and the resources placed at your disposal determined, sometimes by your market share and sometimes by the number of workers you employ in a region; sometimes by your price-earnings ratio and sometimes by your 'strategic importance'; and, when even the absolute size of your losses can be transformed into an asset yielding an income stream, you might be wise to diversify your portfolio, to be able to shift your accounts, to be equally skilled in applying for loans as in applying for job creation subsidies, to have a multilingual command of the grammar of credit worthiness and the syntax of debt forgiveness. To hold recombinant property is to have such a diversified portfolio.

To gain room for manoeuvre, actors court and even create ambiguity. They measure in multiple units, they speak in many tongues. They will be less controlled by others if they can be accountable (able to make credible accounts) to many.[15] In so doing, they produce the polyphonic discourse of worth that is post-socialism.

We can hear that polyphonic chorus in the diverse ways that firms justify their claims for participation in the debt-relief programme. The following litany of justifications are stylized versions of claims encountered in discussions with bankers, property agency officials, and enterprise directors: Our firm should be included in the debt relief programme

> because we will forgive our debtors (i.e., our firm occupies a strategic place in a network of inter-enterprise debt)
> because we are truly credit worthy (i.e, if our liabilities are separated from our assets, we will again be eligible for more bank financing. Similar translations could be provided for each of the following justifications)
> because we employ thousands
> because our suppliers depend on us for a market
> because we are in your election district
> because our customers depend on our product inputs
> because we can then be privatized
> because we can never be privatized
> because *we* took big risks
> because we were prudent and did not take risks
> because we were planned in the past
> because we have a plan for the future
> because we export to the West
> because we export to the East
> because our product has been awarded an International Standards Quality Control Certificate
> because our product is part of the Hungarian national heritage
> because we are an employee buy-out
> because we are a management buy-in
> because we are partly state-owned
> because we are partly privately-held
> because our creditors drove us into bankruptcy when they loaned

135

to us at higher than market rates to artificially raise bank profits in order to pay dividends into a state treasury whose coffers
had dwindled when corporations like ourselves effectively
stopped paying taxes.

And so we must ask, into whose account and by which account will
debt forgiveness flow? Or, in such a situation, is anyone accountable?

An East European capitalism?

How are we to understand these unorthodox forms, these organizational 'monsters' regrouping the seemingly incongruous? In this
concluding section, we reconsider the three aspects of recombinant
property (blurring of public and private, blurring of enterprise
boundaries, and blurring the boundedness of legitimating principles) in terms of three underlying concepts—mixture, diversity, and
complexity.

Mixture

Imagine two economies, each of equal parts public and private. In
one, half the firms are fully private, half are fully public. In the
other, every firm is half public, half private. Each is a 'mixed economy'. Yet it is likely that their dynamics will be the same?[16] No two
economies closely approximate the thought experiment's ideal
types; but it nonetheless puts in sharp relief the question: *What is
the mix of the post-socialist mixed economy?*

My findings of corporate spin-offs and recombinet reorganization
at the enterprise level, and of widespread public ownership combined with inter-enterprise ownership networks among the very
largest enterprises, challenges the assumption, widely held on all
sides of the privatization debate, that post-socialist economies can be
adequately represented in a two-sector model. That analytic shortcoming cannot be remedied by more precise specification of the
boundary between public and private: the old property divide has
been so eroded that what might once have been a distinct boundary
line is now a recombinant zone. Hungary is a post-socialist mixed
economy not because of a simple dualism of well-bounded state
owned firms in one sector and privately owned firms in another but
because many firms themselves exploit aspects of public and private
property relations. What we find are new forms of property in which

136

the properties of private and public are dissolved, interwoven, and recombined. Property in East European capitalism is recombinant property, and its analysis suggests the emergence of a distinctively East European capitalism that will differ as much from West European capitalisms as do contemporary East Asian variants.

The concept of a post-socialist mixed economy is a useful first approximation of an East European capitalism. But its essentialist categories of 'public' and 'private' (and the related dualisms of 'market' and 'redistribution')—even when opened up to the possibility of being mixed together in the same organizational setting—may be more limiting than illuminating.

For decades, capitalism was defined *vis-à-vis* socialism, and vice versa. Their systematic comparison enriched our understanding of both, but the 'methods of mirrored opposition' and similar constructs (Stark, 1986; Szelenyi, 1978, 1988) that worked with these dualisms are no longer fruitful. The demise of socialism challenges that analytically forced choice, and it offers an opportunity for enriching comparative institutional analysis. When we stop defining capitalism in terms of socialism, we see that, in our epoch, capitalism as a construct is only analytically interesting in the plural: *capitalisms* must be defined and compared *vis-à-vis* each other.

Diversity

Our first analytic shift, therefore, must be from the conceptual tools around the concept of *mixture* to those around that of *diversity*. Capitalisms are diverse, and that diversity is manifested in forms that cannot be adequately conceptualized as mixtures of capitalism and socialism.[17] By analyzing recombinant property not only as the dissolution and interweaving of elements of public and private but also as a blurring of organizational boundaries in networks of interlocking ownership, we can escape, for example, the terms of the debate about whether the 'lessons of East Asia for Eastern Europe' are the virtues of neoliberalism or of neostatism (World Bank, 1993; Amsden, 1994). Instead we join economic sociologists who are studying the East Asian economies from a network-centred approach in which not markets, nor states, nor isolated firms, but social networks are the basic units of analysis (Gereffi, 1994; Hamilton, Zeile and Kim, 1990; Hamilton and Feenstra, 1995). In this perspective, the ability of the East Asian economies to adapt flexibly to changes in world markets rests in the interlocking ties characteristic of corporate groups (Orru, Biggart, and Hamilton,

137

1991; Granovetter, 1995), whether these be the patterns of mutual shareholding within the Japanese *keiretsu* (Gerlach and Lincoln, 1992; Hoshi, 1994); the ties of family ownership within the more vertically integrated South Korean *chaebol* (Kim, 1991; Hamilton and Feenstra, 1995); the social ties of the more horizontally integrated Taiwanese *quanxiqiye* 'related enterprises' (Numazaki, 1991); or the dense ties that transgress organizational boundaries in the 'buyer-driven' and 'producer-driven' networks in Hong Kong, Singapore, and elsewhere in Southeast Asia (Gereffi, 1994).

These recent studies of the social embeddedness and local organizational innovation characteristic of East Asian corporate networks suggest that the strategic choice is not plans or markets, or even clans or markets but clans *for* markets. Market *orientation* must be distinguished, from market *co-ordination*: a broad variety of institutions of nonmarket co-ordination are compatible with high performance market orientation (Schmitter, 1988; Boyer, 1991; Bresser, 1993). Many of the most successful forms of network co-ordination in East Asia, moreover, appeared to early observers as highly improbable forms whose atavistic features could not possibly survive beyond the period of post-war reconstruction from which they arose.[18] Our point of departure, it should be clear, however, is not to look to Eastern Europe to find Hungarian *keiretsu* or Czech *chaebol*. Instead of searching for direct counterparts, East Asian/East European comparisons will yield new concepts when we grasp the specificity of the regional variants by explaining the *differences* among the various countries *within a region*.[19]

Complexity

In restructuring assets, we might say that actors are 'identifying' new resources, but this would suggest that the resource was simply hidden or underutilized and only needed to be uncovered. In fact, before recombining resources, they must first redefine them. We call this ability to re-cognize the properties of persons and things *organizational reflexivity*. It cannot be derived from the ambiguity of property claims but is a function instead of the ambiguity of organizing principles (Grabher and Stark, 1997; Stark, forthcoming). The key to adaptability in this view is not simply the diversity of types of organizations but the possibilities for cross-fertilization inside and across organizations where multiply operative legitimating principles collide—or in Harrison White's (1993) phrase, 'values mate to change'.[20]

Some might argue, of course, that multiple orders are fine—provided that each occupies a distinctly bounded domain. Such is the model of modernity in 'modernization' theory: through differentiation, each domain of society would develop as a separate autonomous subsystem with its own distinctive logic. Complexity in this view requires diversity but only as the juxtaposition of clearly bounded rationalities. Marxism, of course, has its own conception of complexity: the temporary overlap of mutually contradictory principles. Both modernization theory and Marxism are deeply grounded in the transition problematic. The noisy clash of orders is only temporary: the revolutionary moment for one, the passage to differentiated domains in the other.

If we break with this transition problem, we can escape from the impoverished conceptions of complexity in both Marxism and modernization theory. In the alternative conception offered here, complexity is the interweaving of multiple justificatory principles on the same domain space. That view, of course, shares with modernization theory the notion of distinctive domains—relatively autonomous fields of action. And it shares with Marxism the notion of the collision of ordering principles. But unlike modernization theory, each domain is a site of heterogeneity; and unlike Marxism, that tension is not consolidated and then released in an all-encompassing revolutionary moment. The noisy clash of orders occurs throughout the social world, and it is not transient but ongoing—punctuated by relative, localized stabilizations but never equilibrium (Latour, 1988).

Post-socialist societies are entering this discordant world. To still that noisy clash by the ascendancy of one accounting, with profitability as the sole metric and markets as the only co-ordinating mechanism, would be to duplicate the attempt of Communism, with its imposition of a unitary justificatory principle, a strict hierarchy of property forms, and a single co-ordinating mechanism. To replicate the monochrome with a different colouring would be to destroy the heterogeneity of organizing principles that is the basis of adaptability.

As this account of recombinant property has demonstrated, post-socialist societies are not lacking in heterogeneous organizing principles. The problem therefore is not a simple lack of accountability but an overabundance of accountability: An actor who, within the same domain space, is accountable to every principle is accountable to none. The adaptability of modern capitalisms rests not simply in the diversity of organizations but in the *organization of diversity*:

139

enough overlap of legitimating principles across domains to foster rivalry of competing accounts within domains and enough bound-edness of rationalities to foster accountability. It is not in finding the right mix of public and private but in finding the right organization of diversity to yield both adaptability and accountability that post-socialist societies face their greatest challenge.

Notes

1 As such it shares many of the shortcoming of 'presentist' history—reading the past as approximations of later outcomes (Somers and Gibson, 1994). In a related critique in the sociology of science, Collins (1982), Latour (1988), and Pickering (1992) turn from outcomes to controversies.

2 East European scholars have long argued that social change is a transformational reshaping of enduring structures exhibiting multiplicity rather than uniformity (Konrad and Szelenyi, 1979; Szücs, 1985; Staniszkis, 1993; Szelenyi, 1994).

3 See, by contrast, Burawoy and Krotov's account of change as retrogression: 'Our case study suggests that with the withering away of the party state the Soviet economy, far from collapsing or transforming itself, has assumed an exaggerated version of its former self' (1992: p. 34).

4 Szelenyi (1978) argued that 'mixture' characterized both East and West: whereas a redistributive welfare state mitigates inequalities produced by markets under advanced capitalism, in state socialism subordinated marketlike institutions miti-gate inequalities produced by the dominant redistributive mechanism. Elsewhere (Stark, 1986) I labelled this analytic method 'mirrored opposition' and used it to analyze differences between capitalist and socialist internal labour markets.

5 In her analysis of 'political capitalism' in Poland, Staniszkis (1991) similarly iden-tifies 'hybrid forms' of 'undefined dual status' in a variety of leasing forms and cost shifting arrangements through which nomenclatura companies enjoy the benefits of property transformation without privatization.

6 Three of these firms are among the 20 largest firms in Hungary and are at the core of Hungarian manufacturing in metallurgy, electronics, and rubber products. Three are small and medium-size firms in plastics, machining, and industrial engineering. This field research was conducted in collaboration with László Neumann, and involved longitudinal analysis of the same firms in which we had earlier studied an organizational innovation of internal subcontracting inside the socialist enterprise (Stark, 1986, 1989, 1990; Neumann, 1989).

7 These data were augmented by ownership data drawn from the files of some 800 firms under the portfolio management of the State Property Agency.

8 A partial list of interviewees includes; the former president of the National Bank; the former deputy-minister of the Ministry of Finance; executives of the four largest commercial banks and two leading investment banks; the former president of the State Holding Corporation; directors, advisors, and officials of the State Property Agency; senior officials of the World Bank's Hungarian Mission; the chief economic advisors of the two major liberal parties; the president of the Federation of Hungarian Trade Unions; and leading officials of the Hungarian Socialist Party (who later ascended to high-level positions in the new Socialist-Liberal coalition government).

9 Such data collection is not a simple matter where capital markets are poorly developed. There is no Hungarian *Moody's* and certainly no corporate directory equivalent to *Industrial Groupings in Japan* or *Keiretsu no Kenkyu* (see, for example, Gerlach and Lincoln, 1992). The labour-intensive solution has been to gather that data directly from the Hungarian Courts of Registry. My thanks to Lajos Vékás, Professor of Law, ELTE, and Rector of the Institute for Advanced Study, Collegium Budapest, for his interventions to secure access to these data and to Szabolcs Kemény and Jonathan Uphoff for assistance in data collection.

10 This 20-owner limitation is a convention adopted in research on inter-corporate ownership in East Asia (Gerlach and Lincoln, 1992; Hoshi, 1994). In the Hungarian economy where only 37 firms are traded on the Budapest stock exchange and where corporate shareholding is not widely dispersed among hundreds of small investors, the 20-owner restriction allows us to account for at least 90 percent of the shares held in virtually every company.

11 See Stark and Kemény (1997) for a detailed analysis of these data on interorganizational ownership ties. Instead of regarding an ownership portfolio as the property of an isolated firm, that paper views portfolios as the properties of networks of firms. Exploiting the double meaning of 'network properties' (as property holdings, on the one hand, and as characteristics such as density, centrality, and extensivity, on the other), it uses a combination of correspondence analysis, cliquing models, and block modelling techniques to identify eight distinctive strategies of network portfolio management by business groups in the contemporary Hungarian economy.

12 Many of these mid-level managers had experiences in the 1980s with an organizational precursor of the present recombinant forms—the intra-enterprise partnerships—in which semiautonomous subcontracting units used enterprise equipment to produce goods or services during the 'off' hours (Stark, 1986, 1989). Like 'second economy' producers who continued to hold a job in state enterprises, these intrapreneurial units were a widespread result of hedging strategies in the Hungarian economy. Some of these partnerships were scarcely disguised rent-seeking schemes that privatized profit streams and left expenses with the state-owned enterprise. Others creatively redeployed resources from diverse parts of the shopfloor and regrouped, as well, the informal norms of reciprocity with the technical norms of the professionals.

13 To put these figures in perspective, for the United States the $105 billion savings and loan bailout represents 1.6 percent of GNP and 7 percent of the projected 1995 federal budget. Venezuela's recent $6.1 billion bank bailout is on a magnitude with the Hungarian programme representing 11 percent of Venezuela's gross national product and 75 percent of the government' 1994 national budget (Brooke, 1994).

14 Those analysts who tend to focus on *strong ties* in an ideational network—that is, where the constituent idea-blocks of a form are tightly coupled and linked in dense patterns—call these forms 'ideologies' (for the classic statement, see Bendix (1956)). Those analysts who emphasize the comprehensible, as opposed to comprehensive, quality of forms focus on the *weak ties* in an ideational network, as stressed in their employment of the term 'stories' and their attention to narrative structure (White, 1992; Sabel and Zeitlin, 1996). Ideologies are like roadmaps, demonstrating the comprehensive connections; stories are like sketched pathways, telling how one got from there to here through a particular chain of connections.

141

David Stark

15 See Padgett and Ansell (1993) for an analysis of such multivocality in another historical setting.

16 In a related path dependent thought experiment: Imagine two mixed economies each with half the firms fully public and half the firms fully private. The first arrived at that sectoral mix from a starting point of only public firms. The other, from a starting point of only private firms. Are their dynamics likely to be the same?

17 My argument, thus, bears no resemblance to 'third road' solutions (i.e., the mistaken notion that there could be some combination of the best features of capitalism with the best features of socialism), and it follows that I am not arguing that recombinant property is a 'best way'. As people living in East Central Europe have known for decades if not centuries, all the best roads to capitalism started somewhere else. I am reminded of the joke in which an Irishman in the far countryside is asked, 'What's the best way to get to Dublin?' He thinks for a minute, and responds, 'Don't start from here'.

18 Incongruity, in itself, neither insures survival nor condemns an organization form to an early death. Kim's (1991) discussion of the combinatory logic of the formation of the *chaebol* in Korea immediately following World War II invites comparison with the formation of recombinant structures during the contemporary period of East European reconstruction.

19 Stark and Bruszt (1998), for example, compare corporate networks in Hungary and the Czech Republic. They find that Hungarian networks are formed predominantly through enterprise-to-enterprise links, sometimes involving banks yet absent ties between banks and intermediate-level institutions such as investment companies. In the Czech Republic, by contrast, ownership networks are formed predominantly through ties at the meso-level in the cross ownership of banks and large investment funds, but direct ownership connections among enterprises themselves are rare. Whereas Hungarian networks are tightly coupled at the level of enterprises but loosely coupled at the meso level, Czech networks are loosely coupled at the level of enterprises and tightly coupled at the meso level.

20 See especially Grabher (1994) for a discussion of how rivalry of coexisting organizational forms contributes to reflexivity and adaptability. For related views on adaptability and complexity, see Landau (1969), Morin (1974), and Conrad (1983).

References

Akerlof, G.A. and Romer, P.M., (1993), 'Looting: The Economic Underworld of Bankruptcy for Profit'. *Brookings Papers on Economic Activity*, 2:1–73.

Alexander, J.C., (1994), 'Modern, Anti, Post, and Neo: How Social Theories Have Tried to Understand the "New World" of "Our Time" '. *Zeitschrift für Sociologie*, 23:165–197.

Amsden, A., (1994), 'Can Eastern Europe Compete by Getting the Prices Right? Contrast with East Asian Structural Reforms'. Pp. 81–107 in *Rebuilding Capitalism: Alternative Roads after Socialism and Dirigisme* edited by Andres Soimano, Osvaldo Sunkel, and Mario I. Blejer. Ann Arbor: The University of Michigan Press.

Bendix, R., (1956), *Work and Authority in Industry: Ideologies of Management in the Course of Industrialization*. Berkeley: University of California Press.

Blanchard, O.J., Froot, K.A. and Sachs, J.D., (1994), Introduction to *The Transaction in Eastern Europe*, Vol. 2, edited by Oliver Jean Blanchard, Kenneth A. Foot and Jeffrey D. Sachs. Chicago: University of Chicago Press.

Bokros, L., (1994), 'Privatization and the Banking System in Hungary'. Pp. 305–320 in *Privatization in the Transition Process. Recent Experiences in Eastern Europe* edited by László Samuely. Geneva: United Nations Conference on Trade and Development and KOPINT-DATORG.

Boltanski, l. and Thévenot, L., (1991), *De la justification: Les economies de la grandeur*. Paris: Gallimard.

Boyer, R., (1991), 'Markets within Alterative Coordinating Mechanisms: History, Theory, and Policy in the Light of the Nineties'. Paper presented to the Conference on the Comparative Governance of Sectors, Bigorio, Switzerland.

Bresser, P. and Carlos, L., (1993), 'The Crisis of the State Approach to Latin America'. Discussion paper no. 1, Instituto Sul-Norte, November.

Bruszt, L., (1988), 'A centralizáció csapdája és a politikai rendszer reformalternatívái' (The Trap of Centralization and the Alternatives of Reforming the Political System). *Medvetánc*, number 1: 171–197.

Bunce, V. and Csanádi, M., (1993), 'Uncertainty in the Transition: Post-Communism in Hungary'. *East European Politics and Societies*, 7(2):240–275.

Burawoy, M. and Krotov, P., (1992), 'The Soviet Transition from Socialism to Capitalism: Worker Control and Economic Bargaining in the Wood Industry'. *American Sociological Review*, 57:16–38.

Collins, H.M. (ed.), (1982), *Knowledge and Controversy: Studies of Modern Natural Science*. Special Issue of *Social Studies of Science*, 2(1).

Conrad, M., (1983), *Adaptability*. New York: Plenum Press.

Cui, Z., (in press), 'Moebius-Strip Ownership and its Prototype in Chinese Rural Industry'. *Economy and Society*.

Denton, N., (1993), 'Two Hungarian Banks Said to Be Technically Insolvent'. *Financial Times*, May 20.

Durkheim, E., (1897), *Le suicide: étude de sociologie*. Paris: Presses Universitaires de France.

Figyelö, (1993), *Top 200: a legnagyobb vállalkozások* [The Top 200 Largest Enterprises]. Special Issue.

Gábor, I., (1979), 'The Second (Secondary) Economy'. *Acta Oeconomica*, 22(3–4):91–311.

Gábor, I., (1986), 'Reformok második gazdaság, államszocializmus. A 80-as évek tapasztalatainak feljödéstani és összehasonlító gazdaságtani tanulságairól (Reforms, second economy, state socialism: Speculation on the evolutionary and comparative economic lessons of the Hungarian eighties)', *Valóság*, no. 6, pp. 32–48.

Gereffi, G., (1994), 'The Organization of Buyer-Driven Global Commodity Chains: How U.S. Retailers Shape Overseas Production Networks'. Pp. 91–122 in *Commodity Chains and Global Capitalism*, edited by Gary Gereffi and Miguel Kornzeniewicz. Westport, Conn.: Praeger.

Gerlach, M.L. and Lincoln, J.R., (1992), 'The Organization of Business Networks in the United States and Japan'. Pp. 491–520 in *Networks and Organizations*, edited by Nitin Nohria and Robert G. Eccles. Cambridge, Mass.: Harvard Business School Press.

Grabher, G., (1994), *In Praise of Waste: Redundancy in Regional Development*. Berlin: Edition Sigma.

David Stark

Granovetter, M., (1985), 'Economic Action, Social Structure, and Embeddedness'. *American Journal of Sociology*, 91:481–510.

Granovetter, M., (1995), 'Coase Revisited: Business Groups in the Modern Economy'. *Industrial and Corporate Change* 4(1):93–130.

Grey, T., (1980), 'The Disintegration of Property'. Pp. 69–85 in *Property*, edited by J. Rolland Pennock and John W. Chapman. New York: New York University Press.

Hamilton, G.G., Zeile, W. and Kim, W-J., (1990), 'The Network Structures of East Asian Economies'. In *Capitalism in Contrasting Cultures*, edited by S.R. Clegg and S.G. Redding. Berlin: Walter de Gruyter.

Hamilton, G.G. and Feenstra, R.C., (1995), 'Varieties of Hierarchies and Markets: An Introduction'. *Industrial and Corporate Change*, 4(1):51–91.

Hirschman, A., (1958), *The Strategy of Economic Development*. New Haven, Conn.: Yale University Press.

Hoshi, T., (1994), 'The Economic Role of Corporate Grouping and the Main Bank System'. Pp. 285–309 in *The Japanese Firm: The Sources of Competitive Strength* edited by Masahiko Aoiki and Ronald Dore. London: Oxford University Press.

Kim, E.M., (1991), 'The Industrial Organization and Growth of the Korean Chaebol: Integrating Development and Organizational Theories'. Pp. 272–299 in *Business Networks and Economic Development in East and Southeast Asia*, edited by Gary Hamilton. Hong Kong: Centre of Asian Studies, University of Hong Kong.

Kogut, B. and Zandur, U., (1992), 'Knowledge of the Firm, Combinative Capabilities, and the Replication of Technology'. *Organization Science*, 3(3):383–397.

Konrad, G. and Szelenyi, I., (1979), *Intellectuals on the Road to Class Power*. New York: Harcourt Brace and Jovanovich.

Kornai, J., (1980), *The Economics of Shortage*. Amsterdam: North-Holland Publishing.

Kornai, J., (1992), 'The Post-Socialist Transition and the State: Reflections in the Light of Hungarian Fiscal Problems'. *American Economic Review*, 82(2):1–21.

Kornai, J., (1993a), 'The Evolution of Financial Discipline under the Postsocialist System'. *Kyklos*, 46:315–336.

Kornai, J. (1993b), 'Transitional Recession'. Institute for Advanced Study/Collegium Budapest, Discussion Papers Series.

Landau, M., (1969), ' Redundancy, Rationality, and the Problem of Duplication and Overlap'. *Public Administration Review*, 29(4):346–358.

Latour, B., (1988), *The Pasteurization of France*. Cambridge, Mass.: Harvard University Press.

Morin, E., (1974), 'Complexity'. *International Social Science Journal*, 26(4):555–582.

National Bank of Hungary, (1992), *Annual Report*. Budapest.

Nee, V., (1992), 'Organizational Dynamics of Market Transition: Hybrid Forms, Property Rights, and Mixed Economy in China'. *Administrative Science Quarterly*, 37:1–27.

Nelson, R.R. and Winter, S.G., (1982), *An Evolutionary Theory of Economic Change*. Cambridge: Cambridge University Press.

Neumann, L., (1989), 'Market Relations in Intra-Enterprise Wage Bargaining?' *Acta Oeconomica*, 40:319–338.

Numazaki, I., (1991), 'The Role of Personal Networks in the Making of Taiwan's *Guanxiquiye* (Related Enterprises)'. Pp. 77–93 in *Business Networks and Economic Development in East and Southeast Asia* edited by Gary Hamilton. Hong Kong: University of Hong Kong, Centre of Asian Studies.

Oi, J.C., (1992), 'Fiscal Reform and the Economic Foundations of Local State Corporatism in China'. *World Politics*, 45:99–126.

Orru, M., Biggart, N.W. and Hamilton, G.G., (1991), 'Organizational Isomorphism in East Asia'. Pp. 361–389 in *The New Institutionalism in Organizational Analysis*, edited by Walter W. Powell and Paul J. DiMaggio. Chicago: University of Chicago Press.

Padgett, J.F. and Ansell, C.K., (1993), 'Robust Action and the Rise of the Medici, 1400–1434'. *American Journal of Sociology*, 98:1259–1319.

Pickering, A. (ed.), (1992), *Science as Culture and Practice.* Chicago: University of Chicago Press.

Powell, W. and DiMaggio, P. (eds), (1991), *The New Institutionalism in Organizational Analysis.* Chicago: University of Chicago Press.

Sabel, C., (1990), 'Mobius-Strip Organizations and Open Labor Markets: Some Consequences of the Reintegration of Conception and Execution in a Volatile Economy'. Pp. 23–54. in *Social Theory for a Changing Society*, edited by Pierre Bourdieu and James Coleman. Boulder, Colo. and New York: Westview Press and Russell Sage Foundation.

Sabel, C., (1990), 'Constitutional Ordering in Historical Perspective'. Pp. 65–123 in *Games in Hierarchies and Networks*, edited by Fritz Scharpf. Boulder, Colo.: Westview Press.

Sabel, C. and Prokop, J.E., (1997), 'Stabilization Through Reorganization? Some Preliminary Implications of Russia's Entry into World Markets in the Age of Discursive Quality Standards'. Conference on Corporate Governance in Central Europe and Russia, World Bank, December.

Sabel, C. and Stark, D., (1982), 'Planning, Politics, and Shop-Floor Power: Hidden Forms of Bargaining in Soviet-Imposed State-Socialist Societies'. *Politics and Society*, 11:439–475.

Sabel, C., and Zeitlin, J., (1966), 'Stories, Strategies, Structures: Rethinking Historical Alternatives to Mass Production'. In *Worlds of Possibility: Flexibility and Mass Production in Western Industrialization*, edited by C. Sabel and J. Zeitlin. Cambridge and New York: Cambridge University Press.

Schmitter, P., (1988), 'Modes of Governance of Economic Sectors'. Manuscript, Stanford University.

Schumpeter, J.A., (1934), *The Theory of Economic Development.* Cambridge, Mass.: Harvard University Press.

Somers, M.R. and Gibson, G.D., (1994), 'Reclaiming the Epistemological "Other": Narrative and the Social Constitution of Identity'. Pp. 37–99 in *Social Theory and the Politics of Identity*, edited by Craig Calhoun. Oxford: Basil Blackwell.

Staniszkis, J., (1991), ' "Political Capitalism" in Poland'. *East European Politics and Societies*, 5:127–141.

Staniszkis, J., (1993), 'Ontology, Context and Chance: Three Exit Routes from Communism'. *Working Papers on Central and Eastern Europe*, Center for European Studies, Harvard University, no. 31.

Stark, D., (1986), 'Rethinking Internal Labor Markets: New Insights from a Comparative Perspective'. *American Sociological Review*, 51:492–504.

Stark, D., (1989), 'Coexisting Organizational Forms in Hungary's Emerging Mixed Economy'. Pp. 137–168 in *Remaking the Economic Institutions of Socialism: China and Eastern Europe*, edited by Victor Nee and David Stark. Stanford: Stanford University Press.

Stark, D., (1990), 'La valeur du travail et sa rétribution en Hongrie'. *Actes de la*

Recherche en Sciences Sociales. (Paris) no. 85, November, pp. 3–19. In English as 'Work, Work, and Justice'. Harvard University, Center for European Studies, *Program on Central and East Europe Working Paper Series*, #5.

Stark, D., (1992), 'Path Dependence and Privatization Strategies in East Central Europe'. *East European Politics and Societies*, 6:17–51.

Stark, D., (forthcoming), 'Heterarchy: Asset Ambiguity, Organizational Innovation, and the Postsocialist Firm'. Paper presented at the Annual Meetings of the American Sociological Association, New York City, August 1996. Forthcoming in a volume edited by Paul DiMaggio, Princeton University Press.

Stark, D. and Bruszt, L., (1998), *Postsocialist Pathways: Transforming Politics and Property in Eastern Europe*. New York and London: Cambridge University Press.

Stark, D. and Nee, V., (1989), 'Toward an Institutional Analysis of State Socialism'. Pp. 1–31 in *Remaking the Economic Institutions of Socialism: China and Eastern Europe*, edited by Victor Nee and David Stark. Stanford University Press.

Stark, D. and Kemény, S., (1997), 'Postsocialist Portfolios: Network Strategies in the Shadow of the State'. Department of Sociology, Cornell University, *Working Papers on Networks and Interpretation*, 1997 #7.

Szelenyi, I., (1978), 'Social Inequalities in State Socialist Redistributive Economies'. *Theory and Society*, 1–2:63–87.

Szelenyi, I., (1988), *Socialist Entrepreneurs*. Madison: University of Wisconsin Press.

Szelenyi, I., (1994), 'Socialist Entrepreneurs—Revisited. *Working Papers*, International Institute, University of Michigan, no. 4.

Szücs, J., (1985), *Les trois Europes*. Paris: Harmattan.

Thévenot, L., (1985), 'Rules and Implements: Investment in Forms'. *Social Science Information*, 23(1):1–45.

Voszka, E., (1991), 'Homályból homályba. A tulajdonosi szerkezet a nagyiparban (From Twilight to Twilight: Property changes in large industry)'. *Társadalmi Szemle*, no. 5, pp. 3–12.

Voszka, E., (1992), 'Escaping from the State, Escaping to the State'. Paper presented at the Arne Ryde Symposium on the 'Transition Problem'. Rungsted, Denmark, June.

Walder, A., (1994), 'Corporate Organization and Local Government Property Rights in China'. Pp. 53–66 in *Changing Political Economies: Privatization in Post-Communist and Reforming Communist States*, edited by Vedat Milor. Boulder, Colo.: Lynne Rienner.

White, H.C., (1992), *Identity and Control: A Structural Theory of Social Action*. Princeton, NJ: Princeton University Press.

White, H.C., (1993), 'Values Come in Styles, Which Mate to Change'. Pp. 63–91 in *The Origins of Values*, edited by Michael Hechter, Lynn Nadel, and Richard E. Michod. New York: Aldine de Gruyter.

World Bank, (1993), *The East Asian Miracle. Economic Growth and Public Policy*. Oxford: Oxford University Press.

The making of an industry: electricity in the United States

Mark Granovetter and Patrick McGuire

1 Introduction: economic sociology and the sociology of industry

Although economic sociology has enjoyed a strong resurgence in recent years, it has focused on relatively low or high levels of aggregation. One central concern has been what determines the actions of individuals and firms, and another the role of government and large-scale interest groups in the governance and evolution of the economy. With some notable exceptions (eg, Hirsch, 1972; Campbell, Lindberg and Hollingsworth, 1992; Dobbin, 1994; Roy, 1997), few have paid close attention to middle levels of aggregation such as industries. Problems of industrial organization have largely been left to economists, who treat industry boundaries as resulting unproblematically from the nature of the product, the state of technology at a given time (as summed up by production functions), consumer demand, and the attempt to reduce production and transaction costs.

Sociologists have reacted to some general arguments on the subject of organizational form, especially those of Chandler (1962, 1975, 1990) and Williamson (1975, 1985), and to some of the other standard assumptions. But these critiques, whatever their merits, have been largely defensive; they have followed and responded to economic arguments rather than setting the agenda with a distinctively sociological position about industry and organizational form. A substantial sociology of industry must be a persuasive alternative based on serious research about particular industries and their evolution, rooted in a coherent view of how people and organizations form and co-operate in such a way as to produce those goods and services that consumers demand.

We do not dispute the convenience of defining industries as sets of firms that produce the same or related products. But we argue that such classifications are deceptively simple and not obvious at the outset; instead it is up for grabs, early on, exactly which products will fall inside and outside an industry's boundaries, and even what will be defined as a product. To understand the outcome, one must analyse socio-economic and institutional links among self-designated competitors, since an industry only becomes a social reality when firms are similarly structured, occupational categories are standardized and extra-organizational structures are created to manage competition and articulate common goals (cf. White, 1981). Thus, which firms are considered to be involved in 'related activities' is a social construction that evolves in ways that cannot be understood only in technical terms, but requires also attention to social processes and interactions among firms.

We stress the role of human agency and social structure in determining which firms become associated into an industry and in defining the scope and structure of the resulting collectivity. Standard economic discussions of industrial organization neglect human agency since they assume that industrial structure is an inevitable and efficient consequence of existing technology and market conditions. At the opposite extreme from this functionalism, in which the activity of individuals is irrelevant because outcomes automatically meet the needs of the economic system, is the argument that certain industries take the form they do on account of the activity of a few 'great' men or women. Such a position is taken by some philosophers and historians (eg, Hook, 1943; McDonald, 1962). We argue that human agency is vastly underestimated in the former argument but overestimated in the latter and that individual and collective action, while critical, operate only within sharply defined historical and structural constraints.

A sociology of industry ought to account for the social structure of an industry, in which we include: 1) the internal structure of organizations comprising the industry; 2) the structuring of relations between firms and their upstream and downstream trading partners, where 'upstream' means not only suppliers of equipment and raw materials, but also of inputs such as labour and capital—eg, unions, professional groups, agencies creating accreditation standards, and financial institutions; 3) relations among industry firms (including formal and informal relations, cross-stockholding and interlocking directorates, trade associations and vertical relations such as those expressed in holding companies); 4) relations between the industry firms and outside institutions or groups that play crucial auxiliary roles—such as political parties, voluntary associations (eg, the National Civic Federation) and, in the case of electricity, the crucial role of the electrical engineering profession; 5) relations between the industry and government at all levels.

The present chapter is part of a larger project on the history of electricity as an industry in the United States, which will attempt to cover all these bases from the beginning of the industry in about 1880 to its stable form, around 1925.

We believe that the way the electricity industry developed was only one of several possible outcomes and not necessarily the most technically or economically efficient. Its particular form arose because a set of powerful actors accessed certain techniques and applied them in a highly visible and profitable way. Those techniques resulted from the shared personal understandings, social connections, organizational conditions and historical opportunities available to these actors. The instruments of this success, in turn, used their personal and organizational resources to trigger pressures for uniformity across regions, even when this excluded viable alternative technologies and organizational forms. By the 1920s, the diversity of organizational and technological forms was much lower than one might expect, given the highly heterogeneous environments in which electricity was produced. We believe that this suppression of diversity hampered the adaptability of the industry in ways that became clear only in the late 20th century.

We attempt to identify the forces that moved the industry in certain directions, and the advantages that those directions achieved simply by being in place; these advantages then helped perpetuate forms that might not have been abstractly optimal, while excluding possibilities that had previously seemed entirely plausible. These new forms then themselves modified the environment in ways compatible with their needs. Later observers, who look only at a snapshot of technology and organization, may note the fit between industry and environment and conclude that the industry has arisen in its present form *in order* to meet environmental needs. Only a dynamic, historical account can break through the functionalist misconceptions resulting from confining analysis to comparative statics. Our argument resembles that made by economists Paul David and Brian Arthur on the 'lock-in' of inefficient technologies (such as the QWERTY keyboard on which this paper is typed— more slowly than it would be on one of better and well-known design), but draws on the sociology of knowledge and of social structure, leading to a generalization from the case of technology to that of institutional and organizational form.

One implication of our approach is that at several historical junctures, quite different outcomes might have emerged and had this occurred it would likely have been argued, as it has for actual outcomes, that *those* were the most economically or technically efficient. Our goal is systematically to analyse the particular conditions within each historical setting and consider the options and factors influencing path selection at each point of decision-making. This method allows us to differentiate between selected and avoided opportunities, between intentional and unintentional outcomes, to provide a more nuanced and realistic depiction of how economic institutions are formed. It removes the need to infer the intentions of firm leaders from known outcomes, or to rely on teleological categories such as technical and economic efficiency to explain all outcomes.

2 Electricity: the initial boundaries of an industry

In 1880 Thomas Edison had only begun to develop the incandescent electric light, and most homes and factories were lit by natural gas. On-site electric lighting systems had been sold and installed as early as 1878 and by 1885 were a booming business involving over 1,500 arc and incandescent systems, operating in homes and factories (American Electrical Directory, 1886). Alongside these 'isolated plants' (as these systems were known), a fledgling industry of privately-owned central electric stations blossomed from less than two dozen firms in 1882 to almost 500 in 1885 and almost 2,000 independent local firms by 1891, using different technologies and organizational structures.[1] These firms were hobbled by local governments and large equipment manufacturers, and wracked by destructive competition. Yet by 1929, isolated generation was receding in importance, and the industry was dominated by a few large holding companies overseeing central station firms using standardized methods of production, sales, and marketing, common organizational structures, and protected by government agencies that regulated them, guaranteeing profits under the concept that electricity provision was a 'natural monopoly' (Bonbright and Means, 1969; Rudolph and Ridley, 1986; FTC, 1935; McGuire, 1986: 526–529; American Electrical Directory, 1892).

We have reviewed the histories of 80 central station firms and the careers of over 200 one-time employees of Thomas Edison, analysed the participation of 1,500 executives in for-profit firms in industry trade associations, and studied several hundred other secondary and archival sources. We find that the boundaries, composition, and dynamics of the U.S. electric utility industry were constructed by identifiable social networks. We will use the content of several industry contests to demonstrate how and why these networks acted to construct and shape industry development and boundaries in particular ways, and not in others of apparently equal viability.

Central station electric systems were a major commitment for Thomas Edison, who mobilized his personal financial and patent-based resources and those of his subordinate co-workers and their families to create and manage the Edison (later General Electric) electrical equipment manufacturing firms (McGuire, Granovetter, and Schwartz, 1993). He strongly argued that electricity should be the primary commodity, and that electric equipment should be built for and sold to central stations, rather than to each building owner who would generate his own electricity (in a process similar to systems producing heat for a single building).[2] Edison also mobilized long-standing associates to sell and/or invest in several central station firms. They secured funding for several additional central station firms by exploiting antagonisms and fears among financiers. And by exchanging equipment for securities of local firms, Edison created shared ownership between the patent-owners, equipment manufacturing firms, and central station firms.

Edison was establishing the initial boundaries among electric industries. Again drawing upon the collective resources of himself and associates and their families, and upon a production monopoly secured by exclusive contracts, they separated electric light current business from the manufacture of electric devices, electric trolleys, electro-plating, telephone, etc. each of which preceded the incandescent lighting system and involved millions in invested capital and sales by 1881 (Bright, 1972:33). Edison also worked to retain the separation between incandescent lighting (mostly indoor) systems such as his own, and the well-established arc lighting (mostly street and public spaces) systems, keeping them separate industries and markets.

Through 1884 Edison also argued the need to differentiate between firms selling electric current for lighting and those supplying it for motors (Conot, 1979:207), given his own lack of personal investment in devices run by electric power, and his strained personal relations with innovators of such applications (Conot, 1979:Ch. 18).[3] But for a series of reasons, he was unsuccessful at and soon drew back from insisting on this separation. First, some of his friends and investors in his manufacturing and central station firms came to own crucial patents related to power, tailored the equipment derived from these patents so as to operate on his central station system, and signed exclusive production contracts with the Edison manufacturing firms (Passer, 1962, 1953:238–239, McGuire, 1990, McGuire, Granovetter, and Schwartz, 1993). As a result, many local utilities began to simultaneously serve both arc and incandescent lighting systems as well as power customers. Given the different but compatible applications of these technologies, and the technical possibility of serving all customers from common equipment, it became difficult for Edison to argue that separation was efficient.

Moreover, Edison was preoccupied with struggles against his own financiers for the control of his firms and patents, and was distracted from this issue. Thus, in this period, friendships, family connections, personal fears, mobilized collective knowledge and resources, scarcity of capital as well as vested interests and technical possibilities, all shaped the inclusion of various proto-industries within what became the electric utility industry.

While Edison had created the basis for central station firms, it was not inevitable that they would survive or become the dominant form of electric service. Isolated systems (in individual homes and factories) were viable and would be the most common supplier of electricity to consumers through 1915 in most cities (cf. Platt, 1991:209). While economic arguments were mounted on behalf of each type of service, it appears that isolated systems in a factory or apartment building were at least as viable as other decentralized amenities, including home furnaces, water wells, and personal automobiles, each of which became a norm (Gilchrist, 1940:I, 21–32; Adams, 1900). Isolated systems had significant first mover advantages: thousands had been sold before Edison ever opened his first central station—(Brush, 1882, Stout, 1909) and they had the support of major financial houses, such as that of J.P. Morgan. We even found examples of co-ordinated distribution systems involving many isolated stations (Marvin, 1988:170).[4]

Two other industry boundaries—the selection of the preferred form of current, and the standardization of current frequency at 25 and 60 cycles (for power and light, respectively)—also resulted from personal insights, compound historical accidents, longstanding friendships, and corporate interlocks (McGuire, 1990). AC and DC current each had advantages and disadvantages (Passer 1953:

164–166) but neither was intrinsically preferable or dominant. AC became the principal U.S. current form because both General Electric and Westinghouse, the two major manufacturers, had AC equipment and their leaders had no personal stake in promoting an exclusively DC system, and because J.P. Morgan had a lingering antagonism toward Edison who held and could have reaped a handsome profit from continued use of crucial DC patents (David, 1987).

There was no overwhelming technical or economic imperative driving the selection of AC or of 25 and 60 cycles as the industry norm. The 'rotary converter' that transformed AC into DC current also worked in reverse. Systems in which current was generated and transmitted in AC and then converted to DC for distribution were feasible, and indeed were typical in Europe through most of the 20th century and in most U.S. central city areas through the 1920s. Motors and appliances for each current type were manufactured and sold here, and so each current type could have had its own niche. Further, the initial selection of two frequencies of current as a norm (rather than one as occurred in Germany and in parts of Britain and of California—Hughes 1983:129) embedded a technical and economic inefficiency that lingered generally through 1950 when most of the remaining 25 cycle engines were rewired at utility expense (McAfee, 1947:19, Bush, 1973:501).[5] Social factors including involvement of decision-makers in multiple firms (corporate interlocks), personal friendships and animosities guided these decisions and helped to lock in these technical and economic inefficiencies.

3 The stabilization of boundaries and practices in private central station firms

Through 1890 the definition of the electricity industry included both the equipment manufacturing firms and all the local operating utilities. In 1885 the owners of non-Edison electric current sales firms met and formed a trade association, the National Electric Light Association (NELA). The NELA included firms making, selling, operating, and repairing (especially arc) light and power systems. By 1888, it was dominated by the leaders of the Electric Club, a New York organization with a national roster (Nye, 1990:173, NELA, 1888) that constituted a primarily non-Edison social network. In response, Samuel Insull, secretary to Thomas Edison and an executive who helped Edison sell and open central station firms, formed the Association of Edison Illuminating

Mark Granovetter and Patrick McGuire

Companies (AEIC) in 1885. Early AEIC members were mostly personal friends of Edison and/or Insull who were also executives of
small Edison central station incandescent lighting systems.

Beginning in about 1890 both trade associations began to redefine the boundaries of the electricity industry by denouncing city-
owned electric firms, even though such firms used the same
equipment, sold the same commodity, and operated in a similar way
(NELA, 1890:164–179, 1898, 1900: 1:412, Rudolph and Ridley,
1896:23–34, and Toledo Edison 2:83 2/14/1897). The associations
tried to exclude them from their organizational meetings, proposed
boycotts of manufacturers who supplied them, and mobilized to
oppose and impede their creation. They also sought and secured
state legislation that limited not-for-profit systems to street lights in
some cities, such as Detroit (Wilcox, 1908). This new industry
boundary was being built based on form of ownership, contrary to
the logic of the Bureau of the Census and its SIC codes which officially define industries (McGuire, 1986).

A second boundary was being constructed simultaneously during
the early 1890s as local utilities sought to separate themselves from
the electric equipment manufacturing firms. NELA members
included firms selling and operating all types of electric devices
involving several proto-industries, such as electric arc light and
electro-plating, telephone, electrical medicine, and electric motor
devices. In fact the first major electric light company in Chicago—
Chicago Arc Light—emerged from a combination of electric medicine and central station service (Platt, 1991:268). Many of these
industries were in place and had millions of dollars in investments
and/or sales before Edison even invented the incandescent light bulb
(Bright, 1972:33). The NELA's concept of electric light service (and
by extension the composition of the industry) involved vertically
integrated firm components, including manufacturers, operating
utilities, contractors, and repairmen, similar to Bell Telephone.[6]

AEIC membership was limited to people from the Edison-
affiliated central station electric lighting firms and their associated
Edison manufacturing firms (first Edison Manufacturing, then
Edison General Electric). Through 1893 the AEIC promoted a limited notion of industry involving a two-level vertically integrated
industry of equipment manufacturers (GE) and Edison incandescent central station firms. The central stations had exclusive contracts with the manufacturing firms, and depended on them for
financing, supplies, and innovations, factors that in effect left them
as subordinate cheerleaders in the AEIC. This changed when, in

154   © The Editorial Board of The Sociological Review 1998

1892, J.P. Morgan and his allies wrested full control of Edison General Electric from Edison and his supporters, in a leveraged buyout through competitor Thomson-Houston; the resulting firm was renamed General Electric. Beginning in 1893, the owners of early but small Edison central station firms became less prominent in the AEIC, and the organization was increasingly dominated by a small group of former Edison employees. Samuel Insull left General Electric after the buyout to become a utility executive in Chicago; he and other urban executives mobilized to counterpoise their central station firm interests to those of General Electric, redefining the electric utility industry boundary to exclude manufacturers.

There were numerous conflicts of interest between the equipment suppliers and the central stations. Exclusive contracts locked the central stations into purchase from one supplier. In return, the suppliers were supposed to refrain from selling isolated generation equipment within the franchised territory of the utility companies. That they often ignored this provision is evidenced by sharp exchanges at AEIC meetings. Rival central station firms still operated within the same areas, and expected their suppliers to pursue patent infringement suits against other such firms using different equipment; but this was a low priority for the manufacturers. The exclusivity of contracts gave equipment suppliers market power which they used to keep prices higher than seemed reasonable to central stations. Service issues, such as delivery time, were frequent bones of contention. Manufacturers, for their part, considered the central stations unreliable customers, whose often strained financial condition made them delay payment for equipment or issue new securities, to meet this obligation, which might then be drastically devalued in the next recession.

Personal distrust between these groups, in part resulting from past history of conflict and resulting animosity between the J.P. Morgan interests who dominated General Electric after 1892 and the Edison/Insull group, might, in a transaction-cost account, have presented a need for vertical integration between manufacturers and central stations, so as to achieve consummate rather than perfunctory co-operation (Williamson, 1985). But central station executives were pulling forcefully in the opposite direction, to preserve their independence and assert their own interests, through collective action.

The crucial group in this emerging industry is what we will call the 'Insull circle', consisting initially of men who had worked in the drafting room of the Edison Electric Light Company's Goerck

Street (Manhattan, New York) equipment manufacturing plant between 1882 and 1885, at a time when Samuel Insull was Edison's most trusted confidant and head of the Edison manufacturing operations (cf. McDonald, 1962). While hundreds of others worked for Edison during this era, a small group of four who had both worked in the Goerck Street plant in the early 1880s, and had attended special classes together, were especially influential. They had also been among the men sent out by Insull and Edison to help set up and initially operate central station light systems. The four were Samuel Insull, John Lieb, Charles Edgar, and Louis Ferguson. They, along with another set of—gradually shifting but probably never larger than eight—close associates of Samuel Insull, would become the key to industry development for the next 40 years. One of their first efforts was to distance themselves from GE domination in the AEIC, and to create a certifying board—the Electrical Testing Laboratory—to assure GE quality and innovation—and in effect assert their (and central station in general) control over the AEIC. The board of ETL consisted of Lieb, Edgar, Insull and William Barstow, who began working for the Edison manufacturing operations after they moved to Schenectady in 1887.

We refer to this as the Insull circle because of its domination by Insull, and in our ongoing research, we examine Insull's company, Chicago Edison and detail his access to U.S. and European capital. We explain how his personal knowledge, his connections to the European technical and financial community, and a group of very talented friends and associates created both autonomy and innovative opportunity for Chicago Edison.

Insull brought European innovations (including the Wright rate system, load building, and turbines) to the U.S., and actively promoted emulation of and adoption of these techniques and devices among the other principal firms within the AEIC (Hughes, 1983:217–233). His circle identified, deliberated upon, and mobilized to promote these and other technical and organizational changes among AEIC members and then the rest of the central station utility industry. The over-arching theme linking their efforts was the pursuit of what we have called a 'growth dynamic' approach—scrap and replace old technology with new, create and expand a territorial monopoly, increase total and per capita load and establish load balance—as an industry-wide development strategy.[7] They used their personal and trade organization relationships to promote adoption of this strategy and associated technology. As we will detail, alternatives that involved more decentralized and smaller-scale provision of electricity, separation of generation, transmission and distribution, provision combined with the production and sale of other products (such as heat in co-generation arrangements), or provision by not-for-profit companies, were effectively attacked and discouraged by the Insull group.

Crucial to the embedding of their collective template of industry development was domination of the AEIC as a method of transferring technical and organizational norms. Insull's circle held over 90 per cent of the AEIC officer and committee positions, and from 1892 to 1897, in combination with the technical experts from what we will call the 'Six Cities' firms they led (New York, Philadelphia, Brooklyn, Detroit, Boston, and Chicago Edison) delivered almost all the paper presentations at AEIC annual meetings. Leaders of firms in other large cities—Buffalo, Providence, St. Louis, Baltimore, and Pittsburgh—did not participate in the AEIC leadership, despite their having large populations and loads. Regardless of firm or load size, we find that through 1910 most firms only joined and/or became active in the AEIC after hiring other former Goerck St. employees and/or family members of the inner circle's executives.

Our analysis of the composition of AEIC committees from 1897 to 1910 shows that personal networks and firm domination of the AEIC became institutionalized as executives from Insull's circle were replaced. Twenty-three out of 28 times that one of these left a committee position, he was replaced by a subordinate executive from his own firm, an 80 per cent rate of re-constitution of 'broken ties' (cf. Palmer, 1983). Men from the Six Cities firms occupied 275 of the 287 committee positions on AEIC committees and presented 71 per cent of all papers between 1901 and 1910. Direct, almost monolithic, control over the AEIC by this group continued, albeit through firm subordinates.

But important as the AEIC was on its own it was not sufficient to dominate the industry; it was a highly self-selected group associated with large urban firms and it worked closely with General Electric. The other industry trade association, the National Electric Light Association (NELA) was broader, bringing together many smaller firms, those not dependent on General Electric equipment, and in close contact with contractors, jobbers and workers. It held the potential for industry dominance that could not be assured from an AEIC base.

Correspondingly, an informal system of industry-wide self-governance emerged after several Six Cities firms joined the NELA. While several AEIC firms joined the NELA in the early 1890s, they were rarely involved in the NELA leadership before 1896. However in 1897 Insull's circle, aided by leaders from a few other long-standing AEIC firms, became a major bloc in the NELA. Rather than having a straightforward system of unilateral domination as in the AEIC, their *modus operandi* in this trade association was different.

Analysts such as McMahon (1985) and McDonald (1962) have suggested that the AEIC acted as the directing and co-ordinating committee for the remainder of the industry. A brief examination of the committee assignments of the NELA from 1901 to 1910 supports that insight. Insull's circle, their firm subordinates, and executives of other urban firms involved in the AEIC, occupied a majority of seats in two-thirds of the 75 NELA committees existing during the 1901–1910 period.

However, something much more significant was occurring beneath this process. Samuel Insull (President of both the AEIC and NELA in 1898), and his circle gained a substantial minority (13 of 40 positions 1901–1910) in the NELA officerships and executive committees. They, their firm subordinates, and long-standing AEIC supporters together occupied 32 of the 40 seats. In effect they established an important system of significant and strategic influence over the NELA, rather than overt domination.

These leaders, their subordinates and those AEIC firms that had long-standing membership and a former Goerck Street employee as a top executive were a majority in only 19 of the 75 committees (six to ten per year) operating between 1901 and 1910. While rare, those majorities were important, occurring mostly when the committee was new or when its policy focus was initially being established. After policy was initially set, the inner circle and its supporters left the committee, leaving behind a significant minority presence of their subordinate Six Cities executives. In effect, they and their long-standing AEIC supporters created precedent. Afterward, they used their subordinates to scan or monitor the committee deliberations for continued compliance with their initial policy precedents (consistent with the theory of Useem, 1985). When the standing NELA committees did stray from the original policy decisions, committee membership changed soon after and several AEIC associates returned to that committee, re-establishing AEIC-supported policy.[8] Following-up upon this initial insight, Chi-nien Chung (1997) has developed a social network analysis that supports these deduced patterns, showing the high centrality of Insull's circle in the AEIC and their emergence in the NELA after 1895.

Consequently, preferred technologies—including turbines, meters, organizational entities (such as the Contract, Statistical, and Appliance Departments—Insull, 1934: 51; Gilchrist, 1940:8–18; Platt, 1991:89) organizational relations, strategic goals, and even dirty tricks (Gilchrist, 1940: 14–16, 50, 32), were identified, implemented, promoted, and transferred uniformly throughout the industry. Acting through their informal/formal governance structures, the inner circle mobilized their own firms to adopt similar technology, organizational format, or goal (Gilchrist, 1927:472–473). They and/or their Six Cities executive experts then promoted this before the AEIC (Gilchrist, 1940:18; AEIC, 1901:197–209), and in turn they (and/or other AEIC members) did the same before the NELA (NELA, 1905:116–135). They invited executives from other cities to their facilities and taught them about new technologies (Flynn, 1932b:36). They loaned their firm executives (NELA, 1900:412–413; Seymour, 1935:126–127) and consultants[9] to smaller firms so as to enable them to reproduce these policies and/or install new technologies. These efforts and outcomes were then trumpeted in the trade association papers and discussions as trends or rational necessities and subsequently adopted by other central station firms. Significantly, this emerging isomorphism coincided with a decline in industry earnings through 1907 (USDCL, 1910:50). This is not surprising since Insull and other industry leaders acknowledged that their expansion crated some diseconomies (Platt, 1991:178, 342 ft. #37).

This system of industry self-governance had been actively constructed based on friendships, family relations, and social network participation, which were subsequently augmented by actions of formal organizations. Such relations and decisions reverberated throughout the industry via the medium of existing formal organizations that came to be dominated by the inner circle's social network supported by their firm subordinates and former Goerck Street associates. Elements of the preferred template of industry relations became institutionally-embedded through replacement by firm subordinates and/or leaders of other AEIC firms who supported both the organizational and technical policies of the leaders and the system of industry self-governance.

4 Deflecting alternatives to the preferred template of industry development

The success of industry self-governance under the leadership of Insull's circle was most apparent in the containment of alternative forms. There were several viable alternatives to the dominance by urban central station systems and to the 'growth dynamic' strategy during the 1890–1910 era. Isolated systems in individual apartment buildings and/or factories continued to grow in size and in number until by 1902 they produced half of all the horsepower from electricity in the U.S. (USDCL, 1905:3, 1910:14). They were so successful that more U.S. customers (homes and factories) were served by isolated than by central station systems through 1918 (Gould, 1946:21). As late as 1912, more than half of all electricity produced and distributed in the United States was attributable to industry rather than to electric utilities (DuBoff, 1979:41, 219). Even in an urban centre such as Chicago central stations only produced 70 per cent of the electricity consumed in 1922 (Platt, 1991:213). In much of rural America, isolated stations were the only form of electric service available before 1930 (Nye, 1990:296–297).

There were also neighbourhood systems serving small geographic territories. Some were dedicated co-generation systems supplying a neighbourhood with both electricity and steam for heat. Entrepreneur Homer Yaryan, for example, built and operated dedicated steam and electric neighbourhood plants in 35 cities stretching from Cleveland to LaCrosse Wisconsin, including Chicago, Detroit, Toledo, and Fremont Ohio (Scribner, 1910; Cyclopedia of American Biography; Meyer, 1972: 102–103; Porter, 1986). Prominent financier and electricity/natural gas magnate Henry Doherty argued that these multi-use systems involving steam were the hardest to displace because of their efficiency: waste heat from electricity generation could be cycled back into the heating operation, rather than requiring additional energy for cooling the equipment as in traditional generation (cf. Hirsh, 1989), or being dissipated into streams and thus upsetting the local ecosystem by raising temperatures. Investor-owned utilities were in fact so determined to dispose of this competition that they often built otherwise unneeded steam plants to meet the full need of the customer, and ran them at a loss, just to eliminate the competition for electricity (Doherty, 1923:I, 125, 140).

Other neighbourhood systems originated in a 'base' factory, hotel, or trolley firm, and then sold 'surplus' current to other nearby customers (Greer, 1952:14). Some of these were dedicated electric systems while others involved selling electricity in combination with ice, irrigation, pneumatic air, water pumping, and trolleys. For example, 47.4 per cent of all electricity sold to the U.S. public in 1902 and 44.9 per cent in 1907, were sold by 251 and 330 street railroads respectively (USDCL, 1910:14). Such multi-purpose and/or decentralized systems were common in the U.S. through 1910 and they became the norm in Scandinavia, Canada and most of northern Europe and Russia (Nye, 1990: 384; Armstrong and Nelles, 1986:101–104; USDCL, 1910:13–27.

Some such systems sold off current continuously and others sold surplus current during off-peak periods. This type of firm was especially common in areas with hydro-electric potential and/or geographically diffused, energy-intensive factories such as the Carolinas, Georgia, the Rockies, New York, Minnesota, and Michigan. Through the 1920s these factories served their own needs and after normal closing time, when the electrical equipment would have otherwise been idle, they sold their spare current to utilities that engaged only in transmission and distribution. This practice, revived in the late 20th century under the rubric of wholesale 'wheeling', promoted more efficient capital utilization and load balance.

Another common decentralized schema during this era involved separation of the functions of the typical vertically-integrated central station firms. Generation, transmission, and distribution activity could each (or in combinations of two) be performed by distinct firms and by extension could be distinct industries. For example, Niagara, Lockport and Ontario Electric Company in New York State was only a transmission firm (USDCL, 1910:103). The factory-based generation systems noted above sold to a separate (but often co-owned) electric firm that re-sold current during the evening (Horn, 1973). There are even examples of a city-owned generating and transmitting firm that sold current only to street railroads and factories during this early period (BOC, 1912:198). Bulk sales (ie, of current from one utility to another, some of which were sales among integrated firms and others of which were sales to and/or from non-integrated firms) became so common that by 1907 they were described as 'a special branch of the electric industry' (USDCL, 1910:84). Similar separations between generating, transmitting, and distribution firms in various combinations developed subsequently among U.S. Rural Electrification Administration co-ops from 1930 to now, and in Canada and Britain (Doyle and Reinemer, 1979:253–263, Nelles and Armstrong, 1986; Hannah, 1979). Most equipment sales to these 'alternative' neighbourhood, railroads, and city-owned firms between 1895 and 1906 were by Westinghouse rather than by General Electric (Westinghouse, 1898, 1906: 15–16, Coffin, 1909).

The technical merits and limits of such alternative constructs are variable, locally-specific, and debatable. In some cases they were technically- and energy-efficient (especially if combined with new

161

investment in generating technology) and, given sunk capital costs, were often cost-effective.[10] In fact, Moody's (1995) and Sparks (1995) recently predicted that only firms that unbundle their generation from a transmission and/or distribution firm, and firms that co-generate and sell to dedicated transmission/distribution firms, will survive deregulation.

Yet by 1915 most of these decentralized and multi-purpose firms were subsumed, or undermined by technical licenses and patent monopolies (Passer, 1953:56–57, 158–168; Bright, 1972:82–89) and these alternative constructs for the boundaries of the electric current industries had begun to wither. A cross-licensing agreement between General Electric and Westinghouse, for example, severely limited competition in electrical equipment, leading to their 1911 prosecution for anti-trust violations (Bright, 1972:103). Moreover, regulatory bodies weighed in against these decentralized alternatives with prejudicial rulings. The Massachusetts Gas and Electric Commission, for example, prohibited firms from sending current across streets or alleys unless they were regulated utilities; this prevented neighbourhood or surplus sales.

If technology and organizational form actually followed from efficiency considerations, we should have seen considerable variation by area, since what was efficient varied dramatically according to local circumstances. One key puzzle we seek to explain is how such variation was suppressed in favour of a uniform set of technologies and organizational forms. It appears that the usual mode of suppression and homogenization was that the inner circle mobilized its own firms (as exemplars), discussed the 'problem' at the AEIC and after reaching consensus presented their opinion to the NELA. For example, 72 per cent of NELA papers presented between 1901 and 1910 were from Six Cities firms and 4 per cent by other AEIC central station firms. The leaders used their control of the NELA conference paper topics and committees to marginalize advocates of and information about decentralized energy systems. After dominating NELA presentations from 1890–1896, Westinghouse and other decentralized advocates occupied only two officer and three executive committee positions (of 40 and 80 respectively) between 1901 and 1910, presented only 15 per cent of all papers, and only once for one year had two of their advocates on a committee (public policy committee, 1906). Even in this later case they did not hold a majority. They were joined by three men whose firms were AEIC members—one from a Big Six urban firm and the other two long-time supporters of Insull's policies and agenda.

Insull's circle, their firm associates, and their AEIC supporters presented papers advocating the elimination of isolated systems and the integration, centralization and state-level regulation of production. They influenced the content, agenda, and goals of (both sets of) trade association committees toward load building and balancing and other 'growth dynamic' attributes. They also actively promoted the reconfiguration of suppliers and dependent downstream constituencies to match those 'emerging trends'.

Our research identifies friendships, family connections, shared travel, co-authorship, and site visits among the executives of the inner circle affecting the timing and selection of the various elements of this preferred template of industry development. Absence of individuals not affiliated with them on trade association committees and paper presentations might be argued to be merely a matter of friends selecting other friends for committee assignments. But our review and analysis demonstrates instead that their omission corresponds also to a conspicuous absence of voices advocating alternative (decentralized) paths of firm and industry development, despite the continued and increasing material success of such alternative systems (USDCL, 1910:13; Gould, 1946:21; Bergman, 1982:67 table #7, 68 table #9).[11]

Many of the more energy and cost-efficient technologies introduced in the 1890–1910 era by central station firms could have rendered comparable advantages to non-central station systems, as for example did the installation of turbines in neighbourhood and rail-based systems. (Indeed, the average size of an isolated generator quadrupled between 1904–1914 as they sought and gained economy of scale advantages—USDCL, 195:36). Yet discussions of such alternatives are essentially absent from trade association discussions and publications; similarly omitted was the strong growth, and increasing importance of municipally-owned firms (USDCL, 1910, 1915).

Critics could argue that the dominant market position of the inner circle, which included their leadership of six large urban firms, was the key factor motivating convergence of the industry and standardization of technology. But in fact, isolated systems purchased from 35 per cent to 50 per cent of all electrical equipment, and were thus hardly a negligible market factor. Of the remaining electric production for public sale, railroad firms produced over 45 per cent of all electric current in the U.S. and thus were major purchasers of generating equipment roughly equal to the combined purchases of all investor-owned electric firms (USDCL, 1910:14). The six largest urban central station electric firms in the U.S. (two of which were not among Big Six firms) constituted only 20 per cent of the central station equipment purchases (itself less than half of public sales—a category involving barely more than half of all electric sales) and generated 25 per cent of all central station profits (USDCL 1905:10–11). In fact, the largest 73 central station firms held only 56 per cent of installed central station capacity (USDCL, 1910:67–68). Thus the market position of the Six Cities firms was important but it certainly did not represent an overwhelming portion of customer demand for equipment such that it could result in their having leverage on manufacturers for this reason alone.

5 Restructuring the market: institutionalizing the growth dynamic model

Insull's circle often had to mobilize and re-organize the market to help lock in their preferred template. We detail how they altered the internal dynamics, standards and content of the trade press, unions, college officials, and professional associations. We repeatedly find that several of them were also officers in these groups, and/or that individuals from the larger Goerck Street group, and/or AEIC committees were the principal advocates of change in the direction of a growth dynamic, and/or sat on committees charged with securing such change. These extra-industry groups and others including suppliers and organized customer groups (again often involving Goerck Street *alumni*) typically established legal/contractual obligations and created vested interests that influenced firms involved in sales of electric current.

Groups also emerged that promoted organizational and occupation-related changes among relatively autonomous and diffused industry firms. These included NELA sub-groups, occupational/fraternal clubs (that included initiation, parades, and picnics), corporate welfare and employee clubs (that promoted loyalty through ritual social activity), and/or professional associations (with annual conferences emphasizing social and professional obligation). Here again we note the participation and leadership of the inner circle and of AEIC -associated firms.

In one case, four key figures (Lieb, Edgar, Insull and Barstow) constituted the board of a collectively-owned lab, the Electric Testing Laboratory, that created the technical criterion and standards for production of bulbs and other end-use devices (cf.

McMahon, 1985:17–20). This allowed them to monitor, license (nor not), and potentially to discipline major manufacturers including GE. It also allowed them physically to create the basis for technical continuity and integration among the central station firms of the industry. Their friendships with GE manufacturing executives and important consulting firms (several members of whom had also been at Goerck St.), their personal and/or firms' subsequent ownership of smaller investor-owned firms after 1905, and their long-established and institutionalized policy of loaning of executives to other firms (often through the aegis of the NELA), helped to promote the transfer of preferred policies that rendered disproportionate benefit to their capital-rich, integrated, urban central station firms.

The most important external issue was the passage of state regulation as a method for diffusing the growing challenge of public takeover and ownership of central station urban electric firms. Unable to mobilize support among industry firms for state regulation, or to impose it through informal governance or social peer pressure, Insull's circle turned to friends outside the industry with whom they shared membership in men's clubs, business groups, and/or corporate interlocks.

Several of the circle, Board members from their Six Cities firms, and General Electric, encouraged the National Civic Federation to study this issue and individuals including Samuel Insull and Charles Edgar became members of the study committee. After the introduction of multiple anti-public ownership biases into the study process, and despite mixed findings generally more favourable to public- than privately-owned firms, the NCF adopted the specific provisions that had been proposed by Insull and promoted by his circle for almost a decade—provisions favouring state regulation that protected investors and (to some limited extent) the public specifically by rewarding the pursuit of a 'growth dynamic' strategy and not decentralized alternatives, and rewarded firms with the greatest access to investment capital. These provisions transformed bankers (dependent upon the knowledge of and often sharing interlocks with Insull's circle) and holding company executives (which included several of the circle, and others of whom were former Goerck St. employees) into agents of industry standardization. The bankers and the NELA policy committee (dominated by Insull's circle) then secured support from other investor-owned electric firms for state regulation that had previously been resisted (McGuire, 1989).

The NCF promoted 'its' plan to state governments, several of which were directly lobbied by Insull's circle. Analyses then and now

Mark Granovetter and Patrick McGuire

uniformly show that regulation, in the form adopted, promoted merger and rewarded urban, capital-rich IOUs, while disadvantaging publicly-owned firms by locking in their territorial limitations and prohibiting their operating rules. As a result, the Wisconsin utility commission approved 50 of 52 IOU rate increases, while denying 28 of 39 rate reductions sought by public firms between 1908–1914 (Jones, 1914). These criteria also impinged upon the operations of decentralized systems, creating bureaucratic and other conditions that burdened their profitability.

Critics of our argument might perceive Insull's circle as Chandler-esque (1977) characters—uniformly insightful, proactively exercising initiative, pursuing efficiency, and achieving rational outcomes. In fact, technical, organizational and/or economic inefficiencies were created and often locked in due to their efforts. We find that they were overwhelmingly reactive in their efforts: reactive to the potential alternative systems, to public ownership and to challenges to specific elements of the growth dynamic strategy. They were backing into the future as much as or more than striding into it.

Acting through informal governance processes, for example, they had pressured firms to select inefficient paths (such as boycotting Nernst and fluorescent bulbs, over-extending their territories, ignoring street light service, investing in DC equipment, and entering the stand-alone steam heating business) and repeatedly to select the less efficient between two paths of potential development. For example, because of the threat of electric railroads as sellers of surplus current, industry firms sought contracts to supply electricity and/or merger with trolleys, which in fact were in decline and would actually force numerous central station companies into bankruptcy between 1915 and 1935. Correspondingly, after 1902 they essentially ignored electric cars (then 60 per cent of all cars in operation—Volti, 1990), that drew almost all their current at night and could have drastically improved the IOUs load balance. The making of policy through defensive reaction was so pervasive that several of Insull's circle even ignored their personal investments in electric car companies while pursuing trolley loads, hurting their industry, their firms, and themselves.

6 Summary: the social construction of the Electricity industry

We conclude that the electric utility industry was born not of Benthamite Equations or optimizing rationality, but longstanding friendships, similar experiences, common dependencies, corporate interlocks, and active creation of new social relations. Samuel Insull and his circle of collaborators socially constructed their firms in similar ways, and then promoted a system of industry governance and template diffusion. They drew upon their local and national contacts to re-frame the market and the political system in ways that pressured utility firms toward technical, organizational, economic, and legal conformity. Yet, isomorphism among firms was never fully achieved because this was a system of influence and not of direct control, and because of the varying resources and market attributes in each firm's locale.

This study directly examines only one industry, and one with an unusual combination of highly diffused production and highly intensive capitalization. The largest firms did not directly compete, and there are virtually no international market or trade concerns. Further, we have only examined industry development occurring from 1880 to 1925. These attributes limit generalization of our findings to other industries. Nevertheless, most major industries are similar in having important trade associations, interacting with government and regulatory bodies, and seeking capital from bankers and the public through debt and equity markets. More specialized aspects of electricity have commonalities with the products of other important industries; telephone, telecommunications, transportation and computing service firms, for example, face comparable issues of peak-load pricing, load-balancing, and issues of expansion in relation to optimal utilization of capital. Communications, transportation and entertainment industries are similar in having highly decentralized consumers, and are currently going through consolidations reminiscent of those in the early period of electricity.

More generally, we believe our approach allows us to identify industries whose outcomes are typically attributed to economic and technical rationality, individual achievement and omniscience. When the case is carefully examined within its historical context, all these may turn out to be socially constructed by the mobilization of resources and influence through social networks. Industries are constantly re-negotiated, re-framed, and re-mobilized in response to their environment.

Finally, our story, is empirically and theoretically incomplete. While we find a tight web of friendship, shared experience, club activity, and domination through an industry governance structure in the process of industry formation, we do not believe that such concentrated patterns necessarily continue indefinitely; a fuller theory of industry would specify under what conditions all this shifting of boundaries would solidify. Were we to follow the industry past its formative years chronicled here, we would find that processes and relationships once shaped by individuals became institutionalized in more formal organizations, institutional alliances, standardized practices, and industry norms. As in other industries, we argue, such patterns become embedded as norms, unless and until an industry-wide crisis occurs.[12] At that point, a new social network of firm leaders has the potential to re-define and re-construct a new industry based upon various elements of the old.

Acknowledgements

The authors are listed alphabetically. We acknowledge the financial support of National Science Foundation Grant SBR 96–01437, the Urban Affairs Center and Office of Research of the University of Toledo which helped to underwrite the collection of archival data, and the Center for Research on Social Organization of the University of Michigan which provided other material resources. We are also grateful for the comments of Chi-nien Chung, Valery Yakubovich and members of a seminar on the electricity industry that meets periodically in the Department of Sociology at Stanford.

Notes

1 Of the central station firms existing in 1882, only a handful powered incandescent lights, the rest providing arc lighting for outdoor illumination, or for hotels, factories or large public buildings. The first incandescent station was brought on line by Edison himself, on October 1, at Pearl Street, in New York's financial district; it served no more than about a square mile. Arc lighting stations existed from 1879 on, but it was only incandescent stations that provided residential service and which eventually displaced arc lighting stations entirely. Thus it is common, if not literally correct, to describe Pearl Street as the 'first' central station installation.

In the early period of the industry, arc and incandescent systems ran on different cycles and frequencies, and each product line or system of lighting had its own distinctive current and frequency for operating its devices.

2 Ironically, however, in this period, an Edison firm was also the main provider of generators to homes and businesses. Despite Edison's distaste for this option, its substantial profits and consequent approval by investors discouraged him from curbing it.

3 The first central stations were oriented almost entirely to lighting, and Edison, like most others, underestimated the subsequent demand for current used to power motors. The capacity of central stations in the 1880s was rated by the number of lamps they could support.

4 In fact, until the early 20th century, it was not even inevitable that electricity would displace natural gas as the dominant lighting medium for home use. Many homes in which electricity was installed through 1900, had dual systems: using gas for daily light and the more expensive option, electricity, only when entertaining guests (Platt, 1991:80,154–155).

5 Inefficiencies continue. For example, Toledo (Ohio) Edison, until 1996, operated a generator producing 25 cycle current in an otherwise abandoned power plant in order to serve a single customer, which, consequently, did not have to rewire its motors (Sharp, 1995).

6 One NELA member—Western Electric—manufactured telephones and sold them to Bell as its main business, but also produced, installed, and repaired electric arc and incandescent equipment (Smith, 1985).

7 By 'growth dynamic' we mean something essentially similar to what Richard Hirsh (1989), in his important account of the impact of technology on the utility industry, calls the 'grow-and-build' strategy.

8 A good example of this is the NELA Public Policy Committee, 1904–8.

9 Many of these consultants were themselves Goerck St. alumni such as Frederick Sargent, (Sargent and Lundy, 1961:15–18; Toledo Edison, 1:19 9/10/1894) or members of Insull's own circle, such as William Barstow (1900–1905 *National Cyclopedia of Biography*).

10 A good indicator of viability of cogeneration is found in the success of such systems in the aftermath of the 1978 PURPA Act which required central station firms to purchase current from such producers at a rate equal to their own (low) production costs. It spurred the rise of over 3,000 independent power generators—many of them co-generators. This has accounted for over half of all new privately-owned electrical generation in the U.S. since 1986 (Hoffman, 1994:10–13). Also, most of the 1,900 public firms in the U.S.A are transmission and distribution, or distribution-only firms: 91 per cent buy part and 75 per cent buy all of their power from generating and/or transmitting firms.

11 Indeed before the advocates of the growth dynamic had won decisively, the differences could even lead to public quarrels. In 1902, Henry Doherty, then president of NELA, and a sceptic about the virtues of unlimited growth, physically tussled on the dais of the meeting with the vice-president, Insull's deputy, Louis Ferguson from Chicago Edison, about who would have the chalk and chalkboard and who would assume the (silent) Chair role at the meeting. Doherty (1924:III, 136–137) had hard feelings for years afterward, and complained about Ferguson's constant promotion of his agenda.

12 Hirsh (1989) provides an excellent account of what precipitated such a crisis for the electricity industry in the 1960s and 1970s: combination of technical stasis— the industry having reached some basic physical limitations in increased economies of scale, inflation, supply shocks for fuel, and a changing political climate that reduced tolerance for pollution while increasing consumers' resistance to rate increases.

References

Adams, A.D., (1900), 'Electric Central Stations and Isolated Plants'.*Cassier's Magazine*, 18 (May):54–57.

Mark Granovetter and Patrick McGuire

AEIC, various years. *Proceedings of the Annual Meeting of the Association of Edison Illuminating Companies*.

American Electrical Directory, (1886), *American Electrical Directory*. Ft. Wayne: Star Iron Tower Company.

American Electrical Directory, (1892), *American Electrical Directory*. Ft. Wayne: Star Iron Tower Company.

American Society of Mechanical Engineers, (1937), *George Westinghouse Commemoration*. New York: American Society of Mechanical Engineers.

Armstrong, C. and Nelles, J.V., (1986), *Monopoly's Moment: The Organization and Regulation of Canadian Utilities, 1830–1930*. Philadelphia: Temple University Press.

Arthur, W.B., (1989), Competing Technologies, Increasing Returns, and Lock-in by Historical Events', *The Economic Journal*, 99:116–131.

Bergman, M., (1982), 'Electric Utility Statistics: 1882–1982'. *Public Power*, 40:5:65–68.

Bright, A. Jr., (1972), [1949] *The Electric-Lamp Industry*. New York: Arno Press.

Bonbright, J. and Means, G., (1969), [1932] *The Holding Company*. New York: August Kelley Publishing.

Brush Electric Company, (1883), *Brush Electric Company Catalog*. Cleveland: Brush Electric Company. In Vertical File 'Power—Electric Companies—Brush Electric Company', in Henry Ford Museum Archives.

Bush, G., (1973), *The Future Builders: The Story of Michigan's Consumers Power Company*. New York: McGraw-Hill.

Campbell, J., Hollingsworth, J.R. and Lindberg, L., (191), *Governance of the American Economy*. New York: Cambridge University Press.

Chandler, A.D., (1962), *Strategy and Structure: Chapters in the History of the Industrial Enterprise*. Cambridge, MA: MIT Press.

Chandler, A., (1977), *The Visible Hand: The Managerial Revolution in American Business*. Cambridge: Harvard University Press.

Chandler, A.D., (1990), *Scale and Scope: The Dynamics of Industrial Capitalism*. Cambridge, MA: Harvard University Press.

Chung, C., (1997), 'Networks and Governance in Trade Associations: AEIC and NELA in the Development of the American Electricity Industry 1885–1910'. *International Journal of Sociology and Social Policy*, 17(7/8):57–110.

Coffin, C., (1909), Letter to Samuel Insull in Insull Papers Box 19, folder #4 5/24/09, in Loyola University Library, Insull archive, Chicago, IL.

Conot, R., (1979), *A Streak of Luck*. New York: Seaview Press.

David, P., (1986), 'Understanding the Economics of QWERTY: The Necessity of History', in W.N. Parker, *Economic History and the Modern Economist*, Oxford, U.K.: Basil Blackwell, pp. 30–45.

David, P.A. (1987), *Hero and the Herd in Technological History: Reflections on Thomas Edison and the Battle of the Systems*. Stanford, Ca.: Center for Economic Policy Research, LEFR Pub. #100.

Dobbin, F., (1994), *Forging Industrial Policy*. Princeton: Princeton University Press.

Doherty, H., (1924), *Principles and Ideas for Doherty Men: Papers, Addresses and Letters by Henry L. Doherty*. Compiled by Glenn Marston, six volumes. No publisher or city indicated.

Doyle, J. and Reinemer, V., (1979), *Lines Across the Land: Rural Electric Cooperatives*. Washington: Environmental Policy Institute.

Du Boff, R., (1984), 'Networks of Power: A Review'. *Business History Review*, 58:283–284.

Federal Trade Commission, (1935), 'Investigations of Utility Companies—Laws and Regulations'. Part 73 a of 70th Congress, 1st session, Senate Documents Volume 12.

Flynn, J.T., (1932b), 'Up and Down with Sam Insull'. *Collier's Magazine*, 12/10/32. pgs. 18–19, 35–36.

Gilchrist, J., (1927), *A Course in Departmental Organization and Function*.Chicago: Commonwealth Electric.

Gilchrist, J., (1940), *Public Utility Subjects, 1910–1926*. Chicago: Privately Published.

Gould, J.M., (1946), *Output And Productivity In The Electric And Gas Utilities*. National Bureau Of Economic Research, Boston: Harvard University Press.

Granovetter, M., (1985), 'Economic Action and Social Structure: The Problem of Embeddedness', *American Journal of Sociology*, 91:481–510.

Granovetter, M., (1990), 'The Old and New Economic Sociology: A History and an Agenda', in *Beyond the Marketplace: Rethinking Economy and Society*. Roger Friedland and A.F. Robertson (eds), New York: Aldine de Gruyter.

Greer, R.C.L., (1952), *Electric Power and History In South Eastern New Hampshire*. New York: Newcomen Society.

Hannah, L., (1979), *Electricity Before Nationalization*. London: Macmillan.

Hirsch, P., (1972), 'Processing Fads and Fashions: An Organization-Set Analysis of Cultural Industry Systems'. *American Journal of Sociology*, 77 (January): 639–659.

Hirsh, R., (1989), *Technology and Transformation in the American Electric Utility Industry*. Cambridge: Cambridge University Press.

Hoffman, M., (1994), 'How You Can Get Cheaper Power' *Consumer Research*. 10/94.

Hook, S., (1943), *The Hero In History*. Boston: Beacon Press.

Horn, C., (1973), *The Duke Power Story: 1904–1972*. New York: Newcomen Society.

Hughes, T., (1983), *Networks Of Power: Electrification In Western Society 1880–1930*. Baltimore: Johns Hopkins University Press.

Insull, S., (1915), *Central Station Electric Service*. Edited by William Kelly, Chicago: Private Printed.

Insull, S., (1934), *Memoirs of Samuel Insull*, Chicago: Privately Published.

Jones, S., (1914), 'State Versus Local Regulation'. *Annals*, 53:94–107.

Leupp, F., (1919), *George Westinghouse: His Life and Achievements*. Boston: Little, Brown.

McAfree, J.W., (1947), *St. Louis and the Union Electric Company*. New York: Newcomen Society.

McDonald, F., (1962), *Insull*. Chicago: University of Chicago Press.

McGuire, P., (1986), 'The Control of Power: the Political Economy of Electric Utility Development in the United States 1870–1930'. Unpublished Ph.D. dissertation, Department of Sociology, SUNY-Stony Brook, Stony Brook, NY.

McGuire, P., (1989), 'Instrumental Class Power and the Origin of Class-Based State Regulation in the U.S. Electric Utility Industry', *Critical Sociology*, 16:2–3:181–204.

McGuire, P., (1990), 'Money and Power: Variance in Support by Financiers and the Electrical Manufacturing Industry 1878–1896'. *Social Science Quarterly*, 71:3:510–530.

McGuire, P., Granovetter, M. and Schwartz, M., (1993), 'Thomas Edison and the Social Construction of the Early Electricity Industry in America', in *Explorations in Economic Sociology*, Richard Swedberg (ed.), New York: Russell Sage Foundation.

McMahon, A.M., (1983), *Reflections: A Centennial Essay on the Association of Edison Illuminating Companies*. New York: Association of Edison Illuminating Companies.

Marvin, C., (1988), *When Old Technologies Were New: Thinking About Electrical Communication in the Late Nineteenth Century*. New York: Oxford University Press.

Meyer, H., (1972), *Builders of Northern States Power Company*. Minneapolis: Northern States Power.

Moodys' Investors Service, (1995), *Stranded Costs Will Threaten Credit Quality of U.S. Electrics*. New York: Moodys' Investors Service. 9/95.

National Electric Light Association, (various years), *Proceedings of the National Electric Light Association*. New York: NELA.

Nye, D.E., (1990), *Electrifying America: Social Meanings of a New Technology*. Cambridge: MIT Press.

Palmer, D., (1983), 'Broken Ties: Interlocking Directorates, The Inter-Organizational Paradigm and Intercorporate Coordination'. *Administrative Science Quarterly*, 28:1:40–55.

Passer, H., (1953), *The Electrical Manufacturers, 1875–1900: A Study of Competition, Entrepreneurship, Technical Change, and Economic Growth*. Cambridge: Harvard University Press.

Passer, H., (1962), 'Frank Julian Sprague: Father of Electric Traction, 1857–1934', in William Milled (ed.), *Men In Business: Essays on the Historical Role of the Entrepreneur*. New York: Harper Torch Books. pp. 211–237.

Piore, M. and Sabel, C., (1984), *The Second Industrial Divide*. New York: Basic Books.

Platt, H., (1991), *The Electric City: Energy and the Growth of the Chicago Area 1880–1930*. Chicago: University of Chicago Press.

Porter, T.M., (1986), 'Steam Heat in the Old West End'. *Toledo Metropolitan Magazine* June 2:16–6, 22.

Riley, J., (1958), *Carolina Light and Power Company: 1908–1955*. Raleigh, NC: Carolina Light and Power.

Roy, W., (1997), *Socializing Capital: The Rise of the Large Industrial Corporation in America*. Princeton: Princeton University Press.

Rudolph, R. and Ridley, S., (1986), *The Hundred Year War Over Electricity*. New York: Harper and Row.

Sargent and Lundy, (1961), *The Sargent & Lundy Story*. Chicago: Sargent and Lundy.

Seymour, H.A., (1935), *History of Commonwealth Edison Company*. Chicago: Commonwealth Edison.

Scribner, H., (1910), *Memoirs of Lucas County and the City of Toledo*. Volume 2. Madison, WI: Western Historical Association.

Sharp, L.A., (1995), 11/13/95 Telephone Interview between Lou Ann Sharp— Spokesperson for Toledo Edison—and Patrick McGuire.

Smith, G.D., (1985), *The Anatomy of a Business Strategy: Bell, Western Electric, and the Origins of the American Telephone Industry*. Baltimore: Johns Hopkins University Press.

Sparks, D., (1995), 'Blocked Energy', *Financial World*, 7/18/95:24–27.

Stout, G., (1909), *Bulletins of Edison Electric Light Company of New York 1882–1884: A Memento of the Early Days in the Electric Service Business*. Edited by George H. Stout. Chicago Privately Published. Samuel Insull Collection, E.M. Cudahy Library, Loyola University at Chicago. Box 98.

Toledo Edison, (various years), 'Scrapbook Collection', Toledo Edison Papers. Ward Canaday Center, University of Toledo, Toledo Ohio.

U.S. Dept. of Agriculture, (1916), *Electric Power Development In U.S.* 64th Congress, 1st session, Document #316, Senate, V-V-8, 9, 10. Washington: Government Printing Office.

U.S. Bureau of Corporations, (1912), *Water Power Development in the United States*. Washington, D.C.: Government Printing Office.

U.S. Department of Commerce and Labor, (1905), *Special Census of the Electrical Industries*, 1902. Washington, D.C.: Government Printing Office.

U.S. Department of Commerce and Labor, (1910a), *Special Report on Central Electric Light and Power Stations, 1907*. Washington: Government Printing Office.

U.S. Department of Commerce, (1915), *Special Report on Central Electric Light and Power Stations and Street and Electric Railways, 1912*. Washington: Government Printing Office.

Useem, M., (1984), *The Inner Circle: Large Corporations and Business Politics in the U.S. and the U.K.* New York: Oxford University Press.

Volti, R., (1990), 'Why Internal Combustion?: Invention Technology', *Invention and Technology*, Fall. Pg. 42–47.

Westinghouse Electric and Manufacturing Company, (1898), *A Quarter Million Horse Power of Polyphase Electric Transmission Apparatus*. Pittsburgh: Westinghouse Electric and Manufacturing Company.

Westinghouse Electric and Manufacturing Company, (1907), 'Report of the Board of Directors to the Stockholders of Westinghouse Electric and Manufacturing Company'. Pittsburgh: Westinghouse Electric and Manufacturing Company.

White, H., (1981), 'Where Do Markets Come From?' *American Journal of Sociology*, 87 (November):517–547.

Williamson, O., (1975), *Markets and Hierarchies: Analyses and Anti-Trust Implications*. New York: Free Press.

Williamson, O., (1981), 'The Economics of Organization: The Transaction Cost Approach', in *American Journal of Sociology*, 87(3):548–577.

Williamson, O., (1985), *The Economic Institutions of Capitalism*. New York: Free Press.

Wright, W., (1957), *History of the Georgia Power Company, 1885–1956*. Atlanta, Ca.: Georgia Power Company.

The margins of accounting

Peter Miller

Accounting is most interesting at its margins. For it is at the margins that we see new calculative practices added to the repertoire of accounting. It is at the margins that accounting as a body of legitimated practices is formed and re-formed by the adding of devices and ideas of various kinds. It is at the margins that accounting intersects with, and comes into conflict with, other bodies of expertise. And it is at the margins that accounting comes to be linked up to the demands, expectations and ideals of diverse social and institutional agencies.

The term margins is used here to refer to that part of the terrain or surface of accounting that, at a particular point in time, is immediately within its boundaries. Categories of fixed and variable costs, principles of discounting, and practices of standard costing, were all initially located at the very boundary of accounting practice, and only gradually moved towards its centre. To attend to the margins of accounting is to attend to the ways in which these calculative practices and their related rationales have, in certain countries, initially permeated accounting at its boundaries, and gradually come to occupy a dominant position.

To attend to the margins of accounting is to emphasize that there are different margins at different points in time, and in different places (Hopwood and Miller, 1994). The margins of accounting change as the boundaries of accounting are redrawn. The margins are fluid and mobile, rather than static. What is on the margins at one point in time can become central or taken-for-granted, relatively fixed and durable, at a later date. Moreover, the margins of accounting vary from one national setting to another.[1] In all these different respects, there is a *multiplicity* of margins to be considered.

This adding of practices to accounting at its margins typically takes place through a process of problematizing (Rose and Miller,

1992). Existing practices are criticised. Claims are advanced that other practices not only remedy these defects, but go substantially beyond them, offer something more, something different, something better. Not all such criticisms result in accounting being transformed and its boundaries redrawn. But from time to time the critics and reformers win. The questioning of a particular technique, the hopes of those seeking to 'modernize' accounting practice, the aspirations of those with new promises and products to sell, result in a relatively enduring alteration in the contours and boundaries of accounting. This problematizing of existing practices is itself an accomplishment. 'Problems' have to be made recognizable, a particular perception has to form, people have to be convinced that problems are intrinsic to a particular device rather than contingent, a measure of agreement has to be reached as to the nature of the problems identified, a consensus has to form that something needs to be done, and another way of calculating that fits the problem identified has to be made available. Then, and only then, do things change.

Sometimes, this problematizing of existing practices is done by accountants themselves. Indeed, over the last decade and more, and particularly within management accounting, there has emerged an industry of self-criticism. This may turn out to be little more than an intensification of a perpetual process of critique and reform, of dream and disenchantment, a process that no doubt is not limited to accounting. None the less, it is in particularly sharp relief at present within accounting. Accountants are busy denouncing existing ways of calculating, and identifying limitations in long-established practices (Hopwood, 1985). A range of 'new' calculative practices and concepts, drawn from beyond the existing boundaries of accounting, and owing more to manufacturing and engineering traditions than to existing ways of calculating, are being celebrated. Devices that had apparently served firms successfully for many years are now seen to be inherently flawed. The boundaries of accounting are being redrawn, and new ways of calculating called for that are currently at the 'margins' of accounting.

Sometimes this problematizing of existing ways of calculating is done by outsiders. People working within a variety of other disciplines or at least drawing extensively from them, including economics, business strategy, engineering and marketing, have, at different times, argued that accounting is lacking in specific respects, that accounting needs to be supplemented or modified in particular areas, or that it needs something wholly new.

Sometimes this problematizing of existing practices is done by regulatory bodies, government agencies, and other institutionalized actors who argue that there is 'a problem', that something needs to be done, and that accounting is the way to do this. Frequently, these alleged problems have nothing immediately or self-evidently to do with accounting. But, with some guidance, people can often be helped or persuaded to recognize hitherto unidentified connections, and to appreciate that an altered way of accounting might help foster or improve such things as national efficiency, economic growth rates, international competitiveness, employee empowerment, the efficiency or value for money of public services, and much else besides. Accounting can be problematized in these ways, and in the process linked up to the big ideas, characters, and macro-actors that have populated political culture and sociological narratives for so long.

All this has not gone unnoticed. Accounting has long been seen, even by accountants, as linked to the attempts by various actors and agencies to promote themselves, to sell their wares, to argue for anything that benefits them, and to get others to follow them or think in their terms. A notion of 'interests' has been invoked as a way of seeking to explain this activity.[2] For is it not self-evident that individuals and organizations will always act and argue in ways that improve their welfare, that they will always be ready to take advantage of situations that will expand their terrain, improve their opportunities, and increase their economic returns? Indeed, is this not the essence of rational decisions and utility-maximizing behaviour?

Notwithstanding the appeal of this model for those who believe that the world is inhabited by such actors and defined by such acts, this search for parsimony has limitations. Most importantly, it can lead to a neglect of 'how' type questions. Studies of the processes by which particular accounting practices emerge in specific contexts can be seen in a less favourable light than studies that draw upon a predictive model. Researchers, we are told, are 'sceptical of anecdotal evidence' and 'prefer large samples that they can use to test their hypotheses for statistical significance' (Watts and Zimmerman, 1986, p. 11). Yet analyses of the claims and counter-claims made in relation to a particular accounting practice, the ideals and aspirations that articulate a role for it, together with analyses of the conditions of emergence of such arguments, can help us to understand and explain why it is that a particular practice comes to appear problematic, and is eventually seen to be in need of modification or replacement. For it is through this activity of problematizing that the definition of what might count as a possible 'solution' emerges. Moreover, this specification of a solution that may come to be deemed acceptable by the participants helps to structure and delimit the field of possible interests, in important part by defining the terms in which debate can take place. 'Interests' emerge, are articulated and modified through the process of problematizing a particular practice. The interests in question do not necessarily pre-exist the activity of problematizing. The problematizing of existing ways of managing is often fostered by a variety of actors and agencies, not necessarily acting in concert or with the same objectives. Relays and linkages have to be formed between a multiplicity of disparate components and ambitions, and temporarily stabilized. A level of agreement has to obtain between distinct and often unrelated actors. It is the emergence of such temporarily stabilized ensembles or assemblages at the margins of accounting that we need to attend to (Miller, 1997). For it is through such processes that accounting as a body of expertise is formed and re-formed. And it is through the accretion of such processes that accounting gradually acquires a 'centre', one that comes to be regarded widely as self-evident, and which in turn becomes the target of criticism during subsequent attempts to bring new calculative practices within the boundaries of accounting.

A concern with the margins of accounting is thus a concern with the conditions and consequences of accounting practices. It is a concern with processes and outcomes. It is a concern with emergence and stabilization. The margins of accounting are produced, rather than given. This puts to the fore the analysis of the ways in which present calculative practices have been formed historically, what conditions made them possible, what ideals and aspirations they embody, and how they seek to programme the world so as to fit these ideals. Such a focus on the multiplicity of conditions that have helped form accounting practices has the advantage that it can deprive existing techniques of their self-evidence. For if a particular calculative technology emerged only recently and under specific conditions, it is reasonable to expect that it may be modified or replaced in due course. In demonstrating that accounting is itself an ensemble of devices and ideas formed at particular times and in particular locales, rather than an immutable and universal starting point, a focus on the margins of accounting can help in the invention of new ways of organizing and administering. More generally, by examining the margins of accounting and the conditions under which these are altered, we can begin to unravel the intrinsic links between accounting and changing modes of governing the enterprise (Burchell *et al.*, 1980; Miller and Rose, 1990).

A concern with the conditions and consequences of accounting practices directs attention to the historically and culturally localized events that have helped define the territory of accounting. Before accountants could think about costs in particular ways, before they could conceptualize income in a specific sense, before they could calculate investment opportunities in certain terms, the boundaries of accounting had to be defined and redefined. It is through this process of creating and recreating boundaries that accounting is actually constituted as a body of expertise. A number of examples will serve to illustrate the point. Let us begin by considering that most basic and apparently self-evident of categories, the notion of costs.

Linking costs to decisions

Cost-volume-profit calculations, break-even graphs, the distinction between fixed and variable costs, and the notion of marginal costs are central to contemporary management accounting. It is difficult to think of these concepts and calculations as existing at the margins of accounting. It is even more difficult to think of them as practices and ideas that once fell outside the boundaries of accounting. But if we look back only as far as the early 1920s, starting at the University of Chicago, we can begin to appreciate how the cost concepts of accountancy were constituted by the extension and elaboration of economic reasoning.

Students at the School of Commerce at the University of Chicago, along with students in the department of Political Economy, were shown what J.M. Clark described as 'an experiment in a type of economic theory which is largely inductive' (Clark, 1923, p. ix). Unused capacity, or costs which do not vary with output, were the central features of Clark's concerns. Indeed, he went so far as to speculate whether 'the whole body of economic thought must become an "economics of overhead costs" ' (Clark, 1923, p. ix). But economic theory was not only for graduate students in economic theory. Such students should study the accountant's conception of costs. Equally, 'the accountant should know the meaning of cost from the standpoint of disinterested economic science', for it was this concept of cost that 'embodies, in a sense, that impossible goal to which his practical devices serve as approximations' (Clark, 1923, p. x).

Clark was not an accountant but thought that 'the unconventional standpoint of an outsider' might help 'throw a useful light upon the question of what cost accounting can and cannot be expected to do' (Clark, 1923, p. 234). Clark argued that costs should be analysed separately from the formal books of account, rather than being constrained by the rules that govern financial accounting. One might include certain items in cost accounting that would be excluded for purposes of making up the income statement.

According to Clark, it was the railways that brought clearly into view the question of the behaviour of costs and the importance of the notion of overhead costs in particular. For it was soon realized that additional traffic could be carried on the railways at little or no additional cost. Price discrimination could be justified on the grounds that added traffic was not responsible for those costs which did not increase as traffic increased. In any case, it was held impossible to determine the proper share of costs traceable to an individual shipment or unit of business (Clark, 1923, p. 10). While it was initially argued that railways were different from other industries because the large part of their costs were 'constant', or independent of the volume of traffic, it was not long before this argument came to be applied to other industries. The distinction between 'constant' and 'variable' costs was soon to become a general principle for the classification of costs.

Clark was concerned with the 'underlying functions' (Clark, 1923, p. 234) of cost accounting. He argued that these were multiple, and that they required 'an elastic technique' which he described as 'cost analysis' or 'cost statistics'. The functions of cost accounting, according to Clark, were: to help determine a normal or satisfactory price for goods sold; to help fix a minimum limit on price-cutting; to determine which goods are most profitable and which are unprofitable; to control inventory; to set a value on inventory; to test the efficiency of different processes; to test the efficiency of different departments; to detect losses, waste and pilfering; to separate the 'cost of idleness' from the cost of producing goods; and to 'tie in' with the financial accounts (Clark, 1923, p. 236). These different functions of cost accounting called for different concepts of costs. These included: the 'total economic sacrifice of production', including interest on all investment; differential costs; complete records of actual costs and also standards of efficient performance against which to compare them; residual costs; and total operating expenses. Summarizing his views on the purposes of cost analysis, Clark argued that 'the purposes of cost analysis require a number of different conceptions and measures of cost' (Clark, 1923, p. 257). The contemporary idea of different costs for different purposes can be regarded as the end point of such a proposal.

On the other side of the Atlantic, a little over a decade later, others argued in similar terms. Again, concepts drawn from economics were appealed to as a way of seeking to alter the accountants' perception of cost behaviour. Here, the key figures were Ronald Edwards and Ronald Coase.

Edwards, a 'Lecturer in Business Administration with special reference to Accounting' at the London School of Economics, had some ten years' experience as a professional accountant. But this did not prevent him from making strong appeals to the language and concepts of economics to formulate what he called the 'businessman's entrepreneurial problem'. The most important issue about costs, Edwards argued, was 'the extent to which they change with output' (Edwards, 1981, p. 75). It was the avoidability or unavoidability of costs that should be the principal concern. He argued that the additional expense to be incurred by producing the unit to be costed should be called the 'variable cost', and the other expenses the 'fixed cost'. Cost accounting, that is to say, should be based on 'differential' or 'marginal' costs, for it is those costs which vary with output (Edwards, 1981, p. 81). Whereas cost accounting typically analysed past costs, it should henceforth direct its attention to future variable costs. Cost accountants should ignore expenses which are unchangeable and not spend their time calculating arbitrary allocations to departmental expenses which fail to address marginal variations in cost and revenue. Cost accounting should address the entrepreneurial problem, which meant a focus on marginal revenue and marginal cost, supplemented by attention to the avoidance of waste.[3]

A further decisive step was to link cost accounting explicitly to the concept of decisions. This was in large part the achievement of Ronald Coase. For while both Clark and Edwards had sought to alter cost accounting by appealing to the concept of marginal cost, neither had explicitly linked these concepts to the notion of decision. As Coase remarked, in setting out what he regarded as the basic concepts of cost accounting:

The first point that needs to be made and strongly emphasized is that attention must be concentrated on the variations which will result if a particular *decision* is taken, and the variations that are relevant to *business decisions* are those in cost and/or receipts. This reasoning applies to every business *decision*, whether it is concerned with the opening or closing of a department, the manufacture of a new product, the introduction of more frequent style changes or an alteration in the volume of production. Whatever the character of the *decision*, one has to inquire into the variations in costs and receipts which will follow. Costs and receipts which will remain unchanged whatever *decision* is taken can be ignored. (Coase, 1981, p. 98; emphases added.)

The repetition of the term decision is an indication of its perceived novelty. Even Coase was aware that he may have over-used the term, commenting that 'it may seem to certain readers that I am flogging a dead horse' (*ibid.*, p. 98). Business decisions, Coase went on to argue, should depend on 'estimates of the future' (*ibid.*, p. 100). But he parted company with Edwards in stating that there was no need to distinguish rigidly between 'fixed' and 'variable' costs. This followed from Coase's insistence on the centrality to be accorded to the notion of decision. For the question of whether a particular category of cost is likely to vary 'depends solely on the decision which is being taken' (*ibid.*, p. 128). By concentrating on the cost variations that result from different decisions, one avoided the necessity of making further distinctions. While costs might vary with some changes in output, they would not necessarily vary with all changes in output.

In putting forward these proposals, Coase had none of the apologetic tone that Clark and Edwards had used in their respective writings. Clark, for instance, suggested that 'business men' might omit chapter 23 of his book, which dealt with the theory of marginal productivity. He hoped, however, that 'they will find the bulk of the argument worthy of their attention' (Clark, 1923, p. xi). Edwards commented that, whilst his arguments might appear 'to be more academic than businesslike', he hoped they would 'not be condemned on those grounds *alone* . . .' (Edwards, 1981, p. 73). In contrast Coase, reflecting many years later on the views he had expressed in the late 1930s, remarked that he thought of them 'simply as an exposition of views which were generally accepted by economists' (Coase, 1981, p. 97).[4] Coase reiterated many of the same themes as those of Clark and Edwards. That is to say, he set out the 'general rule' that a firm should expand production so long as marginal revenue is expected to be greater than marginal cost, and the avoidable costs of the total output less than the total receipts. Even if it was 'utopian' to think that such a position might be reached in practice, he hoped that 'the cost accountant may so refine his technique to take account of variations in costs and thus facilitate the task of the businessman' (Coase, 1981, p. 102).

In addition, Coase argued that the notion of opportunity cost should be the central category of cost accounting. This particular concept of costs, he argued, was the only one that focused attention 'on the alternative courses of action which are open to the business-man' (Coase, 1981, p. 108). Edwards had argued for attention to 'future variable costs', and Coase reiterated this, stating that 'It is useless to look back at the past, except as an object lesson'. But Coase went one step further, in proposing the notion of opportunity costs as a way of encapsulating in a single concept the 'forward-looking' character of 'business decisions'.

It was to be some years before these concepts appeared routinely in the pedagogy of accounting. Moreover, the concept of opportunity cost remains even today at the margins of accounting practice. Yet the proposals of Clark, Edwards, and Coase in the 1920s and 1930s to modernize cost accounting by means of concepts drawn from economics had far-reaching effects. The boundaries of accounting were redrawn. Cost accounting was provided with some of its most basic devices, such as the cost-volume-profit graph and break-even analysis. Also, and equally importantly, cost accounting was provided with a route through which it might move up the corporate hierarchy.[5] By linking costs to the idea of choices, by calling these choices decisions, and by establishing linkages between these concepts and the notion of executive decision-making,[6] cost accounting was given a significance in terms of managerial actions which it hitherto lacked. A new terminology brought with it new ways of calculating and new ways of thinking. This event at the margins of accounting laid the groundwork for the post-World War II transformation of 'cost accounting' into 'management accounting'.

Making the future calculable

The permeability of accounting to the concepts and calculations of economics has contributed to the making of management accounting in a further respect. The evaluation of major capital investments is perhaps one of the most self-evidently 'managerial' aspects of accounting, and has been the focus of considerable and often heated debate over the last half century. Three separate points in time during this period will serve to illustrate the ways in which this aspect of accounting has been modified at the margins: the year 1938; the year 1965; and the decade of the 1980s.[7]

In 1938, in a long series of articles in the pages of *The Accountant*, Ronald Edwards argued that it was essential to use discounting techniques when considering alternative investments.[8] Only in this way could all financial values be translated into present values. The influence of time should, he argued, be eliminated so as to make comparisons possible. A series of seminal articles by Ronald Coase entitled 'Business Organization and the Accountant' in the same journal reinforced the point, and articulated the idea that the time value of money, and principles of discounting, were essential when seeking to express costs and revenues in money terms.

In response, Stanley Rowland, a colleague of Edwards at the London School of Economics, referred to discounting techniques as 'dangerous nonsense' and 'sheer insanity'.[9] Rowland drew up battle lines between economists and accountants. The arguments of Edwards, he argued, had 'the unanimity which is so characteristic of economists'. Edwards, he stated, was 'enjoying for its own sake the sport of bludgeoning the heads of accountants with intent that they shall be both bloody and bowed'.[10] According to Rowland, the domain of the accountant was that of the ledger, 'a world in which cool sanity reigns (. . .) the bed rock on which his whole scheme rests'.[11] The accountant should be content to 'record the present as it flows into the past' and should leave to others 'the risky business of tearing aside the veil which conceals the future'.[12]

By 1965, things had changed fundamentally. The calculus of discounting had become part of accounting. A new mentality reigned. An editorial in *The Accountant* in 1965 provides a convenient marker. This stated confidently that 'No one would deny the utility of the DCF technique relative to other less precise methods'.[13] Much had happened since the fierce debate in the pages of *The Accountant* in 1938. In 1954, Joel Dean had published his massively influential article in the *Harvard Business Review* (Dean, 1954). This appealed to discounting techniques as 'demonstrably superior to existing alternatives in accuracy, realism, relevance, and sensitivity (Dean, 1954, p. 129). Dean argued that management relied to a worrying degree on 'intuition and authority', and that it lacked the 'skilled analysis and the scientific control' needed for intricate, vital capital investment decisions (Dean, 1954, p. 129). An avalanche of words had reinforced this appeal to discounting techniques, and to economic reason as the basis for managerial decisions.[14] 'Science' and 'objectivity' had become the battle cry for accountants and managers.

Discounting techniques and the concept of the time value of money were disseminated throughout the 1950s and 1960s in a number of different locales. They provided a knowledge base for the new business schools in the UK, offering both a calculus and a conceptual foundation that could be taught to managers. Diverse actors, working within the academy, within firms, and often crossing the boundaries between these distinct terrains, extolled the merits of the discounted cash flow technique for making investment decisions. Professional bodies organized talks for those eager to learn this new calculus. Government agencies such as the National Economic Development Council promoted the technique, for the individual investment decisions of managers were seen to be linked to macro-level economic growth. Even a television series in the UK showed DCF techniques in action.

In these different settings, and with a different tempo in the US and the UK, management accounting was to be transformed at the margins in the two decades following World War II. Particularly in the field of investment appraisal, an economic-financial mentality began to replace the existing accounting mentality. Economic expertise was to supplant intuition and rule of thumb criteria, as the concept of the time value of money was incorporated in investment decisions. Personal judgement would henceforth be based, or so it was hoped, on the claimed neutrality and objectivity of a 'scientific' evaluation of investment opportunities.

But things were to change yet again. Across the 1980s, and into the 1990s, a number of commentators inside and outside accounting have criticised the use of discounting techniques for evaluating investment opportunities. They have argued that the use of discounting techniques to evaluate investment opportunities 'is seriously shortchanging the futures of corporations' (Hayes and Garvin, 1982, p. 72). The 'old financial models' based on the time value of money have been held to give 'little consideration to the strategic opportunities and threats presented by technological advance' (Avishai, 1989, p. 112). More generally, the 'entire capital investment system', including shareholders, lenders, investment managers, corporate directors, managers, and employees has been held to have failed. The effect of this alleged failure, according to one influential commentator, is that the most efficient capital markets in the world, coupled with highly sophisticated investors, produces suboptimal investment behaviour (Porter, 1992, p. 68).

It is too early to predict the outcome of these contemporary criticisms of discounting methods for evaluating investment opportunities. One influential textbook advocates greater caution in the use of discounting methods, yet refrains from advocating their abandonment (Kaplan and Atkinson, 1989). Meanwhile, the number of voices criticising the financial mentality that underlays discounting techniques continues to increase.[15] But it is less a question here of seeking to predict the direction such debates will take in the coming years, than of registering the extent to which they have already problematized the dominant role of financial models for the evaluation of investment opportunities.[16] This demonstrates that the modification of accounting at the margins is not a linear process. It is a process that can be stalled, redirected, and even reversed. In the next section, this redrawing of the boundaries of accounting is explored further, this time in relation to engineering and other non-financial expertises.

Governing the factory

The factory has provided one of the principal sites for the emergence and elaboration of cost and management accounting. The factory has also been a key locale in which accounting has been problematized and transformed at its margins, and in relation to other bodies of expertise. Two instances will serve to illustrate: the development of standard costing in the early decades of the 20th century; and the articulation of a 'politics of the product' in the 1980s.

Between 1900 and 1930, cost accounting was transformed, and its domain massively expanded, by the invention of standard costing and budgeting (Miller and O'Leary, 1994). Henceforth, cost accounting would be concerned with the future as well as the past. Cost accounting would no longer be limited to ascertaining only the actual costs of production or activities. Questions of waste and efficiency could be routinely addressed within the enterprise, whether at the level of the profit of the total firm, the level of material or labour use in production, or at the level of every accountable person within the firm. In the first instance, though, it was the government of economic life within the factory that was of principal concern.

Standard costing made possible a new form of government of the factory. It supplemented the traditional concerns of accounting with the fidelity or honesty of the person. No longer would cost accounting limit itself to the calculation of actual costs. Cost accounting would now embrace individuals, and make them accountable by reference to prescribed standards of performance. Cost accounting would be based on predetermined costs, and would seek to quantify the variance of actual form standard. By this means, cost accounting would seek to bring to the attention of management 'preventable inefficiencies' (Harrison, 1930, p. 8) so that these might be eliminated. The individual would be set standards of performance, and variations from these standards would make visible the existence of inefficiencies. Thus might efficiency be made an individual as well as a collective phenomena.

As a way of seeking to foster the calculated government of life within the factory, standard costing was allied to that vast project of standardization and normalization that has been called scientific management. Standard costing and budgeting emerged in a reciprocal relationship with scientific management. Indeed, F.W. Taylor's paper on Shop Management contains many of the elements of standard costing. And the work of Harrington Emerson explicitly envisaged something akin to a standard costing (Emerson, 1919). Scientific management sought to make visible the wastes that it saw as arising from the actions of individuals. A 'scientific' knowledge of the exact extent of such wastes would be the first step. The second would be the systematic elimination of such wastes. Those such as the Gilbreths would join with Taylor in seeking to dissect and analyse the minute components of which diverse productive activities were composed. The actions of the worker, each and every movement of the worker's body, would be studied so as to optimize the efficiency of each individual action. No matter how minute or apparently trivial the activity, scientific management promised a government of the factory that would be based on the objectivity of expertise.

These new proposals for governing the factory did not emerge in a vacuum. They were linked to a variety of practices beyond the factory and beyond the enterprise that took the promotion of efficiency as the objective of government. Indeed, the notion of efficiency helped establish a reciprocal relationship between the factory and the nation as distinct sites for the promotion of individual and collective efficiency. Efficiency was to be problematized and made quantifiable in a multiplicity of arenas, and by means of a plethora of devices, including statistics, industrial psychology, intelligence testing, and much else besides. The notion of efficiency provided a 'convenient label' under which could be grouped a range of activities, assumptions and interventions by diverse actors and agencies.

A discourse of 'national efficiency' articulated a concern with efficiency at a macro-level. But if such concerns were articulated at the level of the nation as a whole, it was held to be in 'private' locales, such as the factory, the school, and the home that the efficiency of the individual could be acted upon and optimised. Such locales were thus to become key sites within which the quest for health, profit and efficiency would be addressed. Experts of varying kinds, including cost accountants, industrial psychologists and others, were to act upon individuals in such locales. Attempts to improve the efficiency of individuals in such settings would, or so it was hoped, foster national efficiency. For if the purpose of government was to promote the 'good life' of its citizens, it would be able to do so successfully only by acting upon the individual in those most 'private' of domains.

The transformation of cost accounting brought about by the invention of standard costing and budgeting was profound, and was part of a wider ensemble of practices that sought to individualize and normalize efficiency, and to make it calculable. The search for efficiency within the factory was reinforced by a wider quest for efficiency, one that took place in diverse locales. Within the factory, ideas and devices that had hitherto been the province of engineers rather than accountants were initially borrowed, and then made the cornerstone of a transformed cost accounting. Cost accounting gave monetary form and visibility to the ambitions and concerns of other bodies of expertise within the factory. Those such as Towne had sought to construe the engineer as an economist. And those such as Emerson had envisaged engineers and accountants collaborating in the task of detecting and analysing inefficiencies. But it was only when these concerns were articulated in the language and devices of cost accounting, when they were made visible and calculable in monetary terms, that they could become central to the government of economic life within the factory.

The redefinition of the boundaries of accounting is an ongoing process, rather than a fixed accomplishment. Cost accounting and management accounting continue to remain permeable to the concerns of those bodies of expertise such as engineering that seek to manage production processes by recourse to non-financial means. This permeability of accounting to other bodies of expertise that

Peter Miller

appear to be closer to the product and production processes has been a particularly notable feature of the past decade.

Across the 1980s, management accounting has been problematized increasingly within an ensemble of arguments and practices that has been termed elsewhere the 'politics of the product' (Miller and O'Leary, 19930. A 'rediscovery of the factory' within American political and economic debates has entailed an indictment of the nation's factories for producing products of low quality. American manufacturing industry has been criticised for inefficiency, for the relatively low educational and skill levels of its workforce, and for seeking short-term profits at the expense of long-term goals. Just as the objects and objectives of cost accounting were redefined in the early years of this century through standard costing, so too is management accounting currently being modified at the margins in relation to an intensified concern with the product.

This 'rediscovery of the factory' has had major implications for management accounting. Whilst management accounting once held out the promise of making enterprises governable at a distance, and according to the financial facts, it is precisely this distant nature of such expertise that is now held to be the problem. The ideal of managing the factory and the enterprise at a distance, through the financial numbers alone, is increasingly questioned. For the preoccupation with short-term cost reduction rather than long-term competitiveness, and with financial restructuring to bolster profits rather than technological innovation, is held to have arisen out of the financial mentality that dominates the management of American manufacturing industry. Accounting has come to be regarded as part of the problem, rather than the solution.

It is difficult to assess the extent to which this questioning of management accounting will transform the government of the factory in western economies. And it is also difficult to estimate the extent to which management accounting will be modified in the process, or will lose out to other bodies of expertise that promise to bring the government of the factory into closer proximity with 'the product'. It is certainly the case that increasing appeal is being made within management accounting to a wide range of non-financial measures, including set-up times, inventory levels, defect and re-work rates, material and product velocity within the factory, and much else besides. Issues of strategy are coming to be seen as part of the legitimate ambit of management accounting. And other ideals and aspirations, such as those of transforming modes of 'economic citizenship', of enabling worker 'empowerment', and of installing 'customer-driven manufacturing' are permeating the domain of management accounting. Even if one recognizes the discrepancy between such ideals and factory life, their transformative potential is considerable.

However, there are also developments which go in the other direction, inwards towards accounting's ideal of producing a factual and financial calculus of economic relations, rather than outwards towards adjacent bodies of expertise. The current enthusiasm for activity-based-costing can be regarded as one such attempt to restore the legitimacy of one key area of cost accounting, without fundamentally transforming its calculative practices or its ideals. The hope seems to be that management accounting might be reinvigorated in this way, by a revival of that elusive dream of getting ever closer to 'true' product costs.

But an attempted recuperation of management accounting's existing apparatus is not necessarily at odds with an extension of its territory. Nor do these developments conflict with the argument here for examining the margins of accounting. For whatever the precise outcome of this current period of intense questioning of management accounting, there seems little doubt that its boundaries are being redefined, its ideals modified, and its calculative technologies supplemented. Management consultants, textbook writers, academics, and commentators of various kinds are appealing increasingly for a more direct and immediate way of grasping and making visible the product and production processes. Once again, management accounting is being modified at the margins.

Conclusions

By looking at the margins of accounting, we can understand how this influential body of expertise is formed and transformed. A number of aspects of this process can be noted. Firstly, the alteration of accounting at the margins takes place in *multiple sites and has multiple sources*. From even the brief discussion provided above, it is clear that accounting innovation is not the preserve of any single group. 'Practitioners' are not the sole or even principal source of innovation. Nor is any other single group the source or origin of a particular accounting practice. Instead, the transformation of accounting as a body of expertise takes place within and through an historically specific ensemble of relations formed between a complex of actors and agencies, arguments and ideals, calculative devices

Peter Miller

and mechanisms. It is such ensembles or assemblages that need to be addressed.

Secondly, a concern with the margins of accounting makes apparent the extent to which accounting is *permeable to other bodies of expertise*. Accounting has been made and re-made by borrowing calculative technologies and rationales from a disparate range of knowledges and associated ideals. Accounting, one might say, has a low epistemological threshold. Even though there are often fierce arguments and disputes when a new way of calculating is introduced, and appeals are made to various matters of principle, the malleability of accounting is quite remarkable. The criteria for what can count as accounting are historically contingent and only temporarily stabilised. Accounting is riven with tensions as to its identity and its boundaries. Proposals for new ways of calculating merely serve to heighten these tensions, and to make them manifest.

Thirdly, and perhaps most fundamentally, the implication of the above is that accounting is *little more than an* ad hoc *accretion of previous margins*. If accounting is made and re-made at its margins, and out of components borrowed from other social practices, then there is no essence or core to accounting. Accounting is instead a form of *bricolage*, an activity whose tools are largely improvised and adapted to the tasks and materials at hand. There are no general principles by which one might be able to arbitrate as to what should be inside and what outside accounting. For what is outside accounting today can be a central and taken-for-granted part of accounting within as little as a decade. There is a lesson here for all those 'postmodernists' who have discovered 'fragmentation', and are busy finding it everywhere, including within accounting. Fragmentation is intrinsic to accounting, to managerial expertise more generally, and no doubt to other socially legitimated bodies of expertise.

Finally, a word of caution may be in order. The above arguments might appear to some to amount to saying that accounting does not really exist, or that the connections between its various practices are so tenuous and insubstantial as to question its rationale and existence. This is certainly not what is intended by my arguments here. The aim instead has been to draw attention to the ways in which the calculative practices and rationales of accounting have been assembled in an *ad hoc* fashion in relation to historically and geographically localized concerns and issues. In this, accounting may have much in common with other bodies of expertise, ranging from the most strongly legitimated ones such as law and medicine, to the more weakly established forms of know-how such as business strategy, psychotherapy and marketing. The aim has also been to offer an historical snapshot of some key aspects of accounting. To the extent that accounting has come to be almost synonymous with management in certain countries since World War II, this historical snapshot hopefully tells us something about the ways in which enterprises have come to be governed over that same period.

Notes

1 The examples provided below are taken from Anglo–American contexts, and thus provide a particular view of the margins of accounting. A study of different national contexts would provide a different set of margins, and a different picture of the changing boundaries of managerial expertise. I take as self-evident that the 'margins' discussed here are not universal.

2 The clearest and most developed example of this is the utility maximizing approach to the choice of accounting methods advocated in Watts & Zimmerman (1986).

3 Interestingly, Edwards stated that contemporary textbooks 'give too much space' to the concern with ways of increasing efficiency (Edwards, 1981, p. 87). He was clearly sceptical of standard costing systems, not least because some of them were 'exceedingly complicated' (*ibid.*, p. 88).

4 Indeed, they required such little effort that each article was typed late on a Wednesday night, and delivered to the office of the *Accountant* by his wife whilst he slept. They appeared in print the following Saturday (Coase, 1981, p. 97).

5 On the development of cost accounting in the UK in the early decades of the 20th century, see Loft (1994).

6 See in particular Barnard (1938) for a clear statement of these links. On these developments more generally, see Miller and O'Leary (1989). On the links between administrative theory and the 'subjective' theory of cost, see Thirlby (1952).

7 My discussion here is deliberately brief, as I have discussed the first two of these moments extensively in Miller (1991).

8 Discounting is a calculation for translating future cash flows (such as those arising from an investment) into present values. It is based on the notion of the time value of money, the idea that £1 today is worth more than £1 in one year's time because the use of money has a cost (called the cost of capital, or interest rate).

9 *The Accountant*, 1938, pp. 609–610.

10 *The Accountant*, 15 October 1938, p. 519.

11 *The Accountant*, 15 October 1938, p. 522.

12 *The Accountant*, 15 October 1938, p. 522.

13 *The Accountant*, 6 February 1965, pp. 145–146. DCF is the commonly used abbreviation for Discounted Cost Figure. On this concept see fn. 8.

14 See Miller (1991) pp. 743 ff. for a more detailed discussion of this literature.

15 For a more extended discussion of these issues, see Miller and O'Leary (1993).

16 See Miller and O'Leary (1997) on the development by a major US corporation (Caterpillar Inc) of a broader framework for evaluating investments in modern manufacture.

Peter Miller

References

Avishai, A., (1989), 'A CEO's Common Sense of CIM: An Interview with J. Tracy O'Rourke', *Harvard Business Review* (January–February).

Barnard, C.I., (1938), *The Functions of the Executive*, Cambridge, Mass.: Harvard University Press.

Burchell, S., Clubb, C., Hopwood, A. and Hughes, ? (1980), 'The Roles of Accounting in Organizations and Society', *Accounting, Organizations and Society*, Vol. 5, No. 1, pp. 5–27.

Clark, J.M., (1923), *Studies in the Economics of Overhead Costs*, Chicago: University of Chicago Press.

Coarse, R.H., (1981 [1938]), 'Business Organization and the Accountant', in J.M. Buchanan and G.F. Thirlby (eds), *LSE Essays on Cost*, New York: New York University Press. Originally published in the *Accountant*, 1938.

Dean, J., (1954), 'Measuring the Productivity of Capital', *Harvard Business Review*, pp. 120–130.

Edwards, R.S., (1981), 'The Rationale of Cost Accounting', in J.M. Buchanan and G.F. Thirlby (eds), *LSE Essays on Cost*, New York: New York University Press.

Harrison, G.C., (1930), *Standard Costing*, New York: Ronald Press.

Hayes, R.H. and Garvin, D.A., (1982), 'Managing as if Tomorrow Mattered', *Harvard Business Review*, May–June 1982.

Hopwood, A., (1985), 'The Growth of "Worrying" about Management Accounting', in pp. 227–235 in K.B. Clark, R.H. Hayes and C. Lorenz, (eds), *The Uneasy Alliance: Managing the Productivity-Technology Dilemma*, Cambridge, Mass.: Harvard Business School Press.

Hopwood, A.G. and Miller, P. (eds), (1994), *Accounting as Social and Institutional Practice*, Cambridge: Cambridge University Press.

Kaplan, R.S. and Atkinson, A.A., (1989), *Advanced Management Accounting*, 2nd edition, Englewood Cliffs, NJ: Prentice-Hall, Inc.

Loft, A., (1994), 'Accountancy and the First World War', pp. 116–137 in A.G. Hopwood and P. Miller (eds), *Accounting as Social and Institutional Practice*, Cambridge: Cambridge University Press.

Miller, P., (1991), 'Accounting Innovation Beyond the Enterprise: problematizing investment decisions and programming economic growth in the UK in the 1960s', *Accounting, Organizations and Society*, Vol. 16, No. 8, pp. 733–762.

Miller, P., (1997), 'The multiplying Machine', *Accounting, Organizations and Society*, Vol. 22, No. 3/4, pp. 355–364.

Miller, P. and O'Leary, T., (1989), 'Hierarchies and American Ideals, 1900–1940', *Academy of Management Review*, Vol. 14, No. 2, pp. 250–265.

Miller, P., and O'Leary, T., (1993), 'Accounting Expertise and the Politics of the Product: Economic Citizenship and Modes of Corporate Governance', *Accounting, Organizations and Society*, Vol. 18, Nos. 2/3, pp. 187–206.

Miller, P. and O'Leary, T., (1994), 'Governing the Calculable Person', in A.G. Hopwood and P. Miller (eds), *Accounting as Social and Institutional Practice*, Cambridge: Cambridge University Press.

Miller, P. and O'Leary, T., (1997), 'Capital Budgeting Practices and Complementarity Relations in the Transition to Modern Manufacture: A Field-Based Analysis', *Journal of Accounting Research*, Vol. 35, No. 2, pp. 257–271.

Miller, P. and Rose, N., (1993 [1990]), 'Governing Economic Life', *Economy and*

Society, Vol. 19, pp. 1–31, reprinted pp. 75–105 in M. Gane and T. Johnson, *Foucault's New Domains*, London: Routledge.

Porter, M.E., (1992), 'Capital Disadvantage: America's Failing Capital Investment System', *Harvard Business Review*, (September–October 1992).

Rose, N. and Miller, P., (1992), 'Political power beyond the State: problematics of government', *British Journal of Sociology*, Vol. 43, No. 2, pp. 173–205.

Thirlby, G.F., (1952), 'The Economist's Description of Business Behaviour', *Economica*, 19, pp. 148–167.

Watts, R.L. and Zimmerman, J.L., (1986), *Positive Accounting Theory*, Englewood Cliffs, NJ: Prentice-Hall.

Another discipline for the market economy: marketing as a performative knowledge and know-how for capitalism

Franck Cochoy

Thanks to various circumstances . . . one discovered how to disconnect experiences from the businesses in which they had been acquired, to gather, keep and transmit them as an objective form of capital. It is this formidable mass of experience that entails, when used, the forwarding of economic rationalism to the highest degree of perfection. (Sombart, 1966)

How does the market economy work? On the one hand, orthodox economists have long argued that market equilibrium depends on the automatic adjustment of supply and demand; on the other hand, heterodox economists (Williamson, 1985; Arthur, 1989), but also historians (Chandler, 1977; Tedlow, 1990) and sociologists (Prus, 1989) have tried to show that supply and demand are socially constructed (Granovetter and Swedberg, 1992), that managerial practice shapes the contours of the market.

Our objective in revisiting this debate is not so much to radicalize the classical opposition between the two camps but, paradoxically, to outline their common ground. Firstly, the arguments of both groups are always rooted in an examination of supply and demand and of their 'natural' or contingent aspect; secondly, their propositions always entail a separation of science (economics) from practice (management) in order to investigate the complex correspondences between the one and the other.

Discussing the foundations of this endless dispute seems to be a good way to resolve it. In order to understand the market economy, one can look somewhere else, and ask other questions: does the functioning of markets rely on *instances* other than supply and demand? does the functioning of markets rest on *processes* other than those of science (economics) and/or practice (management)? In asking those questions, one discovers that, between economics and managerial practices, there lies the relatively unknown set of management sciences. These 'sciences of practices' or 'practices equipped by science' work to perform the whole economic game (both theoretical and empirical).

Let us go a bit further. Among management sciences, among the third parties animating the market, marketers surely deserve a particular attention. We intend to show how marketing experts have long played a mediating role, and have occupied a central position in the history of modern capitalism. Half-way between producers and consumers, half-way between economics and managerial practices, marketing specialists have gradually re-invented the fundamental market actors and processes; they have succeeded in disciplining (mastering/codifying) the market economy.

How have marketers performed the market economy? Our argument is that the progressive 'performation'[1] of the economy by marketing followed a fourfold process. Firstly, marketing pioneers tried to train themselves in the empirical study of markets and to educate similar specialists (performation through peer-formation). Marketers reached that first objective by inventing special human and conceptual frames for market knowledge and practice (performation through pre-formating). From that point onward, the adepts of the discipline of markets played the game of managers and management, of economists and the economy (performation as performance: acting and playing). Eventually, they reshaped their own activity, but also the market and the economy altogether (performation through reformation).

Performation through peer-formation: marketing as learning and teaching

Of course, the *discipline* of marketing (the control of markets) began well before the *discipline* of marketing (the science of markets). From that point of view, speaking of marketing as a contributor to the construction of markets is not particularly innovative. Numerous studies have long documented the fact that the marketing know-how of managers played a decisive role in the rise of contemporary capitalism: since the middle of the 19th century, the progressive internalization of markets in big companies (Cochran, 1972; Chandler, 1977), the recurrent practice of market segmentation (Tedlow, 1990), or even the social construction of demand (McKendrick *et al.*, 1982; Mukerji, 1983; Campbell, 1987; Strasser,

1989; Ohmann, 1996) have confirmed the victory of the 'visible hand' of managers over the invisible hand of the market. As long as marketing is no more than an ordinary weapon of business forces, its study does no more than reinforce the idea of a social construction of markets. As long as marketing is viewed as the simple extension-cord of supply power over demand, one can conclude that the theoretical economy is an obvious by-product of classical economic interactions: ie, interactions between the producer and the consumer.

However, the history of marketing is also that of a progressive separation of marketing knowledge from market practices. The objective of this paper is to show that the birth of marketing as a distinct body of knowledge located half way between supply and demand, but also between science and practice, changes everything: the emergence of marketing as an alternative discipline (rule/reference) of the market economy favours the circulation of knowledge, the improvement of new men and concepts, thus the implementation of new ideas and practices. In turn, these transformations are able to renew not only the social identity of marketing actors but also to modify the general orientation of economic activities.

From economics to marketing: marketing as learning

In order to understand how the emergence of marketing as a management discipline contributed to the functioning of markets, it is useful to observe that, from its very beginnings, the academic study of marketing found its origins in the science of economics itself. The founding fathers of modern marketing theory were economists of the American Middle West who were disciples of the German historical school of economics. They were economists, because at that time economics was the only discipline dealing with market phenomena (Bartels, 1976). But as disciples of the German historical school of economics, their dual education contrasted sharply with the classical orientations of their peers educated in the United States: the German historical school insisted that the approach to economic matters should be simultaneously historical, statistical, and practical; in short oriented toward the empirical study of real markets (Jones and Monieson, 1990). Eventually, they were Mid-West economists who, as members of Land Grant Universities, were exposed on a daily basis in the complex difficulties of agricultural exchanges, which led them to study the functioning of real marketing channels, and more precisely the shipment of perishable commodities from rural areas to urban places (Converse P.D., 1959).

Distanced from classical economics and remote from the business world, the economists who founded marketing were forced to invent everything. This extreme marginality paradoxically was also their source of strength. In order to build a new knowledge, these men undertook to follow physically the movement of commodities along marketing channels; they decided to make an inventory of marketing institutions, procedures and practices. From that point of view, the testimony of L.D.H. Weld, who authored the very first marketing textbook, is particularly enlightening:

> When I began to teach marketing in the fall of 1913 there was practically no literature on the subject. I had to get out and dig up my own information. I studied at first-hand the movement of grain through and the use of future trading in the Minneapolis Chamber of Commerce. . . . I personally followed shipments of butter and eggs and other commodities from the country shipper in Minnesota through the wholesalers, jobbers, and retailers to New York, Chicago, and other cities. I analyzed each item of expense involved in this passage through the channels of trade. I studied the methods of determining price quotations, the operations of butter and egg exchanges, and the auction markets in Eastern cities. I also studied at the first hand the operations of the co-operative shipping associations of Minnesota and issued bulletins on this subject. (Weld, 1941)

As a man from 'nowhere', knowing nothing, the future marketing teacher goes through the domains of others and picks up their knowledge. In visiting other areas, he builds a transversal knowledge. Before him, knowledge existed, but concealed in every link in the chain After him, the knowledge is revealed, integrated, redistributed. The whole picture is eventually ready to be displayed:

> By the end of two years of this work I had written my book, 'The Marketing of Farm Products'. (Weld, 1941)

The academic doesn't know anything, but when he learns something, he tries to teach it. And from that point onward, this outsider, this intruder in the historical competition between private actors, proposes a transversal dissemination of his stolen/new knowledge; he anticipates a possible performance of the economy by his new management science.

Franck Cochoy

From marketing practices to marketing classes: marketing as teaching

But in order to fully perform the market economy, the marketer had still to become the trainer of merchants. In the early years, this was far from obvious: why would businessmen listen to the lessons of teachers who until then knew less than themselves? Why would they give up learning on the spot, through practice? Why would they accept the inventory and divulgation of their precious knowledge, at the risk of losing their expertise and market advantages? Why would they barter a local but improved knowledge for a general but uncertain science.

When trying to answer this fourfold question, one may begin by observing that the invention of academic marketing coincided with the grouping of two important movements. On the business side, at the beginning of the century, executives emerged as a distinctive social group, and gave birth in 1919 to the American Administrative Management Association (in 1925, it became the American Management Association). At the same time, university education developed and unified itself: the Association of American University was created in 1900, the American Association of University Professors in 1915, the American Council on Education in 1918.

Business activities were growing, and *management* became a profession—the profession of executives. Universities were spreading, and higher education became a profession—the profession of academics. The professionalization of the one was indistinguishable from the professionalization of the other. The mission of universities was to carry on the standardization of education and the criteria of careers. Educational institutions were the only bodies which could set up the diplomas that would testify to the skills of the anonymous actors arriving on the new labour market of management specialists. In return the executives, having no other wealth than their exclusive know-how, were the only persons in the business world who were directly interested in the construction of the sciences that could legitimate their action, warrant their jobs, and build a common identity for them well away from the group of stockholders.

Here lie the reasons why the business schools grew and gathered, in 1916, around an American Association of Collegiate Schools of Business. Business schools were the rallying point of the convergent rise of executives and universities. The business schools, as their name implies, allowed the mixing of business and knowledge, a new definition for each side. From that point of view, it is necessary to outline how marketing pioneers were hybrid-men, easily crossing and combining the identities of manager and academic. They went from the university to business, then from business back to the university (Cochoy, 1995).

The first group of men (the group of deviant economists who became marketers: Ralph Starr Butler, L.D.H. Weld, Paul H. Nystrom) was able, through the alternation of academic and business positions, to develop the marginal knowledge of business margins gathered by marginal men, so that it finally reached the centre, the knowledge and power places of the big American Universities (NYU, Columbia) and businesses (Procter and Gamble, U.S. Rubber). Just like the bees that carry pollen from flower to flower, these men could cross-fertilize each of the fields encountered with the knowledge acquired in the others.

The second group of men, by migrating from business to academia, obtained the distant and over-arching position necessary to integrate business experiences, Arch W. Shaw in particular, as a businessman who had interests in *several* companies of Chicago and was thus inclined to compare and synthetize the varied situations he encountered, was successively hired by Harvard and Northwestern University to contribute to the development of business curricula. Shaw took advantage of the broad perspective provided him by the multiplicity of his positions in order to invent the references, devices and methods that could gather and unify the new community of management specialists.

On the business side, Shaw founded *System, the Magazine of Business* (the direct ancestor of our modern *Business Week*), a forum where business professionals could discover general ideas on business conduct, a place where they could share and improve their common wisdom, beliefs, and experiences. On the academic side, Shaw made two decisive innovations. On the one hand, he established the first business laboratory—the bureau of business research. This institution permitted the construction of a systematic, cumulative and transversal body of knowledge and thus made academic business skills superior to individual business visions. On the other hand, Shaw developed the case method. This educational device made it possible to transfer practice to the classroom and thus gave business teachers the privilege of a pedagogy of practice, but also a means to simulate real business operations, to gather business experiences (as knowledge) by the conduct of experiences (as experiments)—to *learn practice* without the risks of a real job.

All these first endeavours aiming at generalizing local business practices and knowledge soon favoured the emergence of some global unifying procedures, and this occurred because the circulation of men in the market economy (the invention of executive careers) demanded the standardization of their languages, qualifications, and skills. In marketing, this standardization followed a double path.

Performation as pre-formating: the discipline of marketing

The first standardization of marketing: from marketing knowledge to marketing people

The first standardization of marketing was ascending and interactive. It was the progressive connection between the observations and knowledge acquired in local fields about marketing commodities, institutions, and functions. We already saw that in order to elucidate the mysteries of marketing channels, the economist-marketer had chosen to follow the movement of products. The following of commodities led to the naming of their origin, transit, and destination places. In the second and third decade of the 20th century, the founding fathers of modern marketing—who received their background education in institutional economics (Brown, 1951)—undertook to describe all the institutions involved in the marketing process, from big wholesale establishments to the smallest retail store (Bartels, 1976). From this double inventory (what circulates: commodities; what they circulates through: institutions) a first generalization became possible. The double entry through products and institutions led to the functional approach, at a time when, precisely, the 'marketing function' began to be institutionalized in American companies (Faria, 1983).

The study of marketing functions was introduced by Arch W. Shaw (1912) who proposed a taxonomy of the 'general functions of middlemen' (*ibid.*). The functions he described were the sharing of risk, transportation, financing, selling. Because it separated men, things, and concepts, the functional approach led to a transversal generalization and integration of local knowledge. Indeed, this approach was reproduced in the first marketing textbooks which, from Weld's *Marketing of Farm Products* (1916) to Clark's *Principles of Marketing* (1922), tried to complete, refine and generalize Shaw's original taxonomy.

Thus, step by step, the knowledge of networks led to a network of knowledge; the empirical and inductive approach going from products to institutions, then from institutions to functions, gave birth to an entirely new body of disciplines and group of specialists. As a consequence, the ascending and decentralized standardization of marketing knowledge was soon furthered by a descending and centralized standardization of marketing people.

The second standardization of marketing: from marketing people to the marketing discipline

The academics interested in the marketing world met in the context of the professional associations they originally belonged to. The Associated Advertising Clubs of the World favoured the meeting of marginal psychologists among the new advertising community; the American Economic Association facilitated the recognition of marginal economists among the crowd of their orthodox peers. Indeed, the meeting of professional associations gave to deviant persons the opportunity not only to discover their marginality among their former community but also to gather together. The two groups of deviant economists and deviant psychologists, because they shared a common interest for marketing activities and a common identity as deviant academics, ended up merging into a National Association of Teachers of Marketing and Advertising (Agney, 1941). Eventually, this first group was soon joined by a third one: the group of executives and technicians specialized in market surveys who, because they felt they were on the margins of business power and academic knowledge, had gathered since 1931 in an American Marketing Society. The marginal specialists of the management of margins decided to merge: on January 1st, 1937, they launched the American Marketing Association (Agnew, 1941).

The appearance of an *ad hoc* professional association helped marketing men to increase their control over business education and management—thus over the American economy as a whole. We have already suggested that the implementation of new knowledge and know-how depended on their generalization and abstraction by means of pedagogic devices. However, this first ascending standardization, because of its iterative and decentralized character, was slow and uncertain; it relied on hazardous encounters, on providential discoveries, on the variable availability of references, or on the goodwill and perspicacity of authors and publishers. On the contrary, a professional association provided the means that were necessary to overcome such difficulties. As early as in the 1920s, the *AMA's* ancestor—the *National Association of Teachers of*

Advertising—set up a *Committee on Teachers' Materials*. This committee was asked to gather pedagogical elements from advertisers and publishers. Later on, the *NATA* launched its own editorial activity: it published the proceedings of its annual meeting through special bulletins (Agnew, 1941). Gathering and publishing texts helped the marketing community to have a simultaneous access to the same type of references: marketers, through these writings, were for the first time able to communicate, to know about the action of the others, to adjust their own positions to the one of their colleagues.

The gathering was eventually possible but it created more problems than it solved. Indeed, the publication of the different works emphasized the heterogeneity of local endeavours, the proliferation of concepts, the extreme polysemy of the 'marketing' word, which was alternatively synonymous with selling, distribution, advertising, and so forth. The comparison was possible, of course, but it produced an impression of cacophony that jeopardized the intellectual and social coherence of the association. That is why the association leaders decided in a second movement on a reordering of the elements they had helped to collect; that is why they undertook to build a common language.

In 1930 they instituted a *Committee on Definitions*, whose members were commissioned to legislate, to standardize, to construct the *official* vocabulary of marketing. Because the *AMA* occupied a central position, it could harmonize, then redistribute, the meaning of words and things, and thus put together a glossary. Because the actors—members and non-members—had other things to do, and because they found it convenient that someone worked on their behalf for them to codify their language, improve their communication and ease both their exchanges and their personal affairs, they became more and more inclined to adopt the *AMA* definitions. Any objections they might have voiced if they had participated directly in the negotiation of marketing terms were waived by delegating the standardization problem, thereby saving time and energy.

But the aim of marketers was not only to produce words and concepts, it was also to make sure that their concepts and words were adopted and adapted in business practices, that this gathering constituted an implementable body of references—that marketing would perform the market economy. To prevent *AMA* definitions from becoming a dead language, one had to show how those tools could play together; one had to quit the paradigm for the syntagm; one had to organize the vocabulary into a coherent whole, so that it could be used by its potential locutors. Meanwhile, because the interest for market surveys was arising, and because *AMA* members were far from becoming the only persons to master this type of surveys, it was urgent to find how to remain in the race, it was necessary to itemize and piece together the knowledge acquired here and there into a coherent whole. In order to do so, the *AMA* launched in 1937 a *Committee on Marketing Techniques*, which all of a sudden published a reference book (Wheeler, 1937). Thanks to this book, the *AMA* could reinforce its role as a reference-institution (but also as an institution that produced references) for the discipline as a whole and for its clients.

However, *AMA* leaders, thanks to their identities as marketing specialists, were well aware that any attempt at acquiring a monopoly position was condemned to failure; they knew that neither language nor knowledge could be fixed for ever. How could they reconcile the reference (the fixed marker) with the upgrading of references (the continuous revision of knowledge)? In order to consolidate their reference position, *AMA* men had to invent a device that could stabilize their disciplinary and institutional identity and enable its ongoing revision. This device was the *Journal of Marketing*. A journal is a place where knowledge is always evaluated and updated. But a journal is also the official outlet of a particular domain, always recognizable as such through its permanent title. Scientific journals are always the same and nevertheless different. They can bring a community together, but they can also register, trigger and communicate the displacements, the movements, the transformations that reach it.

A survey of the first 10 years of the *Journal of Marketing* made it clear that the original themes (agricultural marketing, relations between economic theories and marketing, teaching and marketing) had progressively given way to new orientations, such as sales management or market surveys (Applebaum, 1947). The initial concerns aimed at building the conceptual foundations of the new discipline, describing marketing practices, and finding the proper methods of business teaching. But this first marketing scholarship, which started from the outside to discover the internal knowledge of business, had progressively given rise to a set of concepts, principles and techniques liable to master the relationships between a business and its market.

Marketing texts underwent a thematic evolution through the standardization and generalization of marketing vocabulary and know-how, the spreading of lexicons, directories, textbooks and journals. The resulting maturation of marketing institutions, meetings and human societies—the progressive pre-formating of marketing practice by marketing knowledge and networks—testified to the implementation of a tight link between knowledge and practice. In short, it permitted the performation of concepts through action frames that were both disciplinary and managerial. From that point onward, through the double action of marketing teaching (at the local level) and marketing standardization (at the global level), cognition became synonymous with management. The tight connection between teaching materials and persons was successful in moving the whole marketing world together in spirit if not in totality. In theory and practice, the discipline of marketing influenced the general orientation of the American economy, at both the micro and macro levels.

Performation as performance: playing with and within the economy

A microeconomic performation: on taylorian marketing

At the micro level, the pacing of American marketing by a common spirit and toolkit was prepared and furthered by the progressive interrelation of the new science of markets and the principles of rising taylorism. Since the 'scientific management' of work gave management the means for a better control of production organization, some thought that the taylorian model could be transferred and adapted to the marketing world so that the distribution system could be scientifically mastered (Cochoy, 1994b).

First, as early as 1912, a man named Charles W. Hoyt managed to taylorize the sales department in the same way as Taylor had taylorized the workplace. In Hoyt's proposals, the definition of sales quotas, the description of precise selling routes, and the prescription of a standardized sales education became for the salesmen what production objectives, analysis of working tasks, and planning procedures had been for the taylorized worker (Hoyt, 1912). For the first time in history, the inception of a 'scientific sales management' programme extended the scientific management of work outside the workplace, it spread the optimization of managerial activities beyond the business plant.

Then, in 1927, another author named Percival White radicalized and generalized Hoyt's project. Hoyt had extended the taylorian control of production towards the realm of sales; White proposed to reverse the relation, ie, to start from a 'scientific marketing management' in order to control production as a whole. Foreshadowing the marketing concept and marketing management of the 1950s—which, as we will see, aimed at subordinating the management of the firm to the prerequisites of consumer satisfaction—White proposed putting the entire productive process under the scientific mastery not only of sales, but also of advertising, of distribution, and more generally of the market and the consumer (White, 1927). With this taylorian marketing, the taylorism within was eventually framed by a taylorism without; from one end of the American market to the other, from production to consumption, or rather from consumption to production, the American market was trapped, defined, managed and optimized through the implementation of the same doctrine, the same procedure and the same control.

Between 1912 and 1927, from Hoyt's propositions to White's formulations, in the background of the shift from a simple sales management to a management inspired by the methodical observation and control of the market, there occurred the maturation of marketing knowledge, of marketing glossaries, of marketing techniques, of marketing associations, networks, and institutions. The taylorian marketing of the one and the more descriptive marketing of the other were not the same. But the two forms of marketing went forward on parallel routes, they reinforced each other, they made it possible to *apply* to American businesses a whole set of concepts and devices thanks to which one could conceive each business no longer as a single atom lost in the marketing universe, but as a universe that encompassed its own market. With marketing, the circle of scientific management was closed: the whole economic *circuit*, from each business to the big market, was amenable to a systematic control—marketing was smoothly but surely sliding from microeconomics to macroeconomics.

A macro performation the marketing of the New Deal

At this point of our account, it is important to observe to what extent the rise of company and disciplinary marketing coincides with a sudden weakness of the autoregulative market economy. The decisive affirmation of marketing, both as a management science and as a management technique, is contemporary with the 1929 crisis. In the 1930s, marketers took over a new research domain—the governmental regulation of marketing—and their community welcomed a new type of members—the civil servants of the Federal

State. A few signs show it: during the crisis years, in the *Journal of Marketing* pages, governmental concerns had taken second place (16.7 per cent of the papers) and state personnel represented the third human force of the *American Marketing Association* (15.1 per cent of its members) (Applebaum, 1947). What had happened?

For us, who know the end of the story, the answer is easy: the economic crisis of the 1930s *had gone that way*, the *context* had produced its *effect*, the economy had performed marketing rather than the contrary. But for the actors of the 1930s, things were not as obvious. In those years, it was not the context which imposed its effects on the actors, it was rather the actors who took advantage of the context in order to forward their own position. From this point of view, the very first issue of *The American Marketing Journal*, published in 1934, included a suggestive foreword from its editors:

[1] All of us realize that extremely important problems in business during the next decade or more will almost certainly fall in the field of marketing and distribution. [2] As this first issue goes to press, the National Recovery Administration and the Agricultural Adjustment Administration are making bold attempts to hasten the return of prosperity. [3] Whatever may be their ultimate success and accomplishment, they will certainly have made a lasting impression upon business thinking. [4] Under the descending spiral of the depression, business men have developed a frame of mind which makes them willing to accept leadership along lines which a few years ago they would not have been willing to consider. [5] The Administration assumes that steady employment and adequate wages are of first importance in providing a mass market for our mass production, and the nation is united in a great practical effort to put this conception into universal operation. [6] The results will be watched closely by marketing executives, who will give greater attention to data on wages and hours, as indices of sales possibilities. . . . [7] The purpose of the *American Marketing Journal* is first of all to present worthwhile material which will be of interest to those in charge of marketing operations in business organizations. [8] In other words, we hope to be one factor in helping to sell the results of true market research to management. [9] One of the troubles with much business research is that its practical results are seldom placed before management in such a way that they can be used in modifying the methods of buying and selling commodities. (*The American Marketing Journal*, 1934)

The great depression, because it was disastrous for business, was a fantastic opportunity for the new marketing specialists. The economic chaos jeopardized the beliefs of the old managers, and so it made them more receptive to the implementation of new management principles. Of course, for the new marketers, the crisis was positive only as far its effects favoured the new expertise. That is why they carefully managed to associate the economic disorder with marketing problems [1]. 'Your problems are marketing problems, and you cannot solve them by yourself anymore': this was the way marketers spoke about the crisis to managers—their clients [7; 8]. Actions by the Roosevelt administration gave an ultimate endorsement to marketers. Not only did economic conditions change, but management principles were not the same anymore. The autoregulative economy was being replaced by the Federal interventionism, with its array of codes, rules, specialized agencies, accounting devices, new economic principles [2]. Because the acceptance of the New Deal was universal [5], to the point that the business community itself seemed to accept its fatality [3; 4], one had more or less to 'cope with it', one had to rethink the whole of business life along the lines of an economy giving a larger role to the State regulative action [6]. The new discipline of marketing took note of the New Deal, it formulated concepts adapted to its effects, it offered businesses the means of microeconomic interventionism [8]. The *Journal*, from that point would carry on the job aiming at gathering and codifying these means, and bringing them to its public knowledge [9].

The New Deal, as a macroeconomic context with capital letters, became a new deal, a microsocial complex with small letters. The Federal State project served the formulation of a new discipline. The state rejection of market autoregulation gave marketing the opportunity to quit the economics of its origins (one would take the economic world as it was, and not as what it should be); the setting of the new principles of economic action would serve as a basis for the construction of new marketing techniques.

Just as in the case of the modern welfare state, marketing was built at a time when everything collapsed (Fullerton, 1988b); marketing was dwelling upon the weaknesses of the invisible hand in order to impose its own mediation. For the Prince counsellors as for the management consultants, the jolts of the liberal economy served as foundations for the building of new sciences; the representatives of the public and private sectors advocated the consequences of the lack of an adequate economic science in order to justify the

Franck Cochoy

emergence of macroeconomics on the one hand, of marketing on the other hand. On both sides, a general reappraisal of the market was being proposed—the visible hand of the manager and the provident hand of the State were supposed to gain a decisive control over economic fluctuations, providing that they unified their effort.

The parallelism between the two projects deserved to be noticed. While marketers were trying to organize themselves, by promoting the *AMA* regulation over their profession, the Roosevelt administration was working to master the economy, by putting it under the State regulative action. On the one hand, marketers were defending market surveys as a means to answer the precise wants of consumers. On the other hand, the Federal State was strongly supporting the use of industrial standardization as a tool that could increase market visibility. The definition of industrial codes was particularly close to marketing thought: if the State aimed at the construction of *conventions* that could help a better identification of products (in Lewis' sense [Lewis, 1969]), marketers saw the same device as a strategic weapon for the conquest of competitive advantages: the State opened the door to a technical management of market exchange, the building of conventions (at the global level) was becoming the key-tool of product differentiation and market segmentation (at the local level).

Moreover, State interventionism—the taking over of the economy—contributed to legitimate market studies. The State shifted the emphasis from the study of local markets to the study of the *national market*: it gave a universal implementation and justification to what, until now, had only been a local and peculiar practice. Thus, the launching in 1929 of the first national *Census of Distribution* justified not only the study of marketing phenomena (the completion of the census worked as an implicit recognition of the importance of studying distribution channels) but also its methods (the bureaucratic use of statistics legitimized their increasing use in business [Desrosières, 1993]) and its aims (the State recognized the importance, for businessmen, of the availability of general factual information upon which they could develop their action [Brown, 1951])—as Luc Boyer and Noël Equilbey (1990) put it: 'Marketing found its letters patent of nobility in this market crisis'.

Thus, the parallelism between marketing and the New Deal was shifting into a convergence: marketers wished to rely on the existing connections between their project and the Roosevelt administration policy in order to justify their action; they bet on the success of the macroeconomic regulation in order to promote their own science of

208 © The Editorial Board of The Sociological Review 1998

market regulation. The performation of the market by marketers met the performation of the economy by public management. Thus, from the 1930s, the development of the public statistical apparatus became indistinguishable from the formidable rise of market surveys and corresponding methodologies (correlation measurement, sampling theory, multivariate analysis, panel studies) (Bartels, 1976). Indeed, the contribution of the new *economic policy* to the advancement of marketing was not only symbolic. Firstly, the production of federal data provided useful information for the improvement and development of new techniques and knowledge (Converse J., 1987; Boyer and Equilbey, 1990). Secondly, at a time when business employment was dropping, the development of high technical skill positions within the federal administration offered alternative job opportunities to the young executives educated in the business schools (Cochran, 1972). Thirdly, and foremost, the conceptual renewal of economics led to a radical shift of marketing thought. The New Deal argument justified the discarding of the old knowledge and techniques, which had been developed to master a world now obsolete. The codification of the prevalent practices was no more relevant: why would marketers have pursued the inventory of skills that did not work anymore? Economic matters now being different, marketers soon conceived the project of abandoning the inductive approach of their beginnings for a more deductive orientation—it would be worthwhile to construct, *ex nihilo*, the new *science* of marketing:

> In the future, we may hope for a very high degree of perfection in the development of scientific procedure in research in which the American Marketing Association will certainly lead. But developing technique is not enough—important as it is. What we need most is to get some basic principles which shall be the guidance for marketing processes. . . . We have passed the place where we teach only what business does. We do not hesitate to criticize business where it is inefficient in method or uneconomic in purpose. Those members who are practitioners, with few exceptions, are no longer satisfied merely to get the answer the 'boss' wants. Rather they have reached the position where, if their answer is the one the boss wants, they are dubious of their own accuracy. In short, we are well on our way to become a profession. (Agnew, 1941)

Performation as re-formation: from the reform of management sciences to the reformation of marketing scientists

The reform of management sciences

'In the future': at the end of the interwar period, a few marketers were dreaming of a marketing that would be really scientific; they dreamed of a marketing that would reverse the historical relationship between managerial knowledge and practice. In essence, they wanted to escape from a more or less scientific management in order to build a true management science. Instead of deriving their knowledge from practice (instead of accepting that marketing proceeds from management) they called for knowledge to lead practice (they wished for a science that would precede management).

Of course, the formulation of the first marketing concepts and principles, the improvement of market survey techniques, and foremost Hoyt's and White's proposals had paved the way. But the first notions were only codifying practice and the first studies remained mostly descriptive. Moreover, as can be seen from the literature of the times, although the idea of a scientific marketing management was extremely novel, it nevertheless received rather limited attention from marketing academics.

In the 1950s, however, a further important innovation appeared in the American marketing realm: the so-called 'marketing concept'. The marketing concept proposed a link between profit realization and consumer satisfaction and called for management operations to be submitted to the scientific study of markets in order to place all other business departments under the supervision of the marketing department. The novelty was less the idea itself, which was reminiscent of White's scientific marketing management, but rather its systematic and enthusiastic use within American management circles.

The most striking and perplexing feature of the marketing concept, however, was not its potential performative impact over the American economy but rather its evident lack of cognitive effects upon the community of academic marketers. Although businessmen had been experiencing or celebrating the marketing concept throughout the 1950s, it was only at the beginning of the 1960s that academic marketers implemented it in their own speeches and activities. What is the reason for such a discrepancy? Why did academic marketers resist so long? And why did they eventually give up at the turn of the 1960s?

At first sight, the reluctance of academics to accept the marketing concept may seem surprising: in placing the consumer at the centre

210

of marketing and the producer at the periphery (Keith, 1960), the marketing concept was giving academics the means to fulfill their wishes, ie, to turn marketing into a science in its own right and put practice under its guidance. But we don't have to forget the disciplinary identity of the first marketers, and the particular type of science that the marketing concept was calling for. Let us remember: the pioneers of marketing, educated in institutional economics and in the descriptive analysis of marketing channels, were of course able to conduct market surveys, but they had none of the skills that were necessary to explain the mysteries of consumer behaviour and/or to draw quantitative models of the functioning of markets.

The first marketers were conscious of the vulnerability of their own positions: while observing the business world, they were perfectly conscious that the marketing concept was attracting all sorts of consulting agents, the Ernest Dichter, Burleigh Gardner or Sidney Levy—all those who proposed their 'motivation studies', all those who promoted a psychoanalysis of the consumer as a new way to control the markets (Kassarjian, 1994). In looking at American social science, marketing pioneers saw clearly that the specialists of the new technologies brought by the war—operations research, econometrics, general systems theory—were looking toward management in order to ensure their conversion in a civilian context (Reidenbach and Oliva, 1983), and they saw to what extent a marketing management based on the consumer could serve as an anchor point for the implementation of this kind of techniques. Thus, they concluded that in order to safeguard their position, it was imperative to prevent the 'consumer' object from becoming the Trojan horse of the new specialists by speaking again in terms of markets, products, institutions and functions of marketing—in brief: one had better mistrust the marketing concept.

In 1959, however, the Ford and Carnegie Foundations launched an important funding programme aiming at reforming the management sciences. This programme was conducted by Robert Gordon and James Howell, two economists who were favourable to the new social and quantitative sciences. Their idea was to fund the business schools that would, first, abandon the descriptive and inductive approach of the pre-war period and, second, adopt a perspective grounded in the implementation of both quantitative techniques and behavioural sciences (Gordon and Howell, 1959).

For the old generation, the alternative was cruel: refusing the Ford Foundation's recommendations meant missing enticing grants for their own business school; accepting the reform meant being

Franck Cochoy

superseded by approaches they lacked the skill to implement and
thus losing their professional identity. The alternative was cruel but
was not without a solution. In order to reconcile the irreconcilable,
in order to preserve the contradictory interests of their personal
career and collective institutions, the seniors realized they should
make a little move: renouncing the fields of teaching and research,
they migrated towards administrative positions inside their own
schools. In accepting the role of organizing that which outstripped
them, in becoming the administrators of the reform—in managing
the importation of quantitative techniques and behavioural sciences
to management sciences—the old business teachers were able to stay
at the centre of business schools while firmly implementing the new
orientations (Cochoy, 1995).

In marketing, reform was accepted all the more willingly since it
could be presented as the logical extension of the marketing concept. Once institutional economics was abandoned, quantitative
techniques and consumer psychology could be introduced as the
'natural' tools of a management founded on the 'consumer orientation', and the era of marketing management could begin. Thanks to
the hiring of young specialists trained in the new social, economic
and quantitative sciences, the marketing of the 1960s moved in a
double direction. On the one hand, the implementation of operations research and econometrics led to the birth of so-called 'marketing science': a research stream that could model and optimize
market activities. On the other hand, the importation of statistics,
psychology and behavioural analysis gave birth to the so-called
'consumer research': an approach that introduced a systematic
study of consumer behaviour.

From this double orientation, one could proceed beyond Wendell
R. Smith's intuition, who proposed, well before the reform, to use
the economic theory of imperfect competition developed by the
Cambridge school of economics in order to clarify the old practices
of market segmentation and product differentiation (Smith, 1956;
Alderson, 1957). Thanks to quantitative techniques and behavioural sciences, one could develop the concepts and the procedures
necessary for a true 'marketing management'—for a technical and
integrated administration of markets. More precisely, the marketing
management programme entailed two main proposals. First, it presented the idea of marketing mix (Borden, 1964), which seeks to set
the best marketing policy as an optimal and controlled combination
of price, promotion, place and product strategies (McCarthy, 1960).
Second, it pretended to complete and reinforce this marketing mix

model thanks to the systematic use of the taylorian model of planning, analysis and control (Kotler, 1967).

Around the marketing concept/marketing management/marketing mix triptych, the rising implementation of statistical devices in marketing increasingly showed that, beyond prices, the result of competition depended on the management of the multidimensional aspects of products—above all brands, services, packaging (Green, 1963). It showed that one had to play on these many dimensions in order to shape the markets; the use of computers, econometrics, and modelling methods also led to the construction of real black boxes for a technical management of markets (Little, 1979). The concepts of social science and the systematic study of consumption practices made possible not only the modelling of buyer behaviour, but also the implementation of these models for the conduct of marketing strategies (Howard and Sheth, 1969).

Thus, the consequence of the reform of the 1960s was the rapid implementation of a double performance of economic matters (economy/economics). On the one hand, the reform performed economics, in forcing it to migrate from State to business, in adding to the modelling of the whole economic circuit an analogous framing of managerial practices. On the other hand, the reform performed the economy, since the general implementation of the same frameworks, techniques and devices, from the State to business units, through all distribution channels, was bound to reinforce the efficiency of a management of markets.

The contemporary phrases of 'public management' (Laufer and Paradeise, 1990) or 'business governance' (Gomez, 1996) further demonstrate the extent to which economics and management sciences migrated towards politics/political sciences, and joined economics and management. As the result of a gigantic translation and combination process of modern sciences and practices, economics, management and political sciences ended up being only different dimensions of a single socio-technical network (Callon, 1991). On the one hand, at the national and public level, one had the general macroeconomic regulation, the national accounting and political apparatus; on the other, at the local and private level, one eventually obtained a microeconomic managerial regulation.

However, it has been little noticed that the one did not go without the other: if modern marketing, as we have seen, is the natural child of economic and scientific innovations of the New Deal and post-war years, modern economics is greatly indebted, as far as its relevance is concerned, to its effective performation in and through

Franck Cochoy

managerial sciences and practices. The microeconomic empirical management of markets is the only way to have a 'self-fulfilling economy'; it is only through the generalization of the same approaches, methods and tools—that is: through the action of the double apparatus of economic policy on one side and of marketing management on another—that modern marketing practices could definitely quit the autoregulation of the smithian market and enter the regular frame of political, technical and managerial control.

From new forms of marketing management to the reformation of marketing scientists

By the end of the 1960s, however, the success of the marketing concept, marketing management and marketing mix were producing some unexpected consequences. As previously outlined, if the new orientations were eventually implemented, it was only thanks to the hiring of new individuals; the coming of specialists was the indispensable corollary of marketing quantification and 'socialization'. Now, if the business schools were inclined to favour the use of the new sciences for managerial concerns, the new scientists were often less concerned with the managerial use of their knowledge than with the pursuit, within marketing itself, of their 'original' orientations and disciplines.

In consequence, a split in the ranks emerged during the endemic protest atmosphere of the late 1960s. Whereas some proposed a broadened concept of marketing liable to serve as the basis for a social marketing, that is: for a marketing liable to be applied to non-business organizations (Kotler and Levy, 1969; Lazer, 1969; Kotler and Zaltman, 1971), others saw this programme as a call for a societal marketing, that is: a marketing of a more fundamental character, a marketing that would be more preoccupied with the social role of commercial practices than with the search for profit and managerial efficiency (Spratlen, 1970; Sweeney, 1972; Tucker, 1974; Dixon, 1978). To some extent, the idea of societal marketing helped its adepts not only to establish some political distance from the managerial orientation, but its most significant effect was to restore the relative scientific independence of the psychology, sociology or theoretical economics from which they came. Social/societal marketing thus opened the opportunity for a certain 'disapplication' of applied science.

The marketing of the 1970s–1980s ended up juxtaposing on the one hand the more technical, practical and applied marketing and, on the other hand, a marketing more and more oriented towards social protest and/or towards fundamental research, towards the study of the consumer for its own sake, rather than towards the study of the consumer for the optimization of markets (Hunt, 1976). How should we interpret this drift? Did the liberation of specialists entail a less effective performation of the market economy by the marketing discipline? The double thematic and disciplinary broadening of marketing, the relative disapplication of the applied science, the proliferation of contradictory research streams without any managerial orientation, certainly entailed a loosening of the links between science and management, knowledge and power. A closer look, however, reveals that the slackening of the technical, cognitive and human networks of marketing led more to their reconfiguration than to their rupture, and for three reasons.

Firstly, the invention of social marketing made the spreading of marketing beyond the tiny circle of private business activities possible. The social marketing idea, far from breaking with the managerial roots of the discipline, ensured on the contrary the extension of these roots to a few sectors which, until now, had been outside its influence: the invention of political marketing, of cause-related marketing, of public marketing (etc.) ended up placing under the marketing management umbrella a whole set of institutions which, *a priori*, were totally alien to it. Just as the concept of marketing mix could apply the logic of competition far beyond the unique price variable, the broadened concept of marketing could extend marketing knowledge far beyond the private sector. Secondly, the transformation of social marketing into a societal marketing resulted in a tightening of the links between profit and not-for-profit marketing, thanks to the growing intervention of consumer research specialists in governmental services and agencies designed for consumer protection—Federal Trade Commission, Federal Drug Administration, Consumer Product Safety Commission, Office of Consumer Affairs, Office of Consumers' Education (Bloom and Greyser, 1981). The development of consumerism, paradoxically enough, far from condemning marketing for not meeting its commitments, ratified its efficiency, and thus contributed to reinforce the need and presence of marketers in the economy. Thanks to consumers' protest, marketing specialists and their research methods were called for, as expert witnesses and devices, in order to help courts when they had to examine cases of deceptive advertising, commercial frauds and other marketing abuses against the consumer (Kassarjian, 1994). The faults and virtues of marketing thus contributed to the generalization of marketing methods, concepts and persons inside all American institutions, from private companies to federal agencies and judicial institutions. Thirdly and finally, the interpretation of societal marketing as a 'pure' or 'fundamental' marketing favoured the migration of other specialists or specialities, such as epistemology, anthropology (Sherry, 1986), history (Fullerton, 1988a; Cochoy, 1994a), postmodernism (Firat, 1991) or even semiotics and literary criticism (Stern, 1990; Holbrook and Hirschman, 1992). Just like the segmentation of marketing between business marketing and not-for-profit marketing eventually put all the compartments of the American society under the guidance of the micro-marketing governance, the segmentation of marketing between fundamental marketing and applied marketing resulted in the enrolment of all humanities and social sciences around the systematic analysis of markets.

Conclusion: the two meanings of discipline

As we have seen, the marketing performation of the market economy took four successive and embedded aspects. The first two performations—performation through peer-formation; performation through the double standardization of knowledge and practice—dwelled upon the empirical orientations of German institutional economics in order to develop a network of market knowledge and experts. The third performation—the economic performance of marketing—took advantage both of the great crisis of the market economy and of the technical and economic innovations of taylorism and the New Deal in order to promote a more active management of markets, a micro-marketing policy for company use. Eventually, the fourth performation—the immersion of marketing in an ever-increasing set of disciplines and fields—tried to reverse the first three performations; it aimed at replacing the theories of practices with a practice inspired by theory, along with the double model of quantitative macroeconomics and behavioural sciences.

Here, the bringing together of the four performations is more than a mere concluding device. The historical summary shows that, at each stage, marketing came from economics in order to perform the economy without any direct use of economic frameworks! Former economists left economics in order to observe the economy, and subsequently used the economic collapse in order to reshape along their own lines the new economic interventionism. Then, the same marketers ended up importing the specialists and frameworks of macroeconomics and econometrics in order to develop the tools upon which they could perform a marketing management of business. Meanwhile, the market was more and more embedded in a double set of rules and procedures, of concepts and experts, that both defined and shaped it.

Naturally, the efficiency of marketing is still unclear (Marion, 1995). Its performances are hard to describe, complex to evaluate, and difficult to measure empirically. But in this difficulty lies the distinctive character of performative sciences. These sciences are truly *disciplines*, in the double meaning of the word: in their case, one cannot separate science from practice, the discipline-knowledge from he discipline-control since, by definition, these sciences arise in and through practice (Latour, 1996). Managers go through marketing, marketers go through management. Of course, history shows us that the one and the other can do whatever they want with marketing and management, that the one like the other can overcome or override them. But marketing management, for both of them, is always a reference for action, and its imprints are found wherever the observer of the capitalist economy may go: marketing presence, action and effects are daily evidenced in toll free numbers, market surveys, brand responsibility, consumer culture, and foremost in the extreme generalization of marketing vocabulary, that is: in the constant use, by all sorts of actors in every kind of situations, of the metaphors of segmentation, positioning, advertising, targets and niches.

The best sign of the economic performance of marketing lies perhaps less in its direct effect on the market than in its indirect impact on economists. Economists, ever since the works of the Cambridge School, have theorized imperfect competition, which is itself perfectly managed by marketers. Today, economists, sociologists, and socio-economists examine the many aspects of 'non price competition' (Debonneuil and Delattre, 1987; Guellec, 1990; Lancaster, 1975; Oliveira-Martins, 1990), the 'economics of quality' (Karpik, 1989) and the diverse 'conventions' framing the definition of markets and the qualifying of products (Eymard-Duvernay, 1989). But what did marketing do, long before the economists, if not provide suppliers and consumers with the conventions liable to help them qualify the products? What did marketing do, if not develop the relevant tools to overcome price constraints and play on product quality, services, design, and so on? Contemporary analysts of the market economy are often running, without even knowing it, after the knowledge of marketers. If economics was, from the beginning, the inspiring discipline of marketing, one can speculate if marketing did not become, as time went on, the unseen spirit of both the market economy and economics.

Note

1 The word 'performation' is coined on Austin's notion of 'performative utterance' in linguistics. According to Austin (1962), a performative utterance is an utterance that says and does what it says simultaneously (for example: 'I declare the meeting open'). According to this definition, and thanks to a suggestion by Bruno Latour (1996) and Michel Callon (see introduction of this book), a performative science is a science that simultaneously describes and constructs its subject matter. In this respect, the 'performation' of the economy by marketing directly refers to the double aspect of marketing action: conceptualizing and enacting the economy at the same time.

References

Agnew, H.E., (1941), 'The History of the American Marketing Association', *Journal of Marketing*, Vol. 5, April, 374–379.

Alderson, W., (1957), *Marketing Behavior and Executive Action*. Homewood, IL: Richard D. Irwin.

Applebaum, W., (1947), 'The Journal of Marketing: The First Ten Years', *Journal of Marketing*, Vol. 11, 355–363.

Arthur, B., (1989), 'Competing Technologies, Increasing Returns and Lock-in by Historical Events', *The Economic Journal*, March, 116–131.

Austin, J.L., (1962), *How to Do Things With Words*. London: Oxford University Press.

Bartels, R., (1976), *The History of Marketing Thought* (2nd ed.). Columbus, OH: Grid.

Bloom, P.N. and Greyser, S.A., (1981), 'The Maturing of Consumerism', *Harvard Business Review*, Vol. 59, November–December, 130–139.

Boltanski, L. and Thévenot, L., (1991), *De la justification. Les économies de la grandeur*. Paris: Gallimard.

Borden, N.H., (1964), 'The Concept of the Marketing Mix', *Journal of Advertising Research*, June, 2–7.

Boyer, L. and Equilbey, N., (1990), *Histoire du management*. Paris: Editions d'Organisation.

Brown, G.H., (1951), 'What Economists Should Know About Marketing', *Journal of Marketing*, Vol. 16, January, 60–66.

Callon, M., (1991), 'Réseaux technico-économiques et irréversibilités', in R. Boyer, B. Chavance et O. Godard (dir.), *Les figures de l'irréversibilité en économie*. Paris: Editions de l'EHESS, 195–530.

Campbell, C., (1987), *The Romantic Ethic and the Spirit of Modern Consumerism*. New York: Basil Blackwell.

Chandler, A.D. Jr., (1977), *The visible hand. The Managerial Revolution in American Business*. Cambridge, MA: The Belknap Press of Harvard University Press.

Clark, F.E., (1922), *Principles of Marketing*. New York: Macmillan.

Cochoy, F., (1994a), 'The Emerging Tradition of Historical Research in Marketing: History of Marketing and Marketing of History', in *Research Traditions in Marketing*, Gilles Laurent, Gary L. Lilien and Bernard Pras (eds), Boston, Kluwer Academic Publishers, 383–397.

Cochoy, F., (1994b), 'La gestion scientifique des marchés: marketing et taylorisme dans l'entre-deux-guerres', *Recherche et Applications en Marketing*, Vol. 9, n° 2, 97–114.

Cochoy, F., (1995), *De main en main: trois histoires de médiation marchande, de marketing et de marketers*, thèse pour le doctorat de sociologie, Ecole Normale Supérieure de Cachan.

Cochran, T.C., (1972), *Business in American Life: a History*. New York: McGraw-Hill.

Converse, J., (1987), *Survey Research. United States Roots and Emergence, 1890–1960*. Berkeley, CA: University of California Press.

Converse, P.D., (1959), *The Beginning of Marketing Thought in the United States with Reminiscences of the Pioneer Scholars*. Studies in Marketing, No. 3, Austin, TX: The University of Texas, Bureau of Business Research.

Debonneuil, M. and Delattre, M., (1987), 'La compétitivité-prix n'explique pas les pertes tendancielles de parts de marché', *Economie et Statistiques*, n° 203, octobre.

Desrosières, A., (1993), *La politique des grands nombres—Histoire de la raison statistique*. Paris: La Découverte.

Dixon, D.F., (1978), 'The Poverty of Social Marketing', *MSU Business Topics*, Vol. 26, Summer, 51–56.

Eymard-Duvernay, F., (1989), 'Conventions de qualité et formes de coordination', *Revue Economique, L'économie des conventions*, Vol. 40, n° 2, mars, 329–359.

Faria, A.J., (1983), 'The Development of the Functional Approach to the Study of Marketing to 1940', in: S. C. Hollander and R. Savitt (eds), *First North American Workshop on Historical Research in Marketing*, East Lansing, MI: Michigan State University, 160–169.

Firat, A.F., (1991), 'The Consumer in Postmodernity', in: Rebecca H. H. and M. R. Solomon (eds), *Advances in Consumer Research*, Vol. 18, 70–76.

Fullerton, R.A., (1988a), 'How Modern is Modern Marketing? Marketing's Evolution and the Myth of the "Production Era",' *Journal of Marketing*, Vol. 52, January, 108–125.

Fullerton, R.A., (1988B), 'Modern Western Marketing as a Historical Phenomenon: Theory and Illustration', in: T. Nevett and R. Fullerton (eds), *Historical Perspectives in Marketing: Essays in Honor of Stanley C. Hollander*. Lexington, MA: Lexington Books, 71–89.

Gomez, P.-Y., (1996), *Le gouvernement de l'entreprise. Modèles économiques de l'entreprise et pratiques de gestion*. Paris: InterEditions.

Gordon, R.A. and Howell, J.E., (1959), *Higher Education for Business*. New York: Columbia University Press.

Green, P.E., (1963), 'Bayesian Decision Theory in Pricing Strategy', *Journal of Marketing*, Vol. 27, January, 5–14.

Guellec, D., (1990), 'Quelques analyses de la compétitivité hors-prix', *note de l'INSEE*, n° 43/G142, mars.

Holbrook, M.B. and Hirschman, E.C. (1992), *The Semiotics of Consumption*. Berlin: Mouton de Gruyter.

Howard, J.A. and Sheth, J.N., (1969), *The Theory of Buyer Behaviour*. New York: John Wiley and Sons.

Hoyt, C.W., (1912), *Scientific Sales Management*. New Haven, CT: George B. Woolson and Co.

Hunt, S.D., (1976), 'The Nature and Scope of Marketing', *Journal of Marketing*, Vol. 40, July, 17–28.

Jones, D., Brian, G. and Monieson, D.D., (1990), 'Early Development of the Philosophy of Marketing Thought', *Journal of Marketing*, Vol. 54, January, 102–113.

Karpik, L., (1989), 'L'économie de la qualité', *Revue Française de Sociologie*, Vol. 30, n° 2, avril–juin, 187–210.

Kassarjian, H.H., (1994), 'Scholarly Traditions and European Roots of American Consumer Research', in: G. Laurent, G.L. Lilien and B. Pras (eds), *Research Traditions in Marketing*. Boston: Kluwer Academic Publishers, 265–279.

Keith, R.J., (1960), 'The Marketing Revolution', *Journal of Marketing*, 24, January, 35–38.

Kotler, P., (1967), *Marketing Management: Analysis, Planning and Control*. Englewood Cliffs, NJ: Prentice-Hall.

Kotler, P. and Levy, S., (1969a), 'Broadening the Concept of Marketing', *Journal of Marketing*, Vol. 33, January, 10–15.

Kotler, P. and Zaltman, G., (1971), 'Social Marketing: An Approach to Planned Social Change', *Journal of Marketing*, VOl. 35, July, 3–12.

Lancaster, K., (1975), 'Socially optimal product differenciation', *American Economic Review*, 65, 567–585.

Latour, B., (1996), 'Que peuvent apporter l'histoire et la sociologie des sciences aux sciences de gestion?' *Actes des 13èmes journées nationales des IAE*, Toulouse, ESUG, tiré à part, 3–15.

Laufer, R., and Paradeise, C., (1990), *Marketing Democracy: Public Opinion and Media Formation in Democratic Societies*. New Brunswick, NJ: Transaction Publishers.

Lazer, W., (1969), 'Marketing's Changing Social Relationships', *Journal of Marketing*, Vol. 33, January, 3–9.

Lewis, D.K., (1969), *Convention: A Philosophical Study*. Cambridge: MA, Harvard University Press.

Little, J.D.C., (1979), 'Decision Support Systems for Marketing Managers', *Journal of marketing*, Vol. 43, Summer, 9–26.

Marion, G., (1995), 'Le marketing management en question', *Revue Française de Gestion*, janvier-février, 15–30.

McCarthy, E.J., (1960), *Basic marketing: A Managerial Approach* (1st ed.). Homewood, IL: Richard D. Irwin.

McKendrick, N., Brewer, J. and Plumb, J.H., (1982), *The Birth of a Consumer Society*. Bloomington, IN: Indiana University Press.

Mukerji, C., (1983), *From Graven Images: Patterns of Modern Materialism*. New York: Columbia University Press.

Ohmann, R., (1996), *Selling Culture. Magazines, Markets, and Class at the turn of the Century*. London: Verso.

Oliveira-Martins, J., (1990), 'Comportement d'exportations avec différenciation des produits', *Revue d'Economie Politique*, mai–juin.

Prus, R.C., (1989), *Pursuing Customers: An Ethnography of Marketing Activities*. Beverly Hills, CA: Sage.

Reidenbach, E. and Oliva, T.A., (1983), 'General Systems Theory and the Development of Marketing Thought', in: Stanley C. Hollander and Ronald Savitt (eds), *First North American Workshop on Historical Research in Marketing*, East Lansing, MI: Michigan State University, 170–180.

Shaw, Arch W., (1912), 'Some Problems in Market Distribution', *Quarterly Journal of Economics*, Vol. 26, August, 703–765.

Sherry, J.F., (1986), 'Marketing and Consumer Behavior: Windows of Opportunity for Anthropology', *Journal of the Stewart Anthropological Society*, Vol. 16, No. 1, 60–95.

Smith, W.R., (1956), 'Product Differentiation and Market Segmentation as Alternative Market Strategies', *Journal of Marketing*, Vol. 21, July, 3–8.

Sombart, W., (1966), *Le bourgeois. Contribution à l'histoire morale et intellectuelle de l'homme économique moderne*. Paris: Payot.

Spratlen, T.H., (1970), 'The Challenge of Humanistic Value in Marketing', in: David L. Sparks (ed.), *Broadening the Concept of Marketing*. Fall, Chicago, IL: American Marketing Association, 47.

Stern, B.B., (1990), 'Humanizing Marketing Theory: Literary Criticisms and the Art of Marketing', in: Lichtental, D. *et al.* (eds), *Marketing Theory and Application*, 1990 Winter Educator's Conference, Chicago, IL: American Marketing Association, 24–28.

Strasser, S., (1989), *Satisfaction Guaranteed: The Making of the American Mass Market*. New York: Pantheon Books.

Granovetter, M. and Swedberg, R., (1992), *The Sociology of Economic Life*, Westview Press.

Sweeney, D.J., (1972), 'Marketing: Management Technology or Social Process?' *Journal of Marketing*, Vol. 36, October, 3–10.

Tedlow, R.S., (1990), *New and Improved The Story of Mass Marketing in America*. New York: Basic Books.

The American marketing Journal, (1934), *The American Marketing Journal, A Journal for the Advancement of Science in Marketing*, Vol. 1, No. 1, January.

Tucker, W.T., (1974), 'Future Direction in Marketing Theory', *Journal of Marketing*, Vol. 38, April, 30–35.

Weld, L.D.H., (1916), *The Marketing of Farm Products*, New York: McMillan.

Weld, L.D.H., (1941), 'Early Experiences in Teaching Courses in Marketing', *Journal of Marketing*, Vol. 5, April, 380.

Wheeler, F.C., (1937), *The Technique of Marketing Research*. New York: McGraw-Hill.

White, P., (1927), *Scientific Marketing Management: Its Principles and Methods*. New York: Harper and Bros.

Williamson, O.E., (1985), *The Economic Institutions of Capitalism*. New York: Basic Books.

The unlikely encounter between economics and a market: the case of the cement industry

Hervé Dumez and Alain Jeunemaître

Economics emerged as a social science in the 18th century with the theory of markets. Adam Smith and French economists provided demonstration that free markets were ensuring the optimal allocation of resources in the economy.

At that time their theoretical work was echoing very pragmatic debates on the organization of markets. In particular, there was the sensitive issue of the corn markets. In 1774, the French economist Turgot, then *Contrôleur Général des Finances*, liberalised the corn trade in France, breaking away from the mercantile tradition and putting into practice the free market economy principles.

At the start, the relationship between economics as a social science and the pragmatic organization of markets seemed self-evident. Economists would provide the practitioners with the appropriate analytical tools to decide upon the suitable market arrangements.

But, the dialogue between theory and practice changed. Firstly, the structuration of a scientific field had an impact on the development of economic thinking. Secondly, markets were diverse and complex.

At the end of the 19th century, economic knowledge was produced in academic institutions and published in scientific journals. Gaining in autonomy, the discipline became increasingly isolated from the day-to-day work of markets.

Besides, businessmen have always emphasized the specificity of their activity which they pictured as hard to reconcile with the reductionist approach of the economists. Either investments are said to be capital intensive with a long life expectancy, or immaterial and enabling entry at low-cost. The product is durable, or it is not. The manufacturing technology is regarded as simple or complex. The various production stages necessitate or not the employment of skilled labour. The innovation process is fast or slow. Buyers of the product are themselves either the final consumers or intermediaries such as wholesalers, retailers or other industries. Hence, are the economic concepts adjusted to such diversity? Can they help in formulating guidelines for the organization of markets?

These two points raise a fundamental issue: how and when do economists and their modelling encounter the practicalities of the market economy? In broader terms, how does a given market enter economics textbooks, and how does economic theory impact on its working and organization? The case study approach of the cement industry will provide insights on these issues.

Why the cement industry?

The cement industry is used as a standard material in industrial economics textbooks. The industry is among the most studied and modelled. Yet, in economic terms, the sector is rather negligible. As noted Robert R. Salyard, one of the prominent managers of American Cement Co,:

> Total annual sales volume of the cement industry ($1.45 billion) is the same as that of the retail sales of the greeting card or the carpet industry. This is not a huge industry, and it cannot realistically be thought of as if it were in the same size category as oil, steel, or autos. In 1970, there were 84 U.S. industrial corporations with individual annual sales greater that the total cement industry.[1]

Moreover, the industry is strikingly simple. Lee Cummings of Lehigh Portland Cement Company observed: 'This is an uncomplicated industry we're in. We've got one product sold at one price' (quoted in US District Court of Arizona, 1983). The product has also changed little since it was marketed at the beginning of the 19th century. Cement has well defined technical specifications, and even if there are differences in cement consumption according to climates, the product can be said to be undifferentiated and homogeneous.

Another feature of the industry is that the production process has evolved through technological leaps and the industry itself is capital intensive with high economies of scale in production. In other words, the larger the plant, the lower the unit production cost.

But cement is also a ponderous product with high storage and transportation costs. Therefore, in a given location, a market equilibrium is found between the size of the production capacity and the size of the distribution radius. Thus, competition is oligopolistic and locally oriented. Cement plants are few and deliver most of their output in the near vicinity.

How has such a trivial and simple industry entered economics textbooks and been the focus of economic analysis? The answer lies in the existence of antitrust cases.[2] The economic characteristics of the industry raise a competitive issue, straightforwardly formulated in 1934 by the Chairman of Riverside Cement Co., John Treanor, from an often quoted letter (in particular, Machlup (1949:41n): 'Ours is an industry that cannot stand free competition, that must systematically restrain competition or be ruined.' The sentence, written during the Great Depression of the 1930s, is certainly overstated but it is a good shorthand for expressing the competitive predicament in which producers can find themselves.

The wealth of the cement industry hinges on the business cycles of the construction industry. In times of boom, cement producers invest and compete, simultaneously setting up and acquiring plants and production sites (because of the transportation costs, the producers that control the best locations, the best quarries at close proximity to the urban zones and construction sites have a competitive advantage). In the downward trend of the business cycle, each producer is tempted to take customers away from his competitors in order to improve its production capacity utilization rate and therefore to restore his profitability. As cement is a commodity product type, a few cents difference in the price per ton immediately attracts the attention of buyers. Sales volume can easily be increased by offering secret rebates. Of course, in the end, secret rebates disseminate and become known to all market participants, triggering price wars. The dynamics of such competitive process has been set out by the Chairman of Kaiser Cement in December 1973: 'Generally, falling prices follow an insidious path. They often start with an oral price-cut by one company to a few accounts, and then they spread. Usually, when the new, low level of price is met by all the manufacturers, the downward spiral starts again by a company hoping to secure more volume through pricing.' (US District Court for the District of Arizona, 1983:A–57–58). The outcome of price wars is the collapse of the industry as the total cement consumption cannot be increased by a fall in prices. Consequently, in adverse demand conditions, the cement producers seek to stabilize prices in an orderly manner and to shift competition away from price to other aspects such as cost savings, the rationalizing of plants and locations, the search for productivity gains.

These attempts to stabilize the competitive game are investigated by the antitrust authorities. Since the end of the 19th century, the antitrust device is a noticeable feature of the political and economic US system. Two main institutions, the Department of Justice (DOJ) and the Federal Trade Commission (FTC), are responsible for the antitrust policy. In the American way of thinking about political institutions, one competes with the other. Except for criminal offences for which the DOJ has sole authority, both the DOJ and the FTC deal with the antitrust cases. In practice, they work in co-ordination and share out the review of the various markets. But rivalry between the two institutions remains intense. As regards the cement industry, the FTC has the leading role. In the antitrust cases, the opinion of economists is called for and they testify as experts.

The basing point system

The first key antitrust case started with an inquiry into the competitive effects of the so-called basing point system which regulated cement prices in the 1930s. The case was only definitely settled in 1948 by a ruling of the Supreme Court. The antitrust investigation lasted 15 years and required considerable investment in economic thinking from the defendants and the administration. To grasp the competitive issue at stake, the case shall be looked upon within a historical context.

At the end of the 19th century,[3] the big construction sites were mainly located in the East Coast, close to the largest limestone quarries in the Lehigh Valley, Pennsylvania. The first cement plants were therefore set up in this location. From there, long distance deliveries were made by rail.

The US cement producers priced cement according to the basing point system. They published a base point price in the Lehigh Valley and delivered prices for any location (which were the base point price plus the cost of transport by rail to the buyer's location). Under the basing point system, all buyers were able to reckon the delivered cement prices charged by the cement producers in any location of the US territory. This mechanism ensured full price transparency.

Gradually, the construction activity moved west and new cement plants were set up between the Lehigh Valley and these new markets locations. At the start, the new plants rarely had the production capacity to saturate the surrounding regional markets. In their vicinity, part of the deliveries were still made by the distant producers of the Lehigh Valley. Then, for the newly established plants, it was reasonable enough to carry on pricing according to the base point price, published by the distant producers plus the rail transportation costs from their locations. For example, a small cement plant set up between the Lehigh Valley and Philadelphia. The producer chose not to publish a mill price—i.e., not to be a base point from which a buyer would reckon delivered prices. Instead he aligned his Philadelphia delivered prices to the prices charged by the distant Lehigh Valley cement plants. Thus, the basing point system ended up in a paradoxical situation. A buyer in the vicinity of the small cement plant close to Philadelphia would pay as much as if the cement had been shipped from the distant plants located in the Lehigh Valley. The buyer would be charged a high transport cost corresponding to a long haul while the actual transportation cost was much lower. Such pricing principle was referred to as the 'phantom freight' practice. Even more puzzling, the prices charged by the local Philadelphia cement plant would decrease as fast as he would deliver on the way to the Lehigh Valley while the transportation costs increased. The outcome of such a pricing mechanism was that the basing point system allowed the largest producers to sell in the entire market and the small producers to prosper in their local markets. The latter would thrive in the umbrella of the former.

In dynamics, if the cement demand in Philadelphia increases and becomes highly remunerative, the small producer has an interest in investing in production capacity to capture the whole Philadelphia market. He will then publish his mill price and become a base point himself. In this new competitive environment, if the Lehigh Valley cement producers still wish to sell in the Philadelphia market, they will practice 'Freight absorption' that is to say align to the Philadelphia producer prices and not pass on in full the transportation cost to the customer.

Little by little, new base points appeared in the neighbourhood of highly dense areas of cement consumption in order to make these markets as unattractive as possible to distant cement producers. This is precisely what happened in the US cement market (Loescher, 1959:Ch. 4). New cement plants were set up in southern and western regions following the urbanization of new States, and the Lehigh Valley progressively lost its dominance. In 1902, there was only one base point, the Lehigh Valley. In 1908, two more appeared, in Hannibal (Missouri), and in Iola (Kansas). By 1940, base mills were scattered all over the US territory.

The basing point system did not eliminate price competition but it organized it through a transparent pricing mechanism. If a cement plant was willing to increase its market share, it would lower its published mill price and therefore all its delivered prices in the market place. It could also absorb part of the transportation to compete in distant markets. Therefore, a certain amount of cross hauling occurred within the boundaries of the cement plants markets.

Two key events disrupted the system in the 1920s and 1930s. In the first place, trucking generalized in cement transportation in the 1920s throughout the US territory. The cost of trucking decreased. Buyers asked if they could pick-up and load the cement at the mill preferably to having it delivered by the plant and being charged the rail freight price. This new way of doing business jeopardized the entire price system, the coherence and stability of which was derived from the use of delivered prices reckoned from computerized rail freight prices.

The second event was the Great Depression. The construction sector plunged into economic recession. The rate of capacity utilization of the cement plants dropped dramatically. In 1928, the average national capacity utilisation rate was 72.3 per cent and fell to 28.3 per cent in 1932. At such low activity levels, the cement plants were tempted to offer secret rebates to increase their returns.

The industry was quick to respond to both threats. In many areas, the cement producers started by not allowing the customer pick-up. In addition, they reaffirmed the use of the basing point system, and the cement trade association, the Cement Institute, published rail freight price schedule to make sure that all delivered prices were computed from identical transportation costs. Finally, as soon as a cement producer was suspected of proposing a secret rebate to a buyer, his competitors would retaliate by considering the secret rebate as an official drop in his base mill price. Subsequently, competitors would offer to all his customers a discount of a similar magnitude to that of the secret rebate. Therefore, the pricing mechanism allowed for orderly and foreseeable retaliation and reinforced the discipline and the use of the basing point system.

These measures proved effective. Despite the Great Depression and while the rate of capacity utilization of the cement plants was bumping along the bottom, the cement producers succeeded in stabilizing prices and, for some years, even in making profits.

The New Deal launched under the Roosevelt administration changed the economic environment. It relied upon infrastructure investment to stimulate the economy. New roads were built, and the

Federal government, the State authorities, and the local councils placed cement orders. This created temporary new markets that were frequently situated outside the main urban centres and distant from the plants. In order to reduce costs and to get large volume discounts, they neither placed orders with wholesalers, nor negotiated directly with the producers. They used public procurement procedures. Tenders were submitted under sealed offers and, strikingly, the prices quoted by the producers turned out to be identical, as far as the decimal points, reflecting the use of the basing point pricing. For distant locations, where no market existed, the producers used a more sophisticated formula. In 1933, the governor of Illinois tried a different approach. He publicly announced an order of 3.3 million barrels of cement for the year to come, and requested the cement producers to submit written offers specifying a f.o.b. (free on board) mill price. No submissions were sent to his office.

In 1931, the Senate had already asked the Chairman of the FTC to examine the competitive situation in the cement industry. The FTC reported to the Senate in March 1932 (US FTC, 1932). Her main finding was that the basing point system introduced stickiness in the price system and reduced competition. Meanwhile, complaints had been flooding in from State authorities and the Federal Government. Governor Horner of Illinois played a key role in the legal dispute about the basing point system. In July 1937, a formal inquiry was launched. Four years later, in 1941, the FTC staff made known the results of the inquiry and outlined the anti-competitive effects of the basing point system. On 17 July 1943, the FTC issued an order to 'cease and desist'. The decision was brought before the courts of justice and finally, the Supreme Court published its ruling in 1948.

Throughout the legal procedures, economists were heard as they debated the competitive and anti-competitive effects of the basing point system.

On the side of the FTC was Frank Albert Fetter, Professor at Princeton University, who testified before the Congress Commissions and the courts. Fetter had a clear-cut view about cement pricing practices. In his opinion, only the uniform f.o.b. mill pricing should be allowed. Under this pricing mechanism, each cement plant publishes a mill price and buyers manage their own transportation from the plant. As there is no freight absorption, each plant dominates in its geographical market. The size of the natural market of a plant hinges on its competitive aggressiveness when setting its mill price. If a plant is willing to expand or reduce the size of its geographical market, it simply modifies its mill price. Fetter considered that all other pricing mechanisms should be prohibited. He was backed by two prominent economists, Vernon A. Mund (Washington University) and Fritz Machlup (John Hopkins University).

On the side of the defendants, the cement industry, were Nathaniel H. Engle (Washington University), Melvin T. Copeland (Harvard Graduate School of Business) and above all John M. Clark (Columbia University). In 1934, the board of the Cement Institute appointed Clark as their economic expert, and he remained in that position for four years. He gave a synthesized account of his views in 1938, and years later, in 1949, he issued a comment on the Court ruling. He argued that a multi-basing point system based on the use of railways transport price schedules, but allowing the customer to pick-up cement from the plant, was the optimal solution.

To all appearances, Fetter won the economic contest. He proved very skillful at dealing with the various aspects of the debate. In the first place, he managed to convince key persons in the decision-making process. Many economists in antitrust agencies had been Fetter's students. Moreover, he had rallied Walter B. Wooden, the FTC Chief Attorney to his economic ideas. Walter Wooden occupied this position at the FTC from the early 1920s to the end of the 1940s and was the voice of the FTC in the main antitrust Courts cases—Salt producers, Staley, Corn Products, Pittsburgh Plus, Cement Institute, Malsters, Ice Cream Can, Crepe Paper, and Book Paper. He chaired an internal FTC Committee, the 'basing point committee' which was set up to elaborate the Commission's doctrine on the basing point.

Fetter also made judicious use of his neutral scientific status and discredited the economists supporting the cement industry. During a hearing session of a Congress Commission, in 1936, he introduced himself in this manner:

> I will say, Mr. Chairman, that I speak as a mere theorist. A theorist according to one definition is a fellow who is very much interested in understanding what makes the grindstone turn but hasn't any axes of his own to grind. It is a sort of unpractical attitude, and my interest in this or any other subject of this kind is simply the same as any citizen would have. I am interested in it as a student of the subject and trying to understand it, having no antipathy, no feuds, and no favourites in the matter. (Simon, 1950:22)

A few years later, once again during a Congress Commission hearing, he spoke of his economist colleagues who were at odds with him in the following terms:

> You will observe that every one of them is connected with a business school whose main purpose is to train students to make profits in private business. (idem)

Last but not least, Fetter very cleverly used legal argument to support his economic analysis. Allowing the freight absorption practice would have meant agreeing on price discrimination between customers which was under the suspicion of antitrust authorities. Fetter argued that such a decision would prove unworkable. If freight absorption was to be authorized, the Court would have to review all business practices on a case-by-case approach to determine which of them would be permitted and which of them would not. He noted that it would require an army of investigators which would result in endless bureaucratic controls. By contrast, consent on the uniform f.o.b. mill pricing, a system that eliminates price discrimination, would introduce legal certainty and simplicity.

J.M. Clark adopted a different perspective. In his opinion, the handling of the basing point issue required a two step analysis: 1. To analyse and to reflect upon the pricing mechanism alternatives. Which were they and what were their practical competitive advantages and shortcomings; 2. To study the consequences of the possible Court rulings.

When the Supreme Court decision was finally published, Fetter rejoiced, in a paper published in the *American Economic Review* (Fetter, 1948). However, his achievement was anything but convincing.

The Court ruling prohibited all collective arrangements that would support a rigid implementation of the basing point system: the attempts to get rid of customer pick-up and trucking; the refusal to sell directly to contractors (a way of maintaining the dominance of traditional sales distribution channels consisting of dealers and wholesalers, and a way of avoiding direct price competition); the freight absorption from the systematic use of the basing point formula; the exchange of information between producers.

But, the Court authorized the basing point system when managed on an individual basis, and simply required the producers to agree to sell at the mill gate. It allowed the producer to charge non-systematic and significant freight absorption if aimed at competing with other producers. Indeed, too small or too high freight absorption would have meant too little competition.[4]

The case which dealt with a complex issue is still difficult to interpret and to portray within a short comment. According to the scope of the paper, three points deserve attention.

Firstly, although economics and law were in appearance at the forefront in the dispute, politics also had its say. Neither the FTC, nor the Courts, nor even the Supreme Court, had the power to impose the uniform f.o.b. mill pricing to the US business community. At the end of 1948 and the beginning of 1949, the Interstate and Foreign Commerce Committee launched a thorough study on the merits of the uniform f.o.b. mill pricing. It surfaced—and it was self-evident from the start—that it ensured a monopoly power for each cement plant in the boundary of its natural market, and also that it could help the largest plants to co-ordinate on price. By tacit agreement, they would in the first place lower their price to eliminate the smallest plants, before increasing them once having got rid of the small competitors. Small businesses had such a political weight[5] that the recommendation of Fetter was never implemented.

Secondly, in 1950, two years after the Supreme Court ruling, no one thought that the FTC had seriously considered imposing the uniform f.o.b. mill pricing in the US markets (Simon, 1950:55). In other words, a shift in economic thinking was at work. Already, the view that price discrimination was anti-competitive was out of date and the competitive drawbacks of the uniform mill pricing were widely recognized. As Fetter thought that his ideas were prevailing through the Supreme Court decision, most economists thought that these ideas were actually outdated.

Thirdly, although the J.M. Clark economic contention did not convince the Courts, the case gave him the opportunity to write a seminal article, one of the most prominent papers in economics, on the concept of 'workable competition' (Clark, 1940). The general theme of the article stands as follows. Where there is a need to improve competition in a given market, the working of which has little to do with the perfect atomistic market of the economic theory, there is no added value in assessing competition in the light of the perfect market compilation used in the economic textbooks. When one of the conditions for perfect competition is relaxed, it does not follow that more competition will ensue if the other conditions are implemented. Conversely, to improve competition, it is sometimes necessary to move away from the reference to perfect competition.

Later reworked, the concept of 'workable competition' was to be used as the basis of competition policy in countries such as Germany, and particularly when setting up the *Bunderskartellamt* doctrine.[6]

231

The vertical integration case

The Supreme Court ruling on the basing point system had little practical impact. In the mid 1950s, US economic growth was strong and the cement plants had difficulty in meeting demand. In the economic euphoria, massive investments in production capacity were made. With a time lag, they were operational at the end of the 1950s, by which time cement demand had slowed down, resulting in excess capacity in the industry (the average rate of capacity utilization dropped from above 90 per cent in the mid 1950s to around 70 per cent in the early 1960s).

Reacting to the excess capacity situation, the cement producers began to acquire Ready Mix Concrete (RMC) companies.[7] From 1956 to 1969, 55 vertical acquisitions deals occurred (Allen, 1971). The FTC requested its bureau of economics to report on vertical integration (US FTC, 1966a). Following the report, the Commission organized public hearings, and invited cement producers and concrete companies to comment (*RP*, Stearn, August 1966). The outcome of recent antitrust investigations and findings from the economic report and the hearings, were that, in January 1967, the FTC issued a 'statement of general policy enforcement' prohibiting cement producers from taking over RMC companies.

Once again, economic analysis infringed on business market practices.

The debate focused on the findings of the report of the FTC economists.

The report gathered evidence and put forward an economic interpretation. There was little arguing about the collection of facts and data, but the interpretation stirred up controversy.

The facts were complex. The integration vertical moves were the result of diverse business strategies.

There had been *forward* integration strategies—cement producers taking over RMC companies—and *backward* integration strategies—RMC companies investing in cement production assets. Part of the strategic moves were *defensive*—a cement producer would buy large RMC customers to prevent entry in his market. Others were *offensive*—a cement producer would buy RMC companies to penetrate a competitor's market. The vertical integration moves went from the extreme case of full acquisition to the development of vertical links, for example a cement producer would lend money to a concrete company in return for an exclusive purchasing obligation. All vertical control strategies were entangled and adopted simultaneously by the cement producers in the marketplace, offensive and defensive vertical moves responding to each other, bringing about a flow of vertical acquisitions.

The economic context was as follows. On a national basis, the concentration of the cement market was relatively low but increasing. Although new entries had occurred (particularly from steel and RMC companies—backward integration), the number of cement producers diminished by a quarter between 1950 and 1960. The RMC companies were numerous (4000) and delivered within a short distance radius (rarely above 30 miles). But 12 per cent of the RMC companies accounted for a 60 per cent share of the national market. Therefore, the concrete market was a mix of large Ready Mix groups controlling a substantial share of the US local markets and small RMC companies. Of course, the cement producers targeted in the first place the largest concrete businesses. Actually, cost savings were not expected to follow from acquisitions. There was also no convincing evidence that the returns were higher in the concrete industry than in the cement industry.

The hearings organized by the FTC subsequent to the publication of the FTC economists' report asserted the complexity of the vertical integration circumstances. Ideal, a major cement producer, was on the eve of acquiring Builders Supply Co., a Houston RMC firm when the FTC prohibited the deal. W.J. Conway, executive and Vice-Chairman of Ideal praised the FTC decision. Ideal had bidden for Builders, one of his regular customers, only to prevent one of his competitors from taking it over. Conway was openly in favour of a general ban on vertical integration. Raymond S. Chase, the then marketing Vice-President of Dundee cement, was of the same opinion. He explained that vertical integration moves were used by incumbent producers to prevent the entry of more efficient ones. Other cement producers backed the integration moves. One of them was Lehigh cement. Lehigh resisted buying concrete companies until 1965 and from then onwards, acquired massive holdings in the concrete business. In the following years, Lehigh totalled 50 per cent of the RMC acquisitions. Among the largest deals, in 1965, it acquired two RMC companies in Florida, one in Virginia and in 1966, one in Kentucky. Lehigh hired Merton J. Peck, Professor of Economics at Yale University, to contradict the findings of the FTC report on vertical integration.

As regards the FTC, it gave its view about the moves. As more and more cement producers would integrate the downstream concrete market, the remaining producers would be left with little business opportunities and will not survive. Subsequently, horizontal concentration would increase. The smallest RMC firms that would remain independent would only account for a small share of the market and would not be a significant competitive force. The integrated producers would increase cement prices without facing an important independent bargaining power, the largest RMC firms being taken over. The returns of the smallest RMC firms would therefore be squeezed between a high cement pricing and low concrete pricing by the largest integrated cement producers. As a result, entry in both markets would be less likely due to the lack of business opportunity in the concrete market for new cement entrants and the increasing market power of the incumbent cement producers.

Peck and MacGowan argued that the FTC definition of the relevant market was flawed (Peck and MacGowan, 1967) The FTC had based its findings on State data and in its more detailed analysis on data from what it referred to as the '22 metropolitan areas' From the data, the horizontal concentration ratios were high. But technological innovation, enabling transport in bulk (pneumatic loading and unloading systems) impacted on the relevant geographical market of each cement producer. It enlarged the size of the natural market of the cement plants. Hence, Peck and MacGowan contended that a proper economic assessment should be based on geographical markets that could overlap US States markets. If one would consider these larger markets as the relevant competitive markets, the horizontal concentration ratios would drop dramatically. But Peck and MacGowan argued that anti-competitive issues on vertical integration only arise when horizontal concentration in the cement markets is high. Besides, in their view, the vertical integration wave or the vertical integration reaction chain was not empirically demonstrated. They stressed that the moves were at first backward vertical integration, that is to say, RMC companies investing in cement production. Therefore, it had nothing to do with defensive attempts to foreclose the market.

Other economists pointed out the contradictions in the FTC interpretation (in particular, Liebeler, 1968). The FTC was inconsistent when dealing with the issue of cement price discrimination. On the one hand, it forbade the acquisitions of the large RMC firms on the grounds that, after the acquisitions, the cement producers would price differently between their RMC subsidiaries and the remaining independent RMC firms to get the latter out of the market. On the other hand, it considered it vital to maintain large independent

RMC firms as pro-competitive because of their bargaining power. But precisely, large independent RMC firms make use of their bargaining power to get lower cement prices and therefore introduce price discrimination in the market and benefit from a price advantage to exit the independent smallest RMC firms.

At this point, it remained to get a clear understanding of the flow of vertical integration moves and their economic gains.

Allen (1971) studied the fluctuations of securities of the cement groups on the Exchanges. In most cases, once a takeover bid on an RMC company was announced, the value of the cement security increased. One year later, it was at its highest. But, from then on, the value decreased, below the value prior to the announcement of the bid. The vertical integration strategy proved to be a financial fiasco. Many of the deals ended up in financial losses. Allen put forward the idea that the vertical integration wave had no effect on market foreclosure and had been of no help in the management of the excess capacity production crisis. Ironically, in prohibiting the vertical integration moves, the FTC had protected the cement industry against its own *faux pas*. But was it the role of the antitrust agency?

MacBride modelled the vertical integration wave from the following observation. The cement producers thought that vertical integration would work. The economists of the FTC thought that because it would work it would prove anti-competitive. The academic economists generally thought that it would not be financially successful. To reconcile these opinions, MacBride explained the phenomenon in terms of first-mover advantage. The first to acquire concrete assets would invest in a large RMC company in the most profitable location. The first to duplicate this strategy would still find interesting companies to buy. But the last to join the bandwagon would only get small, scattered and uninteresting RMC companies.[8] Therefore the first producer to make a significant vertical integration move would initiate a race to vertical acquisitions with a fall in profits as a market outcome. Therefore, the cement industry paid a high price for the vertical integration strategy. The costs of acquisitions proved high and excess production capacity remained.

On 6 February 1985, the FTC rescinded its 'Enforcement Policy with Respect to Vertical Mergers in the Cement Industry'. It did not comment on the decision which, actually, did not attract attention. The vertical integration was an issue of the past even if acquisitions in the concrete industry started to pick up again (Huñta, 1990:a&b).

Three main observations deserve to be outlined from the vertical integration case.

In 1967, the FTC ruled on vertical integration not on the basis of a competitive assessment of individual cases[9] but on the basis of the competitive consequences of a flow of vertical moves which would drastically change the market structure. However, it did not have the analytical economic tools to deal with the issue. The economists who backed its ruling did not succeed in formulating clearly the issue at stake and the appropriate economic approach to tackle it (Wilk, 1968; Meehan, 1972). Perhaps it also lacked the legal tools to circumscribe the phenomenon. Therefore it put forward the concept of 'market foreclosure' which proved to have little robustness and little relevance. Then, it was opposed by academics coming from the dominant economic stream (Peck and MacGowan, 1967; Liebeler, 1968). who highlighted the pitfalls of the market foreclosure approach in individual cases of vertical integration. In rescinding the ban on vertical integration, the FTC rallied the view commonly shared by academic economists while some of them were elaborating a theory on waves of strategic business moves (MacBride, 1983).

The shift in the FTC thinking with regard to the working of the cement markets needs to be interpreted in its historical context. From the end of the 1950s to the end of the 1970s, the US antitrust authorities were firmly opposed to vertical integration which they considered anti-competitive. The rulings of the Courts of justice backed this general view. The most well-known decision was the Supreme Court ruling in the Brown Shoe case (Brown Shoe Co. *v.* United States, 1962). The period ended up with another Supreme Court ruling, GTE/Sylvania in 1977. In the economic mainstream, vertical integration was no longer considered *per se* anti-competitive. Instead the view was that it should be individually assessed, according to a 'rule of reason' principle. The view expressed by Peck and MacGowan at the time of the FTC report on the cement industry—that vertical integration was not a competitive issue where the horizontal concentration was little—gained momentum. Johnson and Parkman (1987) commented the 1983 FTC rescind as—at last—the victory of economic analysis over the political approach to antitrust which had prevailed since 1967.

Finally, another factor played an important role. In the mid 1970s, the US cement industry was in deep financial difficulties. Insofar as the FTC prevented horizontal concentration and banned vertical integration, the cement producers diversified their activities (in 1968, Lehigh invested in the furniture, the carpet and the yarn industries). These diversification attempts failed. In the early 1970s, the Clean Air Act increased production costs by 10 per cent by requiring additional plant investment. The industry was no longer able to finance its modernization. From 1974 onwards (starting with the acquisition of National cement by Ciments Vicat, a French producer), foreign producers, most of them European, took over the US cement producers. Foreign ownership accounted for slightly under 5 per cent of the production capacity in 1975; by 1980, it jumped to 22.8 per cent and continued to increase, reaching 46.8 per cent in the mid 1980s (PCA, 1992). In such an economic context, the ban on vertical integration was no longer a main focus of attention.

Conclusion

Economic analysis does not encounter the market in a straightforward dialogue. It weighs on the organization of markets at particular times, specially when a regulatory issue arises. What should be the rules governing markets? How restrictive should they be? Such issues are usually dealt with at the time of litigation cases, and in particular of antitrust cases in the US or competition policy cases in Europe. The encounter between economics and markets is therefore channelled through legal disputes and constrained by the legal dimension.

Important consequences follow.

1. The interaction between economics and markets is a discontinuous process. It is set in motion by the judicial agenda on regulatory issues. In between interactions, markets are cut off from the evolution of academic economics. Another point is that the legal dimension compels the economists to analyse markets in a historical perspective rather than to reflect upon the prospective dynamics of markets and the likely competitive outcome of particular rulings. In the final stages of the basing point case J.M. Clark made the following thoughtful, but disenchanted, remark:

'So the method remains a hybrid, of the baffling sort in which years are spent arguing everything about the case except the effects (legal and economic) of the order that will finally be issued. During the basic litigation, economic considerations are elbowed out or distorted by legalistic exigencies, both sides probably producing about equally bad or irrelevant or one-sided economics. Since serious and realistic consideration of the effects of an order cannot begin until after the order is issued, economic analysis is backward, though the heart of legality in these cases is economic. This is unfortunate, but it seems to be the way our present system works.' (Clark, 1949:431)

2. Since the dialogue between economics and markets is discontinuous—the antitrust cases come out unexpectedly—a gap may develop between the economic thinking of academics and business practices. It has been stressed that the theorization of the vertical integration wave postdated the antitrust cases, and paradoxically occurred when the FTC shifted its attitude towards vertical integration. It is one of the feature of academic economics to re-interpret and debate endlessly on past antitrust cases using new analytical tools and theoretical developments. Thus the competitive effects of the basing point system were still discussed in the 1980s, 40 years after the Supreme Court ruling (Haddock, 1982 and 1990; Benson, Greenhut and Norman, 1990a and 1990b).

3. Because of the publicity in the media, and the judicial form of the investigations, the dialogue between economics and markets takes place through rhetoric and controversy. In the legal process, economists are viewed as experts. When one of them testifies on behalf of the defendants, another one will testify on behalf of the plaintiffs. Therefore, the exchange between economic theory and markets takes place not through direct application of theoretical models to markets situations but rather through the confrontation of contradictory economic analysis. And experts debates before non economists (judges and juries) who decide. So the situation is complicated.

The economist argues in a tricky environment. One economist knows that other economists will deconstruct and oppose his findings. He is also aware that, as expert, he draws his legitimacy from the scientific field. If his contention appears too simple, he can be opposed by more sophisticated analysis from his colleagues. Conversely, if too sophisticated, he will run the risk of burying the case by orienting the debate in a controversy between experts that is obscure to the judges and the juries who make the final decision.[10] The economic analysis will then lose its persuasive power and will be of little impact and added value in the decision making process. It is therefore of vital importance that economists do not trap themselves by sticking to their theoretical perspective and analytical tools. They should allow themselves to grasp the ins and outs of the legal dispute and the thinking of decision makers. Thus, Fetter explained his preference for the uniform f.o.b. mill pricing arguing from a legal perspective. It was a fair and simple pricing rule to implement. In his opinion, allowing price discrimination in particular cases and not in others would mean that an antitrust assessment on a case by case study would prove unworkable. Lawyers and judges are highly interested in economic analytical tools that helped them to delineate and draw clear lines of demarcation in antitrust issues, on admissible business practices, business practices that should be prohibited and business practices that deserve a case by case economic appraisal. Economists can be tempted to play with these expectations, but doing those doing so run the risk of losing their legitimacy.

4. In the legal disputes, economists argue on both sides, the prosecution and the defence. But their status and the way they are perceived, are not symmetrical. A first asymmetry lies in their position. Some of the economists are civil servants of antitrust authorities, or testify on their account. They are supposed to be in charge of the public interest. Others are hired by industries or trade associations. They are connected with private interests and suspected of lacking independent thinking. As a matter of fact, the antitrust economists consider the business practices from an outer perspective. The vision is external to the industry. The economists hired by the industry have an inner perspective which they develop from a reflexive dialogue. The industry looks at itself in the eyes of the economist which acts as a mirror to find out its own substance and potential ways of exonerate itself. The asymmetry and the importance of the economic status were clearly perceived by Fetter, who made use of all the strategies to impose the f.o.b. mill pricing. Paradoxically, J.M. Clark although the economist of the industry, was much less judgmental.

5. Another dissymmetry relates to the legal process, the onus of proof ('*onus probandi*'). In the vertical integration case, the FTC economists had to define a doctrine on vertical integration enabling for indictment. The economists backing the views of the industry did not have to formulate a theory. They would just pinpoint the weaknesses of the FTC argumentation. They were in a cosier situation. Conversely, in other cases, the antitrust authorities stick to the evidence gathered from their investigations and regard the latter as sufficiently convincing to decide upon the existence of an infringement. The economists of the defendants are then left with no other choice than to interpret the seized documents and other pieces of evidence within a theoretical framework in an attempt to exonerate the industry.

Hervé Dumez and Alain Jeunemaître

6. In spite of the ambiguous relationship between economic analysis and legal rulings, the circumstances in which the rules are elaborated provide the economists with material and data to check-proof their models and formulate new economic insights. The concept of 'workable competition' is, as has been illustrated, a direct consequence of the economic debates on the basing point system. And as the basing point and vertical cases illustrate, data and facts on antitrust cases continue to generate new economic analysis in scientific journals long after the Courts' rulings.

Notes

1 'What cement's future hinges on'. *Rock Products*, May 1972, pp. 107.
2 The study will focus on the US antitrust cases although there has been similar cases in Europe (Germany, the UK, the EC) and in Japan. Antidumping cases have come in addition to antitrust cases. See Dumez and Jeunemaître (1997).
3 Previously wood was the main building material and builders made also use of natural cement.
4 The DoJ had, in the very early stages of the case, endorsed a similar view. In its opinion, the two key factors that would enable competition in the cement industry were, the authorization of customer pick-up, which would prevent trucking from being controlled, and non-systematic price discrimination with freight absorption.
5 'Of the more than 100 witnesses heard by the subcommittee, the large majority were small businessmen. The subcommittee was particularly concerned with receiving the views of small-business men in this controversial subject.' (Simon, 1950:50–51)
6 In the earliest 1957 legislation setting up the German competition policy, paragraph 22 states on the control of abuse of dominance and refers to the US concept of 'workable competition'. (Müller-Henneberg and Schwartz, 1958:1166; see also, Kantzenbach, 1966 and Hoppeman, 1967).
7 The RMC companies are the main buyers of cement, concrete being produced from mixing cement with gravel and sand.
8 This view was shared by the business community. As noted the Vice-President of Atlantic cement: 'While perhaps half of the balance [of cement work] is done by contractors buying for state highway work, it is work that is scattered. It is not concentrated. Work on highway jobs may be 75 miles away. It is not the concentrated, high volume tonnage that is easily accessible to the Atlantic Cement Company, for example, its terminals. It forces us into different selling operations—with added transport costs, smaller customers and more salesmen' (US FTC, 1966b:466), or else the opinion expressed by the Chairman of Nicholson Concrete and Supply Co.: 'ease of entry into the concrete business with a few mixers is one thing. Ease of entry into the position on the basis of controlling an important share of markets is something entirely different' (US FTC, 1966b:325).
9 Taken individually, the vertical integration moves involved a small share of the market, adding little credential to the foreclosure market assumption (Johnson and Parkman, 1987).

10 In another cement industry antitrust case, this time in Europe, an economist modelled the competitive game from a game theory perspective. The aim was to give evidence that the decision not to enter the market of a competitor could result from a non-co-operative game between competotprs. The EC Commission in its lengthy decision (158 pages) dismissed the evidence in the following terms: 'The last comment concerns the existence of oligopolies in the various markets, and consequently, the fact that each operator must, before deciding to enter the market of another, take account of the reactions of competitors and of the retaliatory measures which they might take. Without wishing to enter into game theory and the "prisoner's dilemma", it might be pointed out that it is not certain that each operator gains more by remaining on his own market, since game theory also shows that each operator decides to enter the others' market and risk retaliation when it considers that his long-run advantages are greater if he is present on several markets rather than only one. In addition, games between oligopolists are not simple to resolve, since there are many elements of uncertainty involved, and not just the possible retaliation of one operator or another.' (EEC, 1994 § 11.6). The game theory models are complex and according to the various assumptions may result in contradictory findings with potential endless debates among experts.

References

Allen, B.T., (1971), 'Vertical integration and market foreclosure: the case of cement and concrete'. *The Journal of Law and Economics*, No. 4, pp. 251–274.

Benson, B.L., Greenhut, M.L. and George, N., (1990a), 'On the Basing-Point System'. *The American Economic Review*, Vol. 80, No. 4, June, pp. 584–588.

Benson, B.L., Greenhut, M.L. and George, N., (1990b), 'On the Basing-Point System: Reply'. *The American Economic Review*, Vol. 80, No. 4, September, pp. 963–967.

Clark, J.M., (1938), 'Basing point of methods of price quoting'. *Canadian Journal of Economics and Political Science*, November, Vol. IV, No. 4, pp. 477–489.

Clark, J.M., (1940), 'Toward a Concept of Workable Competition'. *The American Economic Review*, Vol. XXX, No. 2, June, pp. 241–256. Fetter, Frank Albert, (1948), 'Exit basing point pricing'. *The American Economic Review*, Vol. 38, December, pp. 815–827.

Clark, J.M., (1949), 'The Law and Economics of Basing Points: Appraisal and Proposals'. *The American Economic Review*, Vol. XXXIX, No. 2, pp. 430–447.

EEC, (1994), Commission Decision of 30 November 1993 Relating to a Proceeding under Article 85 of the EC Treatise (Cases IV/33.126 and 33.322–Cement). *Official Journal of the European Communities*, L343, Vol. 37, 30 December, pp. 343/1–343/158.

Huhta, R.S., (1990a), 'Another look at vertical integration'. *Rock Products*, February, pp. 15–16.

Huhta, R.S., (1990b), 'Another look at vertical integration'. *Rock Products*, March, pp. 13–14.

Johnson, R.N. and Parkman, A.M., (1983), 'Spatial monopoly, Non-zero Profits and Entry Deterrence: the Case of Cement'. *Review of Economics and Statistics*, August, Vol. 65, No. 3, pp. 431–439.

Johnson, R.N. and Parkman, A.M., (1987a), 'Spatial competition and vertical integration; Cement and Concrete Revisited: Comment'. *The American Economic Review*, September, pp. 750–753.

Johnson, R.N. and Parkman, A.M., (1987b), 'The Role of Ideas in Antitrust Policy Toward Vertical Mergers: Evidence from the FTC Cement-Ready Mixed Concrete Cases.' *The Antitrust Bulletin*, Winter, pp. 841–883.

Kamerschen, D.R., (1974), 'Predatory Pricing, vertical integration and market foreclosure: the case of ready-mix concrete in Memphis'. *Industrial Organization Review*, 1974, Vol. 2, pp. 143–168.

Liebeler, W.J., (1968), 'Toward a consumer's antitrust law: the Federal Trade Commission and vertical mergers in the cement industry'. *UCLA Law Review*, 1968, Vol. 15, pp. 1153–1202.

Loescher, S.M., (1959), *Imperfect Collusion in the Cement Industry*. Cambridge (MA.): Harvard University Press.

McBride, M.E., (1983), 'Spatial competition and vertical integration; cement and concrete revisited'. *American Economic Review*, December, Vol. 73, No. 5, pp. 1011–1022.

Machlup, F., (1949), *The Basing Point System* Philadelphia: Blakiston.

Meehan, J.W. Jr., (1972), 'Vertical Foreclosure in the Cement industry: A Comment'. *The Journal of Law and Economics*, Vol. XV(2), October, pp. 461–471.

Moomaw, R.L., (1976), 'Vertical integration, predation and monopolization: the symbiotic relationship between the cement and ready mix concrete industries'. *Industrial Organization Review*, Vol. 4, pp. 117–119.

Müller-Henenberg, H. and Schwartz, G., (1958), *Gesetz gegen Wettbewerbsbeschränkugnen. Kommentar.* Köln/Berlin: Carl Heymanns Verlag KG.

Haddock, D.D., (1982), 'Basing-point pricing: competitive vs. collusive theories'. *The American Economic Review*, Vol. 72, No. 3, June, pp. 289–306.

Haddock, D.D., (1990), 'On the Basing-Point System: a Comment'. *The American Economic Review*, Vol. 80, No. 4, September, pp. 957–962.

Hoppmann, E., (1967), 'Workable Competition als Wettbewerbspolitisches Konzept' in *Theoretische und institutionnelle Grundlagen der Wirtschaftspolitik*, Berlin: Festschrift für Theodor Wessels.

Kantzenbach, E., (1966), *Die Funktionsfähigketi des Wettbewerbs*. Göttingen.

Peck, M.J. and McGowan, J.J., (1967), 'Vertical Integration in Cement: a Critical Examination of the FTC Staff Report'. *The Antitrust Bulletin*, Vol. XII, Summer, p. 505 et seq.

Phlips, L., (1993), 'Parallélisme de compotements et pratiques concertées'. *Revue d'économie industrielle*, n° 61, 1ᵉʳ trimestre, pp. 25–44.

Phlips, L., (1995), *Competition Policy: A Game-theoric Perspective*. Cambridge: Cambridge University Press.

Portland Cement Association, (1992), *US and Canadian Cement Industry: Plant Acquisition and Ownership Report—1974 to Present*. PCA: Skokie.

Simon, W., (1950), *Geographic Pricing Practices (Basing-Point Selling)*. Chicago: Callaghan and Company.

Stearn, E.Q., (1966), 'FTC heeds cement industry pleas'. *Rock Products*, August 1966, pp. 67–120.

US District Court for the District of Arizona (1983), In *Re: cement and concrete antitrust litigation*. Appendix D: *Plaintiffs joint narrative summary of litigation and statement of central facts and legal issues*. MDL docket No. 296, PHX-MLR (MS). September 7.

US Federal Trade Commission, (1932), *Report of the Federal Trade Commission on*

Price Basis Inquiry, the Basing-Point formula and Cement Prices. Washington.

US Federal Trade Commission, (1933), *Cement Industry, Letter from the Chairman of the Federal Trade Commission, Transmitting in Response to Senate Resolution No. 448, Seventy-First Congress, A Report Relative to Competitive Conditions in the Cement Industry*. Washington.

US Federal Trade Commission (1966a), *Economic Report on Mergers and Vertical Integration in the Cement Industry. Staff Report to the Federal Trade Commission*. Washington DC: US Government Printing Office, April.

US Federal Trade Commission, (1966b), *FTC Public Hearings on Vertical Integration in the Cement Industry*. Washington DC: 12 July 1966.

Wilk, D., (1968), 'Vertical Integration in Cement Revisited: A Comment on Peck and McGowan'. *The Antitrust Bulletin*, pp. 619–647.

An essay on framing and overflowing: economic externalities revisited by sociology

Michel Callon

When reviewing the conditions required for the existence of markets, no concept is more useful or appropriate than that of 'externality'. The concept of externality is effectively central both to economies and to economics. So an attempt to clarify its significance and scope represents a suitable point of departure for renewed efforts at co-operation between sociologists and economists. Rather than highlighting the limitations and weaknesses of the concept with a view to attacking the limitations and weaknesses of economic theory, I intend to show just how useful it is as a tool for understanding the dynamics of markets, drawing upon sociology as an additional resource.

I shall approach this task from the perspective of the sociologist of science and techniques. This will allow me not only to highlight the role of investment—in particular technological—in the emergence of economic agents that are capable of strategies and calculation; it will also serve as an incentive to take the 'performative' role of the sciences—and hence also of economics and sociology—more seriously.

I shall start by putting my economist's hat on in order briefly to remind my fellow sociologists of the various ways in which the concept of externality can be defined, together with its practical and theoretical implications. This will lead on to a discussion of the various mechanisms upon which the concept is predicated. I shall then touch first upon what I shall here refer to as 'framing/overflowing' and upon the various issues associated with the identification, measuring and containment of such overflows. I shall subsequently focus my attention on the role played by the technosciences in the proliferation of overflows, highlighting the active role of the social sciences—alongside the natural sciences—in the identification and management of externalities. Finally, I shall draw one of the most important conclusions suggested by this exercise: that the market is not simply expanding, but rather continuously emerging and re-emerging, and that its consolidation requires constant and substantial investments.

1. Definition(s) and issues

1.1. *Definitions*

Since this text is intended as much for sociologists as for economists, I shall start by spending a little time defining the concept of externality, since many sociologists are currently unfamiliar with it.

The simplest approach is to start with an example. A metallurgical factory produces aluminium and emits chlorinated fumes. These spread out over the countryside, representing a threat to neighbouring livestock and crop farmers. In order to combat or eliminate the noxious or toxic effects of these fumes (which cause weight loss in livestock and reduce crop yields), the affected farmers must make certain investments. It is here that the concept of externality becomes pertinent, in the sense that in the absence of any incentives to do so, the chemical company fails to account in its calculations for the costs that it is imposing upon agents (in this case, the neighbouring farmers) who, despite the fact that they are penalized by its activities, remain external to the sphere of economic relationships in which the company itself operates. This failure gives rise to externalities—in this case negative. The farmers' interests are compromised and they are unable to assert their own preferences since, in order to remain commercially viable, they must make investments for which they can not negotiate any compensation.

But externalities can also be positive. Consider the example of a pharmaceutical company with research and development (R&D) laboratories that use screening methods to test large numbers of molecules prior to undertaking clinical tests once the various active substances have been identified. To protect its findings and the potential profits it can expect from related monopolies, the company files patents which disclose some of the information that has ben produced. The latter thus becomes available to competitors and may inspire them to rethink the direction of their own research. Such transpositions are all the more straightforward and productive because they are predicated upon very similar knowledge bases (Richardson, 1972). Competitors may thus benefit, free of charge, from the efforts and investments of a company which has had to bear the associated costs and risks on its own. This case is a classic example of 'positive externalities', the mirror image of the preceding kind. It is easy enough to show that such situations are commonplace wherever business activities result in the production of information with the potential for large-scale application.

It appears that the concept could be extended to include behaviour which is not exclusively economic in nature. Take the case of a teenager living in a terraced house who decides to arrange a birthday party. The celebrations go on late into the night. Driven by a heady mix of booze and bopping, the volume of the music steadily increases. Unfortunately he did not invite his neighbours to the party. If we imagine that there is no legislation banning such late-night festivities, the situation becomes comparable to that of the factory polluting the surrounding environment. The person holding the party maximizes his own well-being, but only to the detriment of his neighbours, who have no legal means of eliminating the source of the nuisance and so must devote a portion of their resources, time and energy to combating the noise. Effects of this kind are not necessarily negative in themselves. If my house is off the beaten track and my neighbour decides to build a service road, my well-being is improved without any related expenditure on my part. If, like me, my neighbour enjoys French Baroque music and plays it loudly enough for me to hear every note clearly, my well-being is enhanced despite the fact that I have not had to make any investment myself.

The analysis could be extended still further. The applicability of such a generalization is clearly demonstrated by the now classic sociological issues underlying the systematic negation of the investment and work required to create a situation which subsequently appears to be an entirely natural 'given'. In this case, certain agents pursue courses of action the costs of which are borne by other agents, with no visible transfer taking place.[1] The concept is strikingly expressed by the American feminist slogan of the '70s: 'Behind every successful man is an exhausted woman'.

I won't discuss such wider applications of the concept of externality, which poses the now classic question of how best to extend economic categories (such as cost, preference or interest) to cover all human activity. I shall restrict the discussion to an issue that is more specific, more technical and also more interesting: namely the indirect (ie, non-commercial) effects of commercial activities unfolding within a framework of market relationships.

The preceding examples and the restriction that I have just imposed on this discussion suggest the following definition of the concept of externality:

Let A, B, C etc. be agents involved in a commercial transaction, or more generally in the negotiation of a contract. In the course of the transaction or contract negotiation, these agents express their preferences or interests and then evaluate the various possible decisions arising from them. The decision they finally take has positive or negative effects, here referred to as externalities, on another set of agents X, Y and Z (as distinct from A, B, and C); the latter are not involved in this transaction or negotiation, either because they have no way of intervening or because they have no wish to do so.

1.2. Issues at stake

In itself, the existence of externalities is not in the least outrageous. That certain people should pay for others or profit from others without bearing the associated costs is not disgusting or disturbing. Such transfers are inevitable: after all, the laws of thermodynamics teach us that you cannot have order without paying the price of chaos. So it is not on moral grounds, but on the grounds of collective efficiency and the optimization of resource allocation that the existence of externalities and various possible ways of eliminating them preoccupy economists to such an extent.

In economics, the concept of externality is linked to a more general category: that of market failures.[2] At this point, it is important to obviate any misunderstandings. The term 'market failure' does not mean that nothing good was produced. Its meaning is more precise: as expressed in terms of efficiency or in terms of the provision of socially desirable goods, the best result that could have been obtained was not achieved in practice.

So what are the consequences of externalities in terms of the role played by the market and prices in the allocation of resources? Within the framework of economic doctrine, the answer to this question is simple. Externalities, whether positive or negative, render the market (at least partially) inefficient, because they are responsible for a gap between private marginal income and marginal social costs. The previous sentence might seem obscure to a non-economist. But the argument is easy to understand. Take the factory mentioned earlier, belching out chlorinated fumes that pollute the surrounding countryside. According to the hypotheses of standard economic theory on this subject, the factory will set the volume of its aluminium production in such a way as to ensure that its marginal income (ie, income corresponding to the last ton or other unit of aluminium sold) is equal to the additional cost incurred in producing this extra ton or unit. According to a number of hypotheses—space, alas, prevents us from discussing them here—economic theory shows that the equilibrium, resulting from the equalization of marginal costs and income, is an optimal one. But if externalities are present, this private calculation, which is supposed automatically to guarantee a social optimum, is biased: it does not take into account the investments which the farmers must make in order to protect themselves from the fumes. In this case, in the absence of appropriate incentives, the market—as a device for obtaining the social optimum—is deficient. This reasoning applies equally to what are known as 'positive' externalities: a medical pharmaceutical company can sit back and wait for its competitors to invest in R&D in the expectation of profiting from the results without spending anything at all. In their anxiety to prevent others from taking advantage of them, players in the sector avoid committing resources, and this in turn means that the collective welfare is substantially lower than it could be if appropriate investment incentives were in place. Negative externalities imply social costs that are not taken into account by private decision-makers; positive externalities discourage private investment by socializing the benefits.

The definition of externalities seems to be clear. In reality, it raises a series of questions which I now propose to examine in more detail, and which will allow me to outline the terms of a new contract of cooperation between economics and constructivist sociology.

2. Framing and overflowing

Beneath the concept of externality lies the more fundamental concept of framing, which implies the possibility of identifying overflows and containing them. Economists do not use this concept, which I am borrowing from Goffman for the purposes of this argument. Once I have reminded my readers of its significance I will emphasize, along with constructivist sociology, the size of the investments required to frame interactions and contain overflows.

2.1. Framing interactions

In his description of interpersonal relationships (of which the relationships involved in arranging the negotiation of a contract represent one archetype), Goffman resorts to the concept of the frame

(Goffman, 1971). The frame establishes a boundary within which interactions—the significance and content of which are self-evident to the protagonists—take place more or less independently of their surrounding context. Goffman emphasizes the dual nature of this framing process. Clearly it presupposes actors who are bringing to bear cognitive resources as well as forms of behaviour and strategies which have been shaped and structured by previous experience: the actors are capable of agreeing (an agreement which does not have to be explicit) on the frame within which their interactions will take place and on the courses of action open to them. But the framing process does not just depend on this commitment by the actors themselves; it is rooted in the outside world, in various physical and organizational devices. This is why framing puts the outside world in brackets, as it were, but does not actually abolish all links with it.

In order to illustrate this definition, Goffman—who loves theatrical metaphors—frequently takes the example of a stage performance. Given the series of interconnected expectations upon which such performances are predicated, they could not take place without the tacit agreement of all those taking part. The spectators know what 'watching a theatrical production' entails and what rules they should obey (so for example they know that as the curtain falls in preparation for the next act, they may break the silence by coughing or clearing their throats). In the same way, the actors on stage know what is expected of them, as do the usherettes and cashiers. But these tacit agreements would swiftly fall apart if they were not contained within a suitable physical framework. A whole series of material means are used to demarcate the theatrical space and the actions that take place within it: the building itself; its internal architecture; the bell, dimmed lights and raising of the curtain that indicate the start of the performance. Similarly, the end of the performance is framed by a series of devices linked in such a way as to make the uncertain spectator aware that this is 'THE END' rather than just another interval. The various elements that form the physical frame are themselves contained within an institutional framework (author's rights, safety regulations, tax incentives etc.) which helps to ensure their preservation and reproduction.

This 'bracketing', which assumes that boundaries are drawn between the actors interacting with one another on the one hand and the rest of the world on the other, does not imply a total absence of relationships. On the contrary: for Goffman, framing would be inexplicable if there was not a network of connections with the outside world: 'We cannot say the worlds are created one spot because, whether we refer to a game of cards or to teamwork during surgery, use is usually made of traditional equipment having a social history of its own in the wider society and a wide consensus of understanding regarding the meanings that are to be generated from it', (Goffman, 1961). Goffman thus emphasizes the fact that everything mobilized in the framed setting guarantees, simply by virtue of its presence, that the outside world is also present. The concept of habitus proposed by Elias and Bourdieu is clearly one way of describing this link and the manner in which it is expressed in the course of the action, but Goffman suggests that over and above the human beings themselves and their disciplined bodies, objects and things, the theatre stage, its walls and sounds, all play a role in setting up these interdependencies.[3]

This concept of framing is easily applied to the interactions that interest economists, whether in the form of classic commercial transactions or contract negotiations. To negotiate a contract or perform a commercial transaction effectively presupposes a framing of the action without which it would be impossible to reach an agreement, in the same way that in order to play a game of chess, two players must agree to submit to the rules and sit down at a chessboard which physically circumscribes the world within which the action will take place.

It is possible to respond to this concept of framing, which is essential to any understanding and description of interactions of whatever kind, by adopting one of two diametrically opposed attitudes which I will now examine in turn. Each of them gives preference to one of the two dimensions of framing, either by emphasizing the closure of the interactions on themselves and the role of the players' mutual agreement in creating this closed situation or, conversely, by highlighting the omnipresence of connections with the outside world and the irrepressible and productive overflows which the latter encourage.

2.2. *When framing is the norm and overflows are leaks*

The first approach tends to believe that framing is the norm—in the double sense of something that is desirable and also statistically predominant—and that overflows are exceptions which must be contained and channelled with the help of appropriate investments.

This position is adopted by micro-sociology, which focuses on interpersonal relationships without considering the factors that sustain these interactions.[4] It is also popular in economic theory, where one of the central preoccupations is to postulate the existence of configurations within which a series of agents develop (commercial) relationships with each other that are sufficient in themselves to account for all co-ordination requirements. The concept of framing indicates that such closure is possible: individuals, whether two or 2,000 in number, whether by communicating through prices or taking turns to negotiate contracts, together regulate problems of resource allocation or property transfer while simultaneously establishing a temporarily impenetrable barrier between themselves and the rest of the world. In this way, any two agents can undertake—in an agreement that depends solely on the exercise of their wills—to interact in a negotiation and then return to anonymity once the transaction is complete. This effectively postulates the actual possibility that a market could exist as a system of relationships between agents (consumers and producers) who reach an equilibrium or harmonious accord.

Framing defines the effectiveness of the market because, in this closed interactional space, each individual can take into account the viewpoint of every other individual when reaching a decision. In this sense, it is possible to assert that externalities are simply the results of imperfections or failures in the framing process. Yet in certain cases framing is either impossible to achieve or is deliberately transgressed by the actors:[5] this produces overflows which cause the barriers to become permeable. Economic theory seems predisposed to the hypothesis that these overflows should be regarded as accidental and consequently that framing should be perceived as the norm towards which everything should tend.

By prioritizing the creation of frames designed to avoid premature overflows, economists are obliged to focus much of their attention on the various forms of overflow that can take place and how best to contain them; ie, on all the repercussions of the contracts linking A, B and C on those not involved in the negotiations (X, Y and Z). This has two consequences. The first is to cause economists to focus their efforts—with evident success—on the identification of leaks and the formulation of devices for creating more effective frames.[6] The second is to facilitate, in certain typical situations, the establishment of tried-and-tested frames: as recently shown by DHL's decision to set up its European hub in Strasbourg, the harmful effects associated with the presence of an airport are no longer simply accounted for after the event; they are brought into the frame in the initial stages of contract negotiation.

2.3. *Overflows are the norm: framing is expensive and always imperfect*

The second attitude, typical of constructivist sociology in particular, takes the view that overflowing is the rule; that framing—when present at all—is a rare and expensive outcome; in short, is very costly to set up. Without the theatre building and its physical devices; without years of training and hours of rehearsal put in by the actors; without the habitual mindset of the audience and carefully written dramas which deliberately limit the range of preprogrammed interactions, the framing of a stage performance would be quite simply inconceivable. This viewpoint is thus the exact opposite of the preceding one: instead of regarding framing as something that happens of itself, and overflows as a kind of accident which must be put right, overflows are the rule and framing is a fragile, artificial result based upon substantial investments.[7] Constructivist sociology does not deny that it is possible to achieve such clarity or put such frameworks in place, nor that such an objective is worth pursuing (see below for a more detailed discussion of this point). But it is primarily interested in showing that such a framing process, in addition to requiring expensive physical and symbolic devices, is always incomplete and that without this incompleteness would in fact be wholly ineffectual.

Let us start by considering the concept of embeddedness first put forward by Polanyi (Polanyi, 1975) and subsequently taken up by Granovetter (Granovetter, 1985). This does not so much represent yet another expression of the implacable hostility between sociology and economics[8] as an affirmation of the omnipresence of overflows. E. Friedberg rightly highlights the habitual misinterpretation of this concept (Friedberg, 1993). Its significance, which is both profound and radical (and incidentally the main theme of Granovetter's celebrated article) centres on the hypothesis that the objectives, intentions, interests and projects of a given actor, and indeed his or her will, are not simply a set of attributes that define his or her own personal, unchangeable identity which the actor could simply by intellectual application, access or express—even unconsciously—if she or he were given the opportunity (this being the meaning of the expression 'to reveal one's preferences'). Nor are they the result of values, norms or institutions which reduce the actor to the status o the 'cultural dope' so justifiably ridiculed by Garfinkel. In fact, they cannot be dissociated from the network of interdependencies in which the actor is enmeshed and to which he or she is continuously contributing (Burt, 1992), (Callon and Law, 1997). In short, the actor's ontology is variable: his or her objectives, interests, will and thus identity are caught up in a process of continual reconfiguration, a process that is intimately related to the constant reconfiguration of the network of interactions in which he or she is involved.

From this perspective, all framing thus represents a violent effort to extricate the agents concerned from this network of interactions and push them onto a clearly demarcated 'stage' which has been specially prepared and fitted out. But their links with the 'outside' world—links that betray their existence simply by the fact that the agents are simultaneously involved in other worlds from which they can never be wholly detached—cannot be reduced to personal relationships alone.[9] Overflows have many sources and can flow in many directions, which tends to indicate that frames are even more problematic than Granovetter suggests.

Take the example of a research contract drawn up between an academic research unit and a commercial enterprise, nowadays a commonplace occurrence. Such a contract does not bind one human being to another, but one legal entity to another legal entity. Each of them is a more or less integrated complex comprised of human beings, equipment (instruments, machinery), libraries and financial resources. The contract provides for the performance of certain actions, defines the terms under which any property rights arising from the results of these actions will be shared, and defines the conditions for monitoring the proper performance of the contract. The text of the contract sets out the joint venture's objectives. The definition of these objectives is frequently—but not exclusively—couched in terms of concepts and ideas borrowed from accepted scientific theory (for example: 'the work shall contribute to the development of an enzymatic electrode capable of functioning in aqueous media' (Cassier, 1995)); it also implies the application and/or possible development of experimental tools or procedures which are mentioned or described in a wealth of technical detail; it generally includes the name(s) of the researcher(s) or research team(s) who will be in charge of the research programme. The contractual undertakings may be more or less specific or complete; clearly all this is dependent on the degree of stability and predictability of the relevant area of research. Clauses providing for the renegotiation of the contract if certain events should take place may also be appended. In short, the aim of the contract is to frame the interaction in as unambiguous a way as possible and/or formulate an agreement on any reframing procedures which may have to be implemented.

253

Michel Callon

But what are the conditions governing the stability (or lack of it) of a contract—or rather, of the framing process that it applies by defining a limited number of actions to be undertaken in an infinite world of possible relationships? As many have remarked since Durkheim, the framing of a contract presupposes the existence of courts of law, as well as the existence of a body of legal texts defining, for example, the content and scope of property rights, as well as the existence of solicitors entrusted with recording the state of knowledge held by each of the contracting parties before the contract comes into force, and so on. But—and this is more interesting for our purposes—such general devices, all of which have a cost, in fact only play a peripheral role, as Williamson clearly perceived. The actual text of the contract introduces a series of tangible and intangible elements (concepts, materials, substances, experimental devices, researchers etc.) which help to delineate and structure the frame within which it will be performed. The contract could not be framed and 'fulfilled' without the participation or requisition of each of these elements: they are involved in the same plot, the same scenario; each of them is obliged to play a predefined role. The actions within the frame are prepared and structured by the equipment, the theoretical statements, the skilled persons of the researchers and technicians, the procedures and reports; all these elements ensure that they are not scattered or dispersed. But—and here we come to the crux of the argument—each of these elements, at the very same time as it is helping to structure and frame the interaction of which it more or less forms the substance, is simultaneously a potential conduit for overflows. The researchers interact with colleagues, take part in conferences, may move temporarily or permanently to different companies or research laboratories. Scientific ideas and concepts circulate on the Internet or through the intermediary of scientific journals, becoming the subject matter for debates and controversies which refine their meaning both within the group and outside it. If theories did not have a public life, they would not exist as certified knowledge. As for the instruments, materials or substances: they are calibrated, standardized and exist in various locations; the way they are modified or perform in one location may have direct repercussions on their performance in other locations.

The different elements constituting the research programme and by extension the research contract are simultaneously resources and intermediaries (Callon, 1991); they frame the interactions and represent openings onto wider networks, to which they give access. It is this dual nature that guarantees the productivity of the entire complex represented by the programme which thus becomes capable of capitalizing to some extent on what is being done elsewhere, on what has been done in the past and on what will be done in the future. No contract is capable of, or has an interest in, systematically suppressing all connections, burning all bridges or eliminating the dual nature of every element involved. Which is why the heterogeneous elements, that are linked together in order to frame the contract and its performance, in reality take part in its overflowing: and it is precisely because they are sources of overflows that they make the contract productive. This can be expressed in terms of a paradox: a totally successful frame would condemn the contract to the sterile reiteration of existing knowledge.[10] It is therefore illusory to suppose that one can internalize every externality by drawing up an all-embracing contract that provides for every eventuality, just as it would be erroneous to equate the incompleteness of the frame with the incompleteness of the contract: the potential sources of overflow are to be found in precisely those elements that give it its solidity, rather than in any areas left unmentioned.

To recap: (i) framing is costly because overflows happen all the time, since they are fed by multiple sources and flow down multiple channels. Framing cannot be achieved by contractual incentives alone, because it is bound up with the equipment, objects and specialists involved in the interaction: it is they who, in their stubborn and obstinate way—to paraphrase a suggestive remark by Whitehead—ensure that certain courses of action are followed and at the same time generate externalities; (ii) this costly framing process is necessarily incomplete: first because a wholly hermetic frame is a contradiction in terms, and second because flows are always bidirectional, overflows simply being the inevitable corollary of the requisite links with the surrounding environment. Without overflows, it would not be feasible to add value locally; thus the only way to stamp out 'reverse engineering' would be to bring all industrial and commercial activity to a standstill! It is because an actor's output gets necessarily beyond her entire control so as to generate profits, that the actor him- or herself is unable to avoid externalities.[11]

3. In order to be framed, overflows must be made measurable

In a recent article, Williamson defines the economic approach as follows: 'Calculativeness is the general condition that I associate with the economic approach and with the progressive extension of economics into the related social sciences' (Williamson, 1993). Without calculative agents and without the minimum level of information that allows such calculations to take place, market co-ordination is bound to fail. This is why economists—and it is one of their great virtues—demonstrate such an obstinate desire to define the conditions in which actions become calculable, and to think up devices that will encourage such conditions to emerge. It is by allowing each agent to have preferences, to hierarchize them, and then to reveal and negotiate them—in a word, to calculate his or her interests, express them and defend them—that transactions are allowed to take place, resulting in a robust and legitimate, if not necessarily, optimal re-allocation of resources and property rights. It is at precisely this point that sociology can make its contribution. By focusing on the omnipresence of overflows, on their usefulness, but also on the cost of actions intended (partially) to contain them, constructivist sociology highlights the importance of the operations required to identify and measure these overflows. It also encourages us to question the mechanisms used to create frames by suggesting ways in which the social sciences might help to develop or to confine such such spaces of calculability.

3.1. Identifying and measuring

The very definition of externalities (see 1.1 above) implies that it is possible to identify not only actors A, B and C but also the effects produced by their activities. Only once this double identification has taken place is it possible to draw up a list of agents who benefit or suffer from these externalities (X, Y and Z).

These processes are often regarded as self-evident and self-explanatory. That this is not in fact the case is clearly shown by the controversies surrounding the reality of the existence of externalities. Three problems arise:

(i) The first is how to identify the effects, ie, how to prove the reality of the overflow. The latter—and this is a point that sociologists will take pleasure in highlighting—cannot be intangible. For something to happen that affects agents outside the frame, it is essential that something should cross or break through the boundary drawn up round the commercial interactions within the frame. Let us call these entities that secretly cross the frame's boundaries intermediaries: they may be chemical substances, sound waves rippling outwards, texts, scientific articles, patents, or researchers or engineers on secondment or moving to other institutions. No externality can exist without relationships; no link can exist unless it follows a trajectory plotted by a material object acting as the medium for the externality. The existence of the latter is predicated upon this simple but unavoidable quality of tangibility: for an overflow to take place, something must overflow. But identifying the actual intermediaries is anything but straightforward.

Some of them, by their very nature, are difficult to identify; others, like spy planes, are deliberately camouflaged by those who send or receive them. Between industrial espionage at one extreme and the publication of patents at the other, for example, there is an entire gamut of intermediate practices which are more or less easy to track down; between the colourful pollutant that indicates the presence of a leak and the odourless, colourless fumes that baffle the most vigilant observer, there is a wide variety of effluents that are more or less easy to identify. In short, with very few exceptions, specific work must be done in order to provide incontrovertible proof of the simple existence of an overflow or leak, implying at the very least the implementation of monitoring procedures and sensors.

Like the natural sciences, the social sciences are obviously involved in these devices, which without them could not exist. When a sociologist demonstrates that hauliers are effectively relying on car drivers to subsidize the cost of their business activities, he is taking part in the process of designing and implementing such sensors. When an economist formulates methods of calculation and constructs proxies designed to test for the existence of technological spillovers (another term for overflows) from one industrial sector to another, he is contributing to this endless tracking process. The aim of the process is to map, as realistically as possible, the trajectories of the various intermediaries which are constantly escaping from the interactional frames that gave birth to them and scattering down a multiplicity of unpredictable pathways. Similarly, a chemist taking and analysing water or atmospheric samples is participating in this immense work of identification; occasionally it turns into a real-life police inquiry, as in the infamous case of the Seveso barrels.

(ii) Providing proof of the tangible existence of overflows is inextricably linked to the identification of their sources and impacts. It is not enough to demonstrate the reality and consistency of overflows; it is also necessary to establish who is responsible for them and who is affected by them. Once again, the effort required is often immense. Various environmental issues provide dramatic evidence of this. It is quite possible to uncover trafficking in toxic waste between Germany and France without necessarily being able to trace the channel back to its source. In some cases, establishing the nature and tangible existence of the effects of overflows presupposes ever-increasing levels of investment. Are CFCs really responsible for the hole in the ozone layer? What are the consequences of global warming, for whom? Does asbestos cause damage to health? Can prions from mad cows be transmitted to human beings and if so, are they communicated through animal feed? Above what levels of atmospheric concentration of dioxin do the lesions caused in cells become irreversible?

In order to draw up these two lists—the list of sources (A, B and C in our earlier definition) and the list of targets (X, Y and Z)—specific studies must be undertaken, sometimes obliging us to create appropriate instruments. The situation is further complicated by the fact that the agents concerned may very well not possess an individual existence or identity until such time as the overflows have been confirmed. In this case, the identity of the group and the awareness of its members that they form a part of it are the outcome of the process of discovering and highlighting the externalities. Riverside farmers in the polluted Loue region; pregnant women under 30 who were prescribed thalidomide; manufacturers of luxury goods who export their products to South-East Asia only to become the 'victims' of counterfeiters: none of them existed as clearly defined groups with interests to defend and a voice to make themselves heard until researchers had succeeded in proving—albeit in ways that are always open to contention—the reality and nature of the overflows involved. There are many other examples of the kind of investigative effort required—involving experts and counter-experts, measuring instruments and diagnostics—in order to arrive at an acceptable description of the externalities and agents involved.

The devices that allow us to visualize the existence of the externalities play a crucial role in this descriptive process. They play a potent part in the formation of the groups concerned and in the growth of their self-awareness: when Parisians read in their daily newspapers that the pollution index has risen above the danger level, or illuminated signs inform the citizens of Florence that ozone concentrations are above the critical threshold, they find it easy to experience themselves either as the victims of motor traffic or conversely, as the drivers responsible for environmental pollution. This real-life experience—sometimes referred to as subjectivity—is largely dependent on the instruments used to identify overflows.

(iii) From the perspective of economic theory, it is not enough to

258   © The Editorial Board of The Sociological Review 1998

record—those familiar with debates within the social sciences unrelated to economics will have gathered that I would prefer to say: perform—these externalities. Overflows are devoid of economic significance unless they give rise to evaluations and measurements. The theory of externalities requires a metrological framework—ie, measuring instruments—that allows the different agents to negotiate an agreement by calculating their respective interests. The possibility and viability of this negotiation both depend on the availability of instruments capable of producing incontrovertible measurements: clearly no negotiation can sidestep the need to respond to issues concerning the extent and scope of the overflows in question. For the farmer working alongside the polluting factory to be able to define his interests and quantify the impact of the overflows on the efficiency of his operation, he must have recourse to legitimate, recognized measuring instruments.

Without calibrated sensors, without epidemiological studies, no negotiation is possible. Agents are unable to establish the cause of their problems or benefits, or the extent of their losses or gains; so it is clear that no compromise can be reached in the absence of such a metrological structure. This is another point at which the natural and social sciences can make a contribution. The chemist who perfects an instrument which is officially approved and can be moved from one place to another without detriment to its performance is providing 'objective' data, usually quantifiable, which allows the agents to measure the externalities and enter into rational negotiation (Mallard, 1996b).[12] The econometrician who uses patent statistics to measure the overflow from one sector to another is clearly taking part in such an exercise, as is the psychosociologist who uses psychometric scales to rank personality disorders that may be due to the sufferers' social environments or the potentially detrimental actions of certain agents.

Once the overflows, source agents and target agents have all been correctly identified and described, and once measuring instruments for quantifying and comparing them have been set up, it becomes possible to reframe the interactions. At this point it is meaningful to assert that X, Y and Z should be allowed to participate in negotiations concerning contracts between A, B and C from which they were formerly excluded. This is the tangible result of the investments we have just described in all their scope and diversity: to give the option of internalizing the externalities, or to put it another way, of reframing hitherto uncontained overflows. These investments apply and produce both knowledge, in that they cause hitherto invisible links to appear, and also a reconfigured collective in which these now visible and calculable links have been renegotiated. The social sciences contribute to this dynamic.

3.2. *Tracing the mechanisms by which controversial situations— where overflowing is the rule—become calculable, in other words capable of being framed*

For calculative agents to be able to calculate the decisions they take, they must at the very least be able to a) draw up a list of possible world states; b) hierarchize and rank these world states; c) identify and describe the actions required to produce each of the possible world states. Once these actions have become calculable, transactions and negotiations can take place between the different agents. In the light of the discussion in the preceding section, I shall now concentrate on the role of the technosciences in the dynamics of overflows and on the possible contributions that could be made by sociology and economics respectively towards framing them and making them calculable.

(i) In 'hot' situations, everything becomes controversial: the identification of intermediaries and overflows, the distribution of source and target agents, the way effects are measured. These controversies, which indicate the absence of a stabilized knowledge base, usually involve a wide variety of actors. The actual list of actors, as well as their identities, will fluctuate in the course of the controversy itself and they will put forward mutually incompatible descriptions of future world states.

A. Rip and myself have suggested that these highly confused situations should be given the name of 'hybrid forums', because facts and values have become entangled to such an extent that it is no longer possible to distinguish between two successive stages: first, the production and dissemination of information or knowledge, and second, the decision-making process itself. Such forums have been proliferating ever since the emergence of the controversy over the hole in the ozone layer in 1974. The crisis relating to mad cow disease is a classic example: here, the turmoil has reached its apogee, foreshadowing situations which will probably become very common in the near future. This hybrid forum is overflowing continuously, with an ever-growing, ever-more-varied cast of characters beside which Leporello's *catalogo* pales into insignificance. By turns we hear from vets, farmers, manufacturers of animal feed, proponents of Thatcherite deregulation, Cordelia (daughter of the British agricultural minister, who appeared on television with her father, eating a beef-burger with evident enjoyment), Brussels, the British government denouncing protectionism, the Germans (accused in passing of 'perfidy' by the British), outraged members of the public, the media, prions (or rather the biologists studying them), butchers frantically acquiring every quality certificate going, politicians losing their heads. The controversy lurches first one way, then the other—because nothing is certain, neither the knowledge base nor the methods of measurement. Not only are the various actors and their interests in constant fluctuation, but even when they enter the debate they are incapable of reaching agreement either on the facts or on the decisions that should be taken. Framing—predicated upon the assumption that actions and their effects are known and measured—is a chaotic process, the implementation and control of which depend directly on the evolution of the controversies involved and on the construction of an agreement regarding the reality and scope of the overflows.

(ii) In 'cold' situations, on the other hand, agreement regarding ongoing overflows is swiftly achieved. Actors are identified, interests are stabilized, preferences can be expressed, responsibilities are acknowledged and accepted. The possible world states are already known or easy to identify: calculated decisions can be taken. The sudden but nevertheless foreseeable—because already experienced—pollution of a watercourse by a chemical factory falls into this category: sensors are already calibrated, analytical procedures are codified; the protagonists already know how to calculate their costs and benefits and are ready to negotiate (if necessary on the basis of clearly formulated insurance contracts) in order to determine the level of compensation payable.

(iii) 'Hot' and 'cold' situations have co-existed ever since the sciences and technology first rose to pre-eminence in Western culture. But the 'hot' source of this mysterious Carnot[1] cycle is becoming increasingly invasive and omnipresent, for at least two reasons:
– The first relates to the growing complexity of industrialized societies, a level of sophistication due in large part to the movements of the technosciences, which are causing connections and interdependencies to proliferate. Here again, the crisis over mad cow disease has a symbolic value. The current situation is the result of the intertwining of a whole series of decisions and interrelated actions, initially autonomous but gradually weaving a web over time that is proving very difficult to pick apart in retrospect, so numerous and heterogeneous are the elements bound up within it.

A regulatory decision (to stop imposing a minimum temperature for the preparation of animal feeds) results following a complex but initially unsuspected—because unheard-of—interplay of interdependencies, in the possible infection of human brains. Within this labyrinth of unexpected and rapidly proliferating connections, establishing the facts (can prions infect human beings?) and interpreting them give birth to widespread debate fuelled by radical uncertainties which can only be resolved by making massive investments, by initiating vast and exceedingly costly inquiries. The local and the global are in constant interaction—the profits of the butcher serving the little town of Antony, where I live, are directly affected by a decision by John Major—and it is very difficult to distinguish between spheres of action or institutions separated by clearly defined boundaries, so complex has the fabric of the social structure become. Reassuring certainties give way to tormented perplexities.

The second relates to the conditions in which knowledge is produced, and more particularly, to methods of experimentation. In a 'cold' situation, it is enough to call upon the experts and their laboratories. But in 'hot' situations, experts or scientists on their own, working in their usual way—ie, shut away in their laboratories—can do nothing. In order to trace links, correlate findings, produce and test hypotheses, they will always be forced to deal with non-specialists. At a stroke, this turns the latter into key players in the production of knowledge and the processing of the measurements required to map out the externalities. Once again, mad cows and their prions provide a useful source of insights. There is no way of establishing the facts without organizing epidemiological studies, without shedding light on the networks for selling and distributing animal feeds, without implementing procedures for tracing animal carcasses etc. Society as a whole must agree to take action in order to produce an officially recognized body of knowledge and measurements—in the metrological sense—in the absence of which the existence and geography of the externalities cannot be regarded as defined; that is to say, without which measurements—in the political sense—cannot be taken with any legitimacy.

(iv) Not only are 'hot' situations becoming more commonplace, more visible and more pervasive, thereby indicating that our societies are now thoroughly permeated by the technosciences; but more importantly it is becoming exceedingly difficult to cool them down, ie, arrive at a consensus on how the situation should be described and how it is likely to develop. Externalities are at the centre of public debates with no obvious conclusions. Firstly, the experts tend to emphasize their differences, because they do not wish to run the risk of making facile commitments. Secondly, economic agents can no longer be kept at a distance from the investigations which by the same token, they help to hamper: some of them have an interest in maintaining the state of controversy and ignorance[13] and do not hesitate to commit substantial resources to doing so because they can influence the content of conclusions by introducing arguments and problems hitherto absent from the debate.

(v) In this 'hot' world, which is becoming increasingly difficult to cool down, the work of economists is becoming ever more arduous because the actors they are tracking are faced by non-calculable decisions. This is the point at which it would make sense to draw up a new contract between sociology and economics. The anthropology of science and technology (AST) has acquired some useful tools for describing the dynamics of these confused situations or 'hybrid forums' (Callon, Law and Rip, 1986; Latour, 1987). Hence it is in a position to keep track of controversies and the experiments they engender without giving precedence to any one point of view, whilst at the same time revealing the socio-technological maps produced by the actors involved as well as the progressive development of instruments for making world states calculable. Thus AST can help with the work of framing interactions by improving the visibility of various efforts to keep track of overflows as well as the visibility of the disagreements or agreements to which they give rise. Like those satellite imaging systems that enable navigators to keep track of their relative positions at all times, the anthropology of science and technology can provide the actors with a cartographical outline of overflows in progress, thereby paving the way for preliminary negotiations.

While the anthropologist of science and techniques and the economist could choose to ignore each other without major inconvenience—the one fascinated by science as it is being brought into existence in laboratories cut off from the world, the other more interested in companies which, out there in the cold world, are applying science already in existence—their insights are becoming complementary and increasingly difficult to treat separately. Wherever they appear, the technosciences breed uncertainty and controversy: our societies are 'hot' thanks to the technosciences, which is why interdisciplinary collaboration is becoming essential to our understanding of them. This is the price we must pay if we wish to keep track of the mechanisms by which social spaces are formed in which decisions taken by actors with recognized identities and interests become calculable.

This does not necessarily mean that sociologists should be slaving alongside their fellow economists in order to ensure that a market can continue to exist whatever happens. Naturally some will decide to do so; others who are more critical or doubtful of the benefits of the marketplace will prefer to invest their energies in the production of charts designed to reveal the ever-expanding network of invisible and increasingly uncontrollable connections. The former will regard framing as the solution and so attach more importance to the effectiveness of cold calculation; the latter will be more interested in overflows and the heat they generate. But whatever they decide to do, they will be unable to evade the logic of framing/overflowing. They are already a part of it.

4. The negotiated market

On several occasions I have used the idea of negotiation to describe the relationships which come into being in hybrid forums: the actors negotiate their own identities and interests as well as the existence, nature and volume of overflows. The concept of negotiation, which lies at the heart of the analysis of science in the making, evokes the theoretical framework proposed by Coase in his analysis of externalities and how we deal with them (Coase, 1960). I intend to discuss this framework in more detail below. My aim is to show that once again, the different approaches are necessarily complementary.

For Coase, who is essentially preoccupied by the conditions governing intervention by the public authorities, agents are quite capable of sorting out the issue of externalities on their own, ie, of internalizing them by means of bilateral negotiations, provided that the two following conditions prevail: (a) property rights are clearly defined and (b) transaction costs are nil. Only in cases where property rights are difficult to establish (so in the presence of indivisible entities, for example: it is quite impossible to establish a property right to the atmosphere with a view to resolving pollution-related issues) is state intervention required. Coase proposes an elegant solution: the existence of an institutional framework which allows negotiations to take place.

This model is beautiful by virtue of its simplicity and the general applicability of the underlying hypotheses, but it presupposes the existence of (i) identified agents (A, B, C and X, Y and Z in my definition), (ii) who are capable of negotiating with each other, ie, of defining their interests and measuring the benefits accruing to them or conversely, the harmful effects of which they are the victims;[14] Coase also needs (iii) overflows that have been confirmed and acknowledged and (iv) property rights allocated in such a way that the identities and responsibilities of the source agents can be established, as can those of the target agents.

We have just seen that these hypotheses, which are straightforward enough in the kinds of situations we earlier described as 'cold', in reality become very cumbersome as soon as we turn our attention to 'hot' situations, where each of these conditions can only be satisfied by making substantial investments in order progressively to accumulate knowledge and create metrological frameworks. They are the result, rather than the starting point, of a lengthy 'cooling' process.

What Coase wants to avoid—and in this he adheres to a tradition with its roots in the political philosophy of the Enlightenment—is that state of nature in which conflicts and antagonisms are resolved by violence. Negotiation and the drawing-up of contracts: these are the methods of co-ordination that he holds up as the ultimate foundation stones of civilization.[15] But in his preoccupation with 'cool' situations in which world states are already known or easy to identify, Coase clearly forgets that this pacification is only possible if it is upheld by instruments that impose upon the agents' subjective (and consequently irreconcilable) viewpoints the transcendence of instruments which—once they have found universal acceptance—guarantee the objectivity of the facts, to which everyone then agrees to submit. The very fact that negotiation is possible—or to put it another way, that human relationships are peaceable—has less to do with laws and institutions (a clear attribution of property rights) than with the existence of this technical infrastructure; ie, to the existence of these instruments and their infallible measurements. In order to achieve such measured behaviour—the word says it all—one must first prove that behaviour is measurable.

Thus Coase's theorem only has a limited value. To fully convey this point it may be useful to draw a parallel with the distinction made between Newtonian physics ('cold') and Einsteinian physics ('hot'): the world views and analytical instruments developed by these two paradigms are different but they are compatible when the ratio of the velocity of bodies in motion to the speed of light tends towards zero. Similarly, Coase's theorem has considerable value in 'cold' situations, ie, when developments only happen slowly or, to

Michel Callon

put it another way, when the actions required to stabilize the actual world states and their descriptions are negligible, in terms of costs and commitments, compared to the difficult and demanding negotiations between agents attempting to reach agreement on the redistribution of resources or exchange of property rights. But things change once controversies start to dominate and situations start to heat up: now actions that involve the identification and measurement of externalities take priority. The emphasis shifts towards the production of an acceptable knowledge base and calibrated, certified measuring instruments that make it possible to map overflows with accuracy. As we have seen, if there is negotiation, it relates to the existence and nature of the overflows, to the identity of the source and target agents. Only once the controversy has been resolved can the other kind of negotiation—involving the transfer of resources, property rights etc.—begin. Those who like to set up family trees would put the negotiation regarding the existence of overflows at the top, because this is the one that determines how actors and externalities are identified. Without it, framing—in this case, the initiation of negotiations on property rights—is impossible. This distinction invites us to differentiate between two different types of negotiations: (a) negotiations aimed at identifying overflows, or 'hot' negotiations, and (b) negotiations aimed at framing them, or 'cold' negotiations. The creation of commercial relationships presupposes that both kinds of negotiations take place, one after the other.

Thus the concept of framing/overflowing helps us to understand why speeches—optimistic as well as pessimistic—on 'the inexorable growth of the marketplace' have no foundation in fact. If only because of the role played by the technosciences in what we are pleased to call advanced societies—technosciences which cause entanglements and networks of interdependencies to proliferate at their leisure—the market must be constantly reformed and built up from scratch: it never ceases to emerge and re-emerge in the course of long and stormy negotiations in which the social sciences have no choice but to participate.

Notes

1 Cf. Strauss's groundbreaking work on the mechanisms by which the imminent death of a terminally-ill patient in hospital is made invisible in the eyes of the patient himself (Glaser and Strauss, 1965). This topic was examined in more detail by L. Star when she studied how 'the prior and ongoing work disappears into the doneness' (Star, 1991).

266   © The Editorial Board of The Sociological Review 1998

2 Externalities only represent one kind of market failure among others, from which they cannot easily be differentiated in their entirety: the public goods (which produce externalities which are generally positive); asymmetries of information and their effects ('moral hazard' and 'adverse selection'); resources which are common property (ie, which are not owned by anyone but can be used by anybody).

3 The most radical presentation of the central role of objects in the framing of interactions is put forward by Latour (Latour, 1994).

4 Certain currents of symbolic interactionism, along with ethnomethodology, take this viewpoint (and support it by reference to arguments that are at once both theoretical and methodological).

5 A very orthodox viewpoint would certainly regard externalities as a purely involuntary—ie, accidental—effect.

6 It would be appropriate here to cite numerous works—in particular on environmental economics—that aim to formulate more effective procedures for framing commercial transactions.

7 Here I am arguing from the standpoint of constructivist sociology—ie, that society is an achievement—rather than that of structuralist sociology, which regards society as the medium in which actors are immersed and sometimes drowned!

8 This antagonism is summed up in masterly fashion by Duesenberry in his oft-cited phrase: 'Economics is all about how people make choices; sociology is all about how they don't have any choices to make' (Duesenberry, 1960).

9 Here we rediscover one of the basic truths intuited by H. Becker and A. Strauss: that actors belong simultaneously to several social worlds and any analysis must take this multiple identity into account in order to trace the dynamics of the interactions.

10 This proposal is merely the consequence of what we should probably call a new theory of action in which what counts are the mediations and not the sources: (Callon, 1991), (Hennion, 1993), (Latour, 1993).

11 It is possible to demonstrate the general applicability of this principle, which relates not just to the commercial transaction but also to the different methods of co-ordination. It is no easier to frame political relationships (between those represented and those who represent them) or personal relationships between people—to take just two well-known and omnipresent forms of interaction.

12 Mallard reminds us of the study undertaken by the monthly journal *Que Choisir* in April 1993: small reactive strips were included with the magazine enabling readers to measure the hardness of their water and its nitrate content for themselves: 'the darker the strip, the higher the level of invisible pollution' read the text accompanying the instrument, and it included a colour-coded list of numerical equivalents. As Mallard clearly demonstrates, the role of these instruments goes far beyond their crucial contribution to the process of calculating respective interests. They also allow us to make the transition from economic space to legal space: a traffic pollution analyzer (CO/CO^2) provides us with more than a figure: as part of a metrological framework in which every element is certified, it allows us to act directly on the legal decision-making process (Mallard, 1996a).

13 Tobacco companies played an important role in sustaining the controversy regarding the ill-effects of cigarettes. By financing the research, they have been actively contributing to the prolongation of a state of doubt and ignorance.

14 Those seeking to show the limitations or suggest a toned-down formulation of Coase's theorem must do more than simply point out the existence of transaction costs relating to the quest for and identification of the source actors, the recon-

struction of the relevant information and finally, the negotiation itself. After all, the transaction costs are based on the assumption that the reality of the phenomena and the existence of the agents involved have been stabilized. But over and above that, what I have in mind are the actual conditions of a negotiation which is only feasible if agreement can be reached on how best to define the overflows. Such an agreement can only be achieved if calibrated measuring instruments are available.

15 It was the same century and the same authors who explored the concepts behind property rights to their limits. The philosophy of the contract and that of property rights are closely interdependent; see for example: Hesse, 1990; Woodmansee, 1984.

References

Burt, R., (1992), *Structural Holes: The Social Structure of Competition.* Cambridge, Mass.: Harvard University Press.

Callon, M., (1991), 'Techno-economic Networks and Irreversibility', in J. Law, *A Sociology of Monsters*, (ed.) pp. 132–164, London: Routledge.

Callon, M. and Law, J., (1997), 'After Individual in Society: Lessons on Collectivity from Science, Technology and Society'. *Canadian Journal of Sociology*, 22(2), pp. 165–182.

Callon, M., Law, J. and Rip, A. (ed.), (1986), *Mapping the Dynamics of Science and Technology*, London: MacMillan.

Cassier, M., (1995), 'Les contrats de recherche entre l'université et l'industrie: les arrangements pour produire des biens privés, des biens collectifs et des biens publics' (Research contracts between universities and industry: arrangements for producing private benefits, collective benefits and public benefits). CSI-EMP thesis, Ecole des mines de Paris.

Coase, E.R., (1960), 'The Problem of Social Costs'. *Journal of Law and Economics* (3): 1–44.

Duesenberry, J., (1960), 'Comment on "An economic analysis of fertility"'. In *Demographic and economic change in developed countries*, ed. The Universities-National Bureau Committee for Economic Research. Princeton: Princeton University Press.

Friedberg, E., (1993), *Le pouvoir et la règle*. Paris: Le Seuil.

Glaser, B. and Strauss, A., (1965), *Awareness of Dying*. Chicago: Aldine.

Goffman, E., (1961), *Encounters: Two Studies in the Sociology of Interaction*. Indianapolis: Bobbs-Merrill.

Goffman, E., (1971), *Frame Analysis: an essay on the organization of experience*. Chicago: Northeastern University Press.

Granovetter, M., (1985), 'Economic Action and Social Structure: The Problem of Embeddedness'. *American Journal of Sociology*, 91 (3): 481–510.

Hennion, A., (1993) *:La passion musicale*. Paris: Métailié.

Hesse, C., (1990), 'Enlightenment Epistemology and the Laws of Authorship in Revolutionary France, 1777–1793'. *Representations 30* (Spring): 109–137.

Latour, B., *Science in Action*. Cambridge, Mass.: Harvard University Press.

Latour, B., (1993), *We have never been modern. Essay in symmetrical anthropology*. London: Harvester Wheatshead.

Latour, B., (1994), 'Une sociologie sans objet? Remarques sur l'interobjectivité'. *Sociologie du Travail* (4): 587–608.

Mallard, A., (1996a), 'Des instruments à leur usage. Aperçu sur la coordination par la mesure'. In *Représenter, Hybrider, Coordonner*, Ecole des mines de Paris, edited by Cécile Méadel and Vololona Rabeharisoa, 179–187.

Mallard, A., (1996b), 'Les instruments dans la coordination de l'action'. Thesis, CSI, Ecole des mines de Paris.

Polanyi, K., (1971) [1957], 'The economy as Instituted Process', in: *Trade and Market in the Early Empires*, K. Polanyi, C. Arensberg, and H. Pearson (eds). Chicago: Henry Regnery Co.

Richardson, G.B., (1972), 'The Organization of Industry'. *Economic Journal*, (September): 883–896.

Star, S.L., (1991), 'The Sociology of an invisible: The Primacy of Work in the Writings of Anselm Strauss', in: D. Maines (ed.), *Social Organization and Social Processes: Essays in Honour of Anselm L. Strauss*, Hawthorme, NY: Aldine de Gruyter.

Williamson, O., (1993), 'Calculativeness, Trust and Economic Organization'. *Journal of Law and Economics XXXVI*, (April): 453–486.

Woodmansee, M., (1984), 'The Genius and the Copyright: Economic and Legal Conditions of the Emergence of the "Author" '. *Eighteenth-Century Studies*, 17 (4): 425–448.

Notes on contributors

Mitchel Y. Abolafia is an Associate Professor in the Graduate School of Public Affairs at the State University of New York at Albany. His research applies the tools of ethnography and organization theory to the study of markets and market regulation. He recently completed a comparative study of financial markets titled *Making Markets: Opportunism and Restraint on Wall Street* (Harvard University Press, 1997) and is currently studying the Federal Open Market Committee of the Federal Reserve Board. He received a Ph.D. in Sociology from the State University of New York at Stony Brook.

Michel Callon is Professor of Sociology at the Ecole Nationale Supérieure des Mines, Paris. Together with Bruno Latour and John Law he took part in the development of the so-called Actor-Network Theory. He has published articles and books on the sociology of science and technology and the economics of research and development He co-edited *Mapping the Dynamics of Science and Technology* and *The Strategic Management of Research and Technology*. He is currently working on the involvement of lay people in the production of scientific knowledge. He is President of the Society for Social Studies of Science.

Franck Cochoy is 'maître de conférences' at the University of Toulouse II and 'chargé de recherches' at the Centre National de la Recherche Scientifique for 1997–1998. A former student of the Ecole des Hautes Etudes en Sciences Sociales in Paris and of the Ecole Normale Supérieure in Fontenay, he earned an 'agrégation' degree and a Ph.D. in Social Sciences. He is working on the technical and human devices which connect/shape supply and demand in the market economy (ie, marketing, packaging, standardization).

© The Editorial Board of The Sociological Review 1998. Published by Blackwell Publishers, 108 Cowley Road, Oxford OX4 1JF, UK and 350 Main Street, Malden, MA 02148, USA.

He is the author of *Discipliner l'économie de marché: une histoire du marketing*, Paris, La Découverte (forthcoming in 1998).

Hervé Dumez is Research Fellow at the Centre de Recherche en Gestion of the École Polytechnique in Paris and Research Director at the Centre National de la Recherche Scientifique. Specialist in European competition policy issues, he is co-author with Alain Jeunemaître of various key publications, among which, *La concurrence en Europe*, Seuil, 1991, 'The convergence of Competition Policies in Europe: Internal Dynamics and External Imposition' in Berger S. and Dore, R. (ed.): *National Diversity and Global Capitalism*. Ithaca (NY)/London (UK), Cornell University Press, 1996. *Understanding and Regulating the Globalization of a Market. The Cement Case* is their latest book to be published by The Macmillan Press, Basingstoke, in 1998.

Bai Gao is an assistant professor of sociology at Duke University. His research interests include economic sociology, law and society, and comparative/historical sociology. He received his Ph.D. from Princeton University in 1994. He is the author of *Economic Ideology and Japanese Industrial Policy: Developmentalism from 1931 to 1965*, which was published by Cambridge University Press in 1997. Currently, he is writing a book on the evolution of competition policy in modern Japan which examines how the legal system, especially the antimonopoly law, influenced the transformation of economic governance.

Mark Granovetter is Professor of Sociology at Stanford University. He is the author of *Getting a Job: A Study of Contacts and Careers*, and a series of articles on economic sociology and social networks, including 'The Strength of Weak Ties' and 'Economic Action and Social Structure: The Problem of Embeddedness'.

Alain Jeunemaître is Research Fellow at the Centre de Recherche en Gestion of the École Polytechnique in Paris and at the CNRS and associate fellow of the Regulatory Policy Research Centre, Hertford College, Oxford. Specialist in European competition policy issues and regulatory policies, he is the editor of *The Regulation of Financial Markets. A Practitioner's Perspective*. Basingstoke, The Macmillan Press, 1997. He is co-author with Hervé Dumez of various key publications, among which, *La concurrence en Europe*. Seuil, 1991, 'The convergence of Competition Policies in Europe: Internal Dynamics and External Imposition' in Berger, S. and Dore, R. (ed.): *National Diversity and Global Capitalism*. Ithaca (NY)/London (UK), Cornell University Press, 1996. *Understanding and Regulating the Globalization of a Market. The Cement Case* is their latest book to be published by The Macmillan Press, Basingstoke, in 1998.

Patrick McGuire is Associate Professor of Sociology at the University of Toledo. He has written numerous articles and chapters on the electric utility and electrical manufacturing industries, and on issues of public ownership of economic institutions in the U.S.

Peter Miller is Professor of Management Accounting at the London School of Economics and Political Science. Originally trained as a Sociologist, he has published extensively in the fields of accounting, management, and sociology. His most recent book is *Accounting as Social and Institutional Practice* (Cambridge University Press, 1994). He is Associate Editor of Accounting, Organizations and Society.

David Stark is the Arnold A. Saltzman Professor of Sociology and International Affairs at Columbia University. He is co-author, with Laszlo Bruszt, of 'Postsocialist Pathways Transforming Politics and Property in Eastern Europe' (Cambridge University Press, 1998) and co-editor, with Gernot Grabher, of 'Restructuring Networks in Postsocialism: Legacies, Linkages, and Localities', Oxford University Press, 1997.

Viviana A. Zelizer is Professor of sociology at Princeton University. She is the author of *Morals and Markets: The Development of Life Insurance in the United States*; *Pricing the Priceless Child: The Changing Social Value of Children*; and *The Social Meaning of Money*.

Index

Abolafia, M. Y., 40
access to market-makers, 78–82
accounting, 23–8, 45, 190
  management accounting, 182–5, 187–9
  margins of, 174–5, 177–8
  problematizing existing practices,
    174–7, 188
accounts, 133
  of recombinant property, 134–6
Act on Financial Institutions 1991
  (Hungary), 130
Actor-Network Theory, 44
agency, 148
  in electricity industry, 149
  networks and, 8–10
Allen, B. T., 235
American Administrative Management
  Association, 198
American Association of University
  Professors, 198
American Council on Education, 198
American Economic Association, 201
American Marketing Association, 201–3,
  206
American Marketing Journal, 206
anthropology, 3, 48
  of markets, 50–1
  of science and technology (AST), 28,
    29, 263
antitrust cases, 225–37, 238–9
Appadurai, A., 18
assets, 132–3
  decentralized reorganization of, 120–9,
    131–2
Associated Advertising Clubs of the
  World, 201
Association of American Universities, 198
Association of Edison Illuminating
  Companies (AEIC), 153–5, 157, 158,
  159

Association of Labour Unions (Japan),
  96
associations of firms, 148, 151
attachments, 35–6
automation, 102
Avishai, A., 184

Baker, W., 10
banking, in Hungary, 130–1
bankruptcies, in Hungary, 130
Bankruptcy Act (Hungary), 129–30
Barstow, William, 156, 164
basing point system, 225–32
Berger, P. L., 106
Biggart, N. W., 101
Block, F., 40
'blood tie', 96–7
bond traders, 72–3, 74, 75
Bourdieu, P., 14, 15–16, 53n
Boyer, L., 208
Bruszt, L., 142n
budgeting, 60–1, 186, 187
Burt, R. S., 9, 11, 44
business cycles, 224
business schools, 198–9, 211–12

calculating tools, 23–6, 45, 50
calculation, 4–5, 12
calculative agency/agencies, 3, 4–12, 32,
  43, 47–8, 50
  and accounting tools, 24, 25, 26
  competition between, 45–6
  and non-calculability, 38–40
  proliferation of, 33
calculativeness, 20–1, 52n, 255–6
  calculating tools, 23–6
  and framing, 16–19
  and gift giving, 12–16
  sources of, 6–12
capitalism, East European, 136–40

Index

Index

Index

variable costs, 180
variation of organization, 162–3
vertical integration, 232–7, 239
vigilance, 75
vocabulary of marketing, 202–3

wage system, in Japan, 87, 93, 104, 107

wages for housework, 63–4
Walder, A., 119
Walzer, M., 38

Watts, R. L., 176
Weber, M., 23, 42–3, 52n
Weld, L. D. H., 196
Westinghouse, 162
White, H., 44
White, P., 204–5
Williamson, O., 13–14, 52n, 89, 255–6
women, and husbands' income, 61–4
Wooden, W. B., 229

Zimmerman, J. L., 176

278